Philippians · Colossians
Thessalonians

Philippians·Colossians Thessalonians

By

H. A. Ironside

LOIZEAUX BROTHERS
Neptune, New Jersey

FIRST EDITION, PHILIPPIANS 1922
FIRST EDITION, COLOSSIANS 1929
FIRST EDITION, THESSALONIANS 1947

COMBINED EDITION, 1982
SECOND PRINTING, AUGUST 1984

ISBN 0-87213-398-2

PRINTED IN THE UNITED STATES OF AMERICA

CONTENTS

PHILIPPIANS

CHAPTER ONE

CHRIST THE BELIEVER'S LIFE, AND THE EVANGELISTIC SPIRIT

CHAPTER TWO

CHRIST THE BELIEVER'S EXAMPLE, AND THE LOWLY MIND

CONTENTS

CONTENTS

COLOSSIANS

PART ONE

DOCTRINAL (Colossians 1:1—3:4)

PART TWO

PRACTICAL (Colossians 3:5—4:18)

CONTENTS

Philippians

PREFATORY NOTE

———

THESE *notes have been jotted down at odd times, over a period of nearly two years, while the writer has been busily engaged in gospel work. They pretend to no literary value, and repetitions may sometimes occur, but such as they are, they are sent forth with the earnest hope that they may be blessed to some of "the quiet in the land" who enjoy simple things, plainly put.*

H. A. IRONSIDE.

July, 1922.

NOTES ON
PHILIPPIANS

Introductory Thoughts

THE account of the labors and sufferings of the apostle Paul and his companions, in Philippi, is given in the 16th chapter of the Acts. They went to Macedonia in response to the vision of the man of that country calling for help, which Paul had seen at Troas. But when they reached the capital, there was apparently no such man feeling his need and awaiting them. Instead, they came first in touch with a few women who were accustomed to gather for prayer n a quiet place, by the riverside, outside the city. There the Lord opened Lydia's heart to attend to the things spoken by Paul. Others too were evidently reached; among them some brethren, as

verse 40 makes clear.   But it was when cast into
prison that the greatest work was done.   The
jailer and his household were won for Christ ere
the messengers of God's grace took their departure for Thessalonica.

The infant church was very dear to the heart of
the apostle, and he was very dear to them.   Their
love and care were shown after he left them, at
various times, and, one would judge, for a number
of years.   But at last they lost touch with him,
apparently during his imprisonment at Cæsarea.
It was when he was in Rome that they again got
into communication with him and fearing he
might be in need, sent him an expression of their
love and care by the hand of a trusted and beloved
brother who was one of themselves,   Epaphroditus.   Having fulfilled his ministry, this faithful
man fell sick, and his illness was of sufficient dur-
ation for word regarding it to reach Philippi, and
the news of the anxiety of the saints there concerning him had come back to Rome about the
time that he became convalescent.   Deciding at
once to return, he was entrusted with the letter
we have before us, which was, one would judge,
dictated to him by the apostle.

It is an epistle of joy, a letter of cheer.   On the

other hand, it contains needful exhortation for a wilderness people, liable to fall out by the way.

It would seem that Epaphroditus had communicated to Paul a certain concern that was weighing upon his heart regarding a misunderstanding or a positive quarrel between two women in the assembly—both much esteemed by the saints and by the apostle himself—which if not checked and healed, was likely to prove a source of sadness, and possibly even division in days to come.

This appears to be much in the apostle's mind as he indites his epistle. He seeks so to present Christ that the hearts of all may be ravished with Him, and thus all selfish aims disappear, and all that is of the flesh be judged in His presence.

This is ever what is needed when the flesh is at work among believers. Therefore the great importance of this portion of the Word of God in the present hour of the Church's history.

The epistle falls very naturally into four divisions, and these are rightly indicated in our common version by the four chapters. The theme of the whole might be put in the three words, *"Christ is all!"* It is the epistle of Christ. It occupies us with Himself; and each separate division presents Him in some different way, and indicates the subjective result in the believer as he is occupied with Christ objectively in the manner presented.

Chapter one sets forth Christ as our Life, and the evangelistic spirit or the gospel mind.

In chapter two we have Christ as our Example, and the lowly mind, or the humble spirit of those who would follow Him.

Chapter three gives us Christ as our Object, and, subjectively, we have the steadfast spirit, the determined mind; that is, the heart and thoughts centered on Himself.

In the last chapter Christ is set forth as our Strength and Supply, and naturally we have with this the confident mind, the spirit of trust that should characterize all who know the resources that are in Him.

It will be readily seen that the epistle is a very practical one. It has to do with our state rather than our standing ; with responsibility rather than privilege; with communion rather than with union. In other words, it is an epistle suited to our wilderness journey. It was written to guide our feet while going through this world. It is a pastoral ministry of a very precious kind.

Others have written very fully and helpfully on this part of the Word of God, whose writings are readily obtainable. It is not the present writer's thought to attempt a labored exposition of the epistle, but simply to jot down some notes which embody the results of his own study, and which it is hoped may be used by the Holy Spirit for the edification and comfort of fellow-saints, particularly such as are becoming discouraged because of the way. Much has been gleaned from what others have set forth, and no pretension is made as to originality of treatment. If Christ Himself becomes a little more appreciated by a few of His own, the object in view will have been attained.

CHAPTER ONE

CHRIST, THE BELIEVER'S LIFE, AND THE EVANGELISTIC SPIRIT

Salutation

(vers. 1, 2.)

"Paul and Timothy, servants of Jesus Christ, to all the saints in Christ Jesus who are at Philippi, with the bishops and deacons: Grace to you and peace, from God our Father and the Lord Jesus Christ."

IT is noticeable how, in many of his letters, the apostle links up younger and less experienced fellow-laborers with himself, as here, in his salutations. He was an apostle by the Lord's call, occupying a unique place as His special messenger to the Gentiles. But he never stands aloof in complacent dignity apart from others who are engaged in the same ministry. He had taken Timothy with him when the latter had not long been in the knowledge and path of the truth, and he testifies later, in this same letter, of the truth that was in him. In his care for the development of the younger brethren, Paul becomes a model for older teachers and evangelists to the end of the

dispensation. If others are to follow on in the
ways that be in Christ, it is well that more experienced men take a personal interest in their
less experienced brethren who manifest a measure of gift, and by associating them with themselves in ministry, lead and encourage them in the
path of faith. It is often the other way, and the
young are disheartened, and permitted to slip
back into business pursuits, who, if wisely ad-
vised, and helped when needed, might become able
ministers of the truth.

Paul and Timothy take no official title here.
They are simply servants of Jesus Christ. The
word means *bondmen.* They were purchased servants, and as such, belonged entirely to Him
whom they gladly owned as their Anointed Master. They were His by right, and they had renounced all title to do the will of the flesh. Nor
is it only ministering brethren who are so designated in Scripture. This is the name that is used
of all Christians. Though sons and heirs we are
also bondmen of love, whose delight it should be
to yield ourselves unto Him as those that are alive
from the dead.

The saints as a whole at Philippi are greeted,
and the elders and deacons specially mentioned.
This is unusual. It evidently implies a particular
sense of obligation to the elders and deacons on

the part of the apostle, probably in connection with ministry of the assembly's gift of love. There may also be the thought of addressing the leaders, or guides, in a special way, in view of the "rift in the lute"— the unhappiness between Euodia and Syntyche, which he desired to rectify.

Elders may, or may not, be official. In the early church they were definitely appointed by apostolic authority. It may be unwise, and going beyond Scripture, for saints in feebleness to-day to set up or ordain official elders. On the other hand, those measurably possessing the qualifications indicated in the epistles to Timothy and Titus, should be recognized by fellow-believers as God-appointed elders, whose counsel should be sought, and who are responsible to watch for souls and to take oversight in the house of God. To fail to own such would be insubjection to the Word of God, but a true bishop or overseer would be the last man to insist upon obedience to him. He would rather lead by serving the saints and by the force of a godly example.

Deacons are those who minister in temporal things, and should be chosen by the saints for this purpose. The word means *servant*, but is different to that used above. It is not "bondman," but a servant acting voluntarily, and in response generally to the expressed desire of others.

Notice the little word "ALL." It is used **very** significantly in this epistle—in a way not found anywhere else in the writings of the apostle Paul.

Observe its use in verses 4, 7, 8, 25 in this chapter, and verse 26 in chapter 2. Is it not plain that Paul desired to bind all together in one bundle of love in this way, refusing to even seem to recognize any incipient division among them? He greeted them *all*, he thought well of them all, *he* prayed for them *all*. He knew it would in the end be well with them *all*. And so he exhorted them *all* to stand fast in one spirit.

As customary in all his letters, he wished them grace and peace. Grace was the general Grecian salutation. Peace was that of the Hebrew. So he links the two together. Grace in its highest sense, favor against desert, could only be known by the Christian. And true peace rests upon the work of the Cross, whether it be that peace *with* God, which is fundamental, or the peace *of* God, which the apostle here would have the saints enter into and enjoy from day to day. Both descend from God, now revealed as Father, and from our Lord Jesus Christ, through whom we have been brought into this place of favor.

The Introduction

(verses 3-11.)

"I thank my God upon every remembrance of you, always in every prayer of mine for you all, making request with joy, for your fellowship in the gospel from the first day until now; being confident of this very thing, that He which hath begun a good work in you will perform it until the day of Jesus Christ: even as it is meet for me to think this of you all, because I have you in my heart; inasmuch as both in my bonds, and in the defence and confirmation of the gospel, ye all are partakers of my grace. For God is my record, how greatly I long after you all in the bowels (or, tenderness) of Jesus Christ. And this I pray, that your love may abound yet more and more in knowledge and in all judgment (or, perception); that ye may approve things that are excellent; that ye may be sincere and without offence (or, blameless) till the day of Christ; being filled with the fruits of righteousness, which are by Jesus Christ, unto the glory and praise of God."

IN these verses we have the apostle's own introduction to this delightful specimen of early Christian correspondence. His interest in the saints at Philippi did not cease with his leaving their city. Through all the years that had passed he had borne them on his heart, and presented them to God in prayer. There were sweet and blessed memories too that filled him with gladness as he looked back on the season of ministry spent amongst them, and as he learned of their continuance in the grace of God in after days.

He thanks God upon every remembrance of them. There was nothing, apparently, in their past history that had caused him pain or anxiety of mind. And so, in every prayer of his for them all, he preferred his request with joy. Their fellowship with him in the gospel had been consistent from the beginning. It will be noticed what a large place "fellowship" has in this epistle, and also how frequently "the gospel" is mentioned. An assembly of saints walking together in the fear of the Lord, exercised about holding forth the Word of Life to the unsaved, is likely to know more of real fellowship than a company of believers occupied chiefly with their own affairs, their own blessings—all about *themselves*. On the other hand, no assembly can prosper that fails to recognize the importance of the divine and holy principles given in the Word to guide believers in this scene.

Fellowship in the gospel may be exercised in various ways: by prayer, by participation in the public testimony, by furnishing the means to enable the laborer to go forth unhindered by perplexities and anxieties as to necessary means to carry on his work. Every servant of Christ going forth for the Name's sake, "taking nothing of the Gentiles," should be entirely cast upon the Lord for his support. On the other hand, it should be esteemed a privilege on the part of those abiding at home, to help them by ministering in temporal things; and such ministry will never be forgotten by Him who has said, "Whosoever receiveth a prophet in the name of a prophet shall receive a prophet's reward."

I remember a brother's definition of fellowship. He was a teamster, and was asked, "What do you understand by fellowship?" He replied, "For each one to pull his own trace and keep it tight." The simile is a crude one, but will be readily understood.

It is noticeable that the apostle had no doubt as to the final outcome for every true believer. He was absolutely confident that the One who had begun a good work in them, would never leave off until He had perfected that which He Himself had commenced. But this would only be attained and manifested in the day of Jesus Christ. A godly old brother used often to say, "The Lord always looks at His people as they will be when they are done." And it is well for us if we can learn to look at them in the same way. An incident is told of an artist who had conceived in his mind a great picture, which he meant to be the masterpiece of his life. He was working on a large canvas, putting in the drabs and grays that were to compose the background, when a friend entered, unnoticed.

The artist worked on with enthusiasm, not aware of the onlooker's presence. But, finally happening to turn, he saw him, and exclaimed, "What do you think of this? I intend it to be the greatest work I have ever done." His friend burst into a laugh, and exclaimed, "Why, to be frank, I don't think much of it. It seems to me to be only a great daub." "Ah," replied the artist, at once sensing the situation, "you cannot see what is going to be there. I can." And so it is with God our Father. He sees in every believer that which will be fully brought out at the judgment-seat of Christ, and He is working now toward that end. We too often see the present imperfection and forget the future glory. But, in the day of Jesus Christ, when all shall be manifested, every believer will be conformed to the image of God's blessed Son. Surely we can join with the apostle even now and say, "It is meet for me to think this of you all." Thus to look upon God's people will deliver from much strife, and from disappointment, when we see crudities and carnalities in those from whom we had expected better things. It is humbling and healthful too to remember that others probably see similar imperfections in us.

Paul carried the saints in his heart, and, though himself in prison, he recognized their fellowship in the defence and confirmation of the gospel, and rejoiced in the manner in which they shared this grace with him. He calls God to witness how greatly he yearned after every one of them in the tender love of Christ Jesus; and in verses 9-11 we have his prayer, which reminds us somewhat of the prayer in Colossians 1. He would have their love abound yet more and more in knowledge and all perception, or discernment. Brotherly love is not a matter of mere sentimentality; it is love in the truth. And this calls for study of the Word of God in order that one may know just how to manifest that love according to each particular occasion. Let us remember there is never a time when we are not called upon to show love to our brother, but we cannot always manifest it in the same way, if subject to the Word of God. Therefore the need of instruction in that Word, and enlightenment by the Holy Spirit, that we may perceive what is in accordance with the mind of God.

The first clause in the 10th verse is sometimes rendered,"That ye may try the things that differ;" or, as given above, "Approve things that are excellent." The meaning is practically the same. For by testing things that differ, we approve what is excellent. Again the test is the Word of God. That Word is given to try all things, and it will manifest what is truly excellent, thus giving the believer to understand how he may walk so as to

please God, that he may be sincere and blameless
in the day of Christ.

Attention has often been called to the striking
fact that we have here the Anglicized Latin word
"sincere," meaning, literally, "without wax"—
used to translate a Greek word meaning "sun-
tested." It might seem at first as though there
is no connection between the two terms. But we
are told that the ancients had a very fine porcelain
which was greatly valued, and brought a very high
price. This ware was so fragile, that it was only
with the greatest difficulty it could be fired without being cracked; and dishonest dealers were in
the habit of filling in the cracks that appeared
with a pearly-white wax, which looked enough like
the true porcelain to pass without being readily
detected in the shops. If held to the light, however, the wax was at once manifested as a dark
seam; and honest Latin dealers marked their
wares "sine cera" (without wax). Thus the apostle would have the saints tested by the sunlight
of God's truth and holiness, and found to be without wax; that is, he would have them straightfor-
ward, and honorable in all their dealings. Anything that savors of sham or hypocrisy is as the
wax used to hide the imperfection in the porcelain.

"Blameless" (see also ver. 15 of chap. 2) refers
to *motive* rather than to act, I take it. It is not

the same thing as "sinless," which would, of course, imply complete moral perfection. "Blamelessness" implies right motives. "The fruits of righteousness" of verse 11 is the same as in Hebrews 12: 11, where "the peaceable fruit of righteousness" is the result of exercise under the hand of God. All is through Jesus Christ, unto the glory and praise of God.

Joy in Gospel Testimony
(chap. 1: 12-20.)

"But I would ye should understand, brethren, that the things which happened unto me have fallen out rather unto the furtherance of the gospel; so that my bonds in Christ are manifest in all the palace [or, Prætorium, *i. e.*, Cæsar's Guard], and in all other places; and many of the brethren in the Lord, waxing confident by my bonds, are much more bold to speak the word without fear. Some indeed preach Christ even of envy and strife; and some also of good will. The one preach Christ of contention, not sincerely, supposing to add affliction to my bonds; but the other of love, knowing that I am set for the defence of the gospel. What then? Notwithstanding, every way, whether in pretence, or in truth, Christ is preached; and I therein do rejoice, yea, and will rejoice. For I know that this shall turn to my salvation through your prayer, and the supply of the Spirit of Jesus Christ, according to my earnest expectation and hope, that in nothing I shall be ashamed, but that with all boldness, as always, so now also Christ shall be magnified in my body, whether it be by life, or by death."

IT is always a sad sign, and an evidence of spiritual decline, when the heart loses its interest

in the message of grace. Some there are so occupied with the deeper truths of the Word of God
that they allow themselves to speak slightingly of
the simplicity of the gospel. Paul was the pre-
eminent teacher of the Church, but to his last
hour, his heart was filled with gospel zeal, and his
sympathies were with the evangelist carrying the
Word of Life to men dead in trespasses and in
sins. Even in his prison-house he rejoiced that
his affairs had really tended to the progress of the
gospel. Satan, doubtless, hoped to hinder that
work by locking up the apostle in a jail, but even
there it became manifest to all Cæsar's court, and
to all others, that his bonds were for Christ's sake.
The very soldiers appointed to guard him were
brought thus to hear the glorious proclamation of
grace to a guilty world; and it is evident, both
from the 13th verse, and the 22nd verse of the
4th chapter, that numbers of them believed. Who
can fathom the joy that must have filled the heart
of Paul as he led one guard after another to the
Saviour's feet! Just as when cast into the Philippian dungeon, he and his companion Silas were
used to the conversion of the jailer and his household, so here, grace triumphed over all seemingly
untoward circumstances, and the prison cell became a gospel chapel, where souls were being born
of God, and stern Roman soldiers became them-

selves the captive servants of One greater than
Cæsar.

In the 14th verse the apostle speaks of another
cause of joy. While he was going about from place
to place preaching the Word, there were gifted
men who held back, feeling, perhaps, that they
were in no sense on a par with him, and so they
permitted the timidity and backwardness of the
flesh to hinder their launching out in a work to
which the Lord was beckoning them. But now
that he is in durance, and can no longer go about
from place to place in this happy service, numbers of these men came forward, and, for the
Name's sake, went forth preaching the Word
boldly, without fear. On the other hand there
were some restless men who had not commended
themselves as fitted for evangelistic work, and
while he was free, were kept in a place of subjection; but now that he was incarcerated they saw
their opportunity to come to the front, and went
forth preaching Christ indeed with their lips,
though their hearts were filled with envy and
strife. But no jealous or envious thoughts entered
the mind of Paul. He rejoiced in those who
preached the Word through good will, out of love,
knowing that he was appointed for the vindica-
tion of the gospel; and, though he could not rejoice in the spirit that moved the others, he, at

least was gladdened to know that it was Christ who was being preached. And so he was thankful for every voice telling out the story of the Cross. Nor would he permit anything to rob him of this joy.

How marked is the contrast between the spirit here exhibited, and that which often prevails to-day. How seldom, in fact, do we see this simple unalloyed rejoicing that Christ is preached, let the aims and methods of the preacher be what they will. Untold harm is often done by harsh, captious criticism of young and earnest men, who often have much to learn, and offend by their uncouthness, by their lack of discernment and understanding of the ways of the Lord, who nevertheless do preach Christ, and win souls. And God has said, "He that winneth souls is wise;" or, as the Revised Version so strikingly puts it, "He that is wise winneth souls." Often have anxious souls been really hindered by the criticism of their elders in matters of this kind. Oh, for more of the spirit of Paul that would lead us to rejoice unfeignedly whenever Christ is preached, even though there be much to exercise our hearts and lead to prayer—and it may be to godly admonition at times, so far as methods and expressions are concerned, which if rightly dealt with now, may soon disappear as excrescences, when the earnest evangelist grows in grace and in the knowledge of the truth.

The 19th and 20th verses show us how the apostle relied upon the prayers of the people of God, and how encouraged he was by this abounding gospel testimony. He felt that it presaged his own deliverance, and pointed to the time when he would again be free according to his earnest expectation, and hope, to preach Christ openly and widely if it should be the will of God, or else to glorify Him in a martyr's death. He had but one ambition, and that, that Christ Himself should be magnified in his body whether by life or by death. No matter what he himself might be called upon to toil or suffer, if the One whom he had met on that never-to-be-forgotten day on the Damascus turnpike were exalted and honored—this would satisfy him.

It is this utter absence of self-seeking that commends any true servant of Christ. We see it strikingly in John the Baptist, who said, "He must increase, but I must decrease." It should be the one supreme characteristic of the evangelist, pastor, or teacher. And where this spirit of self-abnegation for the glory of the Lord is really found, it must commend the ministry, though it makes nothing of the minister. Oh, that one might enter more fully into it!

Christ is all in Life or Death

(chap. 1: 21-26.)

"For to me to live is Christ, and to die is gain. But if I live in the flesh, this is the fruit of my labor: yet what I shall choose I wot not. For I am in a strait betwixt two, having a desire to depart, and to be with Christ, which is far better: nevertheless to abide in the flesh is more needful for you. And having this confidence, I know that I shall abide and continue with you all for your furtherance and joy of faith; that your rejoicing may be more abundant in Jesus Christ for me by my coming to you again."

"To me to live is Christ" is Christian life and experience in its fulness. It has often been remarked, and is well worth remembering, that Christians have many experiences which are not properly Christian experience. The man described in the 7th of Romans is undergoing an experience which will be for his future blessing, but it is not proper Christian experience, though it is clearly enough the experience of a Christian. Christ Himself, so dominating and controlling the believer, that his one object is to live to His glory, is what Paul has before him here. This should be the experience of Christians at all times. But, alas, how few of us enter into it in its entirety. It implies a surrendered will, and the body yielded to the Lord who has redeemed it, that it may be used only to His praise. This is life in its truest sense, and, probably, no one ever entered into it so fully as the apostle Paul.

We may, perhaps, better understand the experience, "For me to live is Christ," if we consider for a moment what life means to many an other. The Christless business man, whose one aim and object is to obtain wealth, might well say, "For me to live is money." The careless seeker after the world's pleasures, if he told the truth, would say, "For me to live is worldly pleasure." The carnal voluptuary given up to self-gratification, would say, "For me to live is self." The statesman, exulting in the plaudits of the people, and craving world-notoriety, might truthfully declare, "For me to live is fame and power." But Paul could say, and every Christian should be able to say, "For me to live is Christ."

And it is only such who can heartily add, "And to die is gain." Death is no enemy to the one to whom Christ is all. To *live* gives opportunity to manifest Christ down here; to *die* is to be with Christ, than which nothing could be more precious.

The apostle himself was in a dilemma as to which of these he would prefer, were the choice left to him. If permitted to continue in the body, he would have further opportunity of service for Him who had claimed him as His own and called him to this ministry. But, on the other hand, he longed "to depart and to be with Christ, which is far better." His had been a life of toil and suffering for Christ's sake, such as only a Spirit-sustained man could have endured without fainting; and as he lay in the Roman prison, his heart longed for release—a release which would mean to be forever with Christ. Labor for Christ was sweet, but rest with Christ would be sweeter. Whitefield used to say, "I am often weary *in* the work, but never weary *of* it," and such was, doubtless, the attitude of our apostle. He loved to serve, yet longed too for the hour of release, with no selfish motive in it, for his one object was Christ, whether in life or in death.

It is amazing how anyone, with words such as these before him, could question for a moment that the Word of God teaches the consciousness of the spirit after death. Paul had no thought that his spirit would be buried in the grave with his body, or that his soul would sleep until the resurrection day. Death to him would be a departure, an exodus, a moving out of the travel-worn earthly tabernacle, and a going to be with Christ, until the first resurrection at the coming of the Lord.

As he weighs everything, the unselfishness of the man comes out strikingly. He sees the need of the Church of God. As it is now, so it was then. There were many evangelists, or gospelers, but few teachers and pastors who really carried the people of God upon their hearts; and he felt that to abide in the flesh was more needful for the flock than rest was for himself. So he says he has confidence that he should abide a little longer, and continue in this scene of labor for the furtherance and joy of faith of the people of God.

It is clear, I think, that he fully expected the Lord would permit him to revisit Philippi, that the rejoicings of the saints there might be more abundant in Christ Jesus on his behalf, through his coming to them again. They were his children in the faith: as a tender father he yearned over them, and longed to see them once more before closing his earthly ministry. We have no record in the Word of God as to whether this desire was fulfilled, but there are early church traditions which indicate that it was. At any rate, we know he was released from his first imprisonment, and allowed to go about in freedom for several years before being again apprehended and martyred for the sake of Christ Jesus, his and our Lord, following Him thus even unto death.

Unity in Gospel Testimony

(chap. 1: 27-30.)

"Only let your conversation (or, behavior) be as it be-
cometh the gospel of Christ: that whether I come and see
you, or else be absent, I may hear of your affairs, that ye
stand fast in one spirit, with one mind striving together
for the faith of the gospel; and in nothing terrified by
your adversaries: which is to them an evident token of
perdition, but to you of salvation, and that of God. For
unto you it is given in the behalf of Christ, not only to
believe on Him, but also to suffer for his sake: having the
same conflict which ye saw in me, and now hear to be
in me."

THE word "conversation," as ordinarily employed by our forefathers, was of far wider scope
than as generally used by us to-day. It meant not
only the talk of the lips, though it included that,
but it took in the entire behavior. The apostle's
exhortation is to the effect that the whole manner
of life of the people of God should be in accordance with the gospel of Christ. No more important message was ever committed to man than
the word of reconciliation, which God has graciously entrusted to His people in this present dispensation of His mercy to a lost world. That gospel tells of the divine means of deliverance from
the guilt and power of sin. How incongruous,
then, if the testimonies of those who undertake to
proclaim it with their mouths deny its power in

their lives! A walk worthy of the gospel is a walk in the energy of the Holy Spirit; it is a life surrendered to Him, whose Lordship that gospel declares.

But it is not merely our *individual* responsibility to walk worthy of the gospel that the apostle here presses. He has rather before him *assembly* responsibility. He desires to hear of the affairs of the Philippians, that, as an assembly, they stand fast in one spirit with one mind, co-operating vigorously for the faith of the gospel. Nothing so mars gospel testimony as contention and self-seeking among God's people. Where jealousies and envyings come in to hinder the fellowship of those who should be standing together heart to heart and shoulder to shoulder for the truth of God, the effect on the world outside is most lamentable. This is particularly so with the unsaved members of believers' families. Nothing is more harmful to them than to find out that their elders are not commending the message they profess to love, by unitedly standing together for the Word of God.

Is there not something here that deserves the careful consideration of many believers in the assemblies gathered to the name of the Lord Jesus Christ at the present time? Have we not allowed personalities, bickerings, and strife to greatly mar and hinder gospel testimony? On the other hand, it must be confessed that some, possessing evangelistic gift, have ignored, to a very marked degree, the importance of assembly fellowship in gospel testimony, launching forth often without the prayerful endorsement of older, more godly saints: they are afterwards surprised and grieved that they do not find heartier co-operation on the part of assemblies whose judgment they ignored to begin with. The evangelist is the Lord's servant, and, therefore, is not subject to human dictation, but, on the other hand, fellowship involves mutual responsibility, and evangelists need to remember that gift is not necessarily piety, nor does it always carry with it good judgment and sound wisdom. Therefore the importance of cultivating humility on the part of the servant, if he would have the hearty fellowship of assemblies in his work.

When there is this lowly, subject spirit manifested by the evangelist, and vigorous co-operation on the part of the assembly, God can be depended on to work in mighty power to the salvation of lost souls, and the blessing of His people; and this, to the enemy, is a condition he most dreads. Where an assembly is walking in love, and exercised about the Lord's things in this scene, they need not fear the attacks of evil powers, natural or supernatural, from without. These unholy hosts read their own doom in the happy fellowship of the saints of God, and see in it a proof of the truth of the Lord's words, "Upon this rock I will build mine assembly, and the gates of hell shall not prevail against it." The thought that many have in mind in reading this scripture seems to be that the assembly of God is as a city *besieged*, beleaguered by the enemies of the Lord, and carrying on a *defensive* warfare, though with the pledge of eventual victory. This, however, is far from fulfilling the picture presented by our Lord. An invading or besieging army does not carry the gates of its cities with it. It is hell, or hades, the realm of darkness, that is being besieged by the forces of light who are carrying on, not a *defensive*, but an *offensive* warfare, and to them the promise is given that "the gates of hell shall not prevail." This is the "perdition" spoken of in verse 28.

Such fellowship as that which the apostle brings before us, cannot be fully entered into apart from suffering, but this is to be esteemed as a privilege by those who fight under the banner of the risen Lord. It is given to such, as it were a guerdon greatly to be desired, in behalf of Christ Himself, not only to trust in Him as Saviour, but manfully to toil and suffer, that His name may be glorified

in the scene where He Himself was rejected and
crucified, and over which He is soon coming to
reign.

How blessedly and how fully had the apostle
entered into this! With what joy did he endure
and suffer that Christ might be glorified! Yea, at
the very time of writing this letter he was the
prisoner of the Lord in a Roman prison, while
saints at Philippi, some of them at least, were
living in comfort and slothfulness, and some even
stooping to quarreling among themselves. The
apostle's words in verse 30 would prove, surely,
a home-thrust to such as these, stirring heart and
conscience, as they contrasted their easy-going
lives with the sufferings of Christ's dear servant,
who was in prison because of his unselfish devotion to the Lord he loved. May we learn to walk
in the same spirit, and mind the same things!

CHAPTER TWO

CHRIST THE BELIEVER'S EXAMPLE

"Others"

(vers. 1-4.)

"If there be therefore any consolation in Christ, if any comfort of love, if any fellowship of the Spirit, if any bowels and mercies, fulfil ye my joy, that ye be like-minded, having the same love, being of one accord, of one mind. Let nothing be done through strife or vainglory; but in lowliness of mind let each esteem other better than themselves. Look not every man on his own things, but every man also on the things of others."

THE last word of this section is the keynote —"*others.*" This was the overpowering, dominating note in the life of our Lord on earth, and because of this He died. "He came not to be ministered unto, but to minister, and to give his life a ransom for"—*others!* He lived for *others;* He died for *others.* Selfishness He knew not. Unselfish devotion for the good of *others* summed up His whole life, and all in subjection to the Father's will. For God, the Father Himself, lives, reverently be it said, for *others.* He finds His delight, His joy, in lavishing blessing on *others.* He pours His rain, and sends His sunshine upon the just and the unjust alike. He gave His Son for *others;* and having not withheld His own Son, but delivered Him up for us all, how will He not with Him also freely give us all things?—we, who are included in the *others* for whom the Lord Jesus Christ endured so much. What wonder then that, if we would follow His steps, we find ourselves called upon to live for *others*, and even to lay down our lives for the brethren!

In the first verse, the "if" does not imply that there might not be consolation in Christ, comfort of love, and fellowship of the Spirit, coupled with tender mercies toward all for whom Christ died; it rather has the force of *since*—it is an intensive form of saying, Since you know there are consolations and comforts in Christ. If these things are blessed realities, how incongruous for a believer to act as though they were non-existent! Drinking in the spirit of Christ, we exemplify the mind of Christ. And so the apostle exhorts the saints to fulfil his cup of joy by likemindedness among themselves, with equal love toward one another, being of one accord, of one mind.

It is very evident that Christians will never see eye to eye on all points. We are so largely influenced by habits, by environment, by education, by the measure of intellectual and spiritual apprehension to which we have attained, that it is an impossibility to find any number of people who look at everything from the same standpoint. How then can such be of one mind? The apostle himself explains it elsewhere when he says, "I think also that I have the mind of Christ." The "mind of Christ" is the lowly mind. And, if we are all of *this* mind, we shall walk together in love, considering one another, and seeking rather to be helpers of one another's faith, than challenging each other's convictions.

This is emphasized in the third verse, "Let nothing be done through strife or vainglory." It is possible, as verses 15 and 16 of chapter one have already shown us, to be controlled by this spirit of strife and vainglory, even in connection with the holy things of the Lord; but Paul himself has furnished us a beautiful example of that lowliness of mind of which he speaks, when he could rejoice even though Christ were preached in contention.

Nothing is less suited to a follower of the meek and lowly Son of Man than a contentious spirit, and vainglorious bearing. Boasting and bitter words ill become one who has taken the place of death with Christ. If, in lowliness of mind, each esteems others better than himself, how impossible for strife and contention to come in. Alas, that it is so much easier to speak or write of these things than to practically demonstrate them!

It is not in the natural man to live out what is

here inculcated. The man after the flesh "looks
out for number one," as he puts it, and is fond of
reminding himself, and his fellows, that "charity
begins at home." But the Christian is exhorted to
look, not on his own things, but on the things of
others. A heavenly principle this, surely, and only
to be attained by a heavenly man, one who walks
in fellowship with Him who came from heaven to
manifest His love for *others*. It is characteristic
of man's deceitful natural heart to suppose that
his greatest pleasure can be found in ministering
to his own desires. But the truest happiness is the
result of unselfish devotion to the things of *others*.
Were this ever kept in mind, what unhappy experiences would many of God's dear children be
spared, and how glad and joyous would fellowship
in Christ become.

"The Kenosis"
(chap. 2: 5-8.)

"Let this mind be in you, which was also in Christ Jesus:
who, being in the form of God, thought it not robbery to
be equal with God, but made Himself of no reputation, and
took upon Him the form of a servant, and was made in the
likeness of men. And being found in fashion as a man,
He humbled Himself, and became obedient unto death,
even the death of the cross."

WE now come to consider one of the most sub-
blime and wonderful mysteries in all Scripture:

what has been called by theologians, "The Doctrine of the Kenosis." The title comes from the Greek expression, rendered in our Authorized Version, "made Himself of no reputation"—an expression which really means "emptied Himself," or "divested Himself." Its full force will come before us as we proceed with our study.

It is a noticeable thing that doctrines are never presented in Scripture merely as dogmas to be accepted by the faithful on pain of expulsion from the Christian company. The most important doctrines are brought in by the Holy Spirit in what we might call an exceedingly natural way. I do not use the word "natural" here in contrast to "spiritual," but rather in the sense simply of sequence to the subject, introduced without special emphasis. In this particular instance before us, the doctrine of our Lord's self-emptying comes in simply as the supreme illustration of that lowliness of mind which should characterize all who profess to be followers of the Saviour. It follows naturally upon the exhortation of the fourth verse, which we have already considered.

"Let this mind be in you, which was also in Christ Jesus" is the way the subject is introduced. This mind is the lowly mind, as it is written, "Even Christ pleased not Himself." And the exemplification of this is at once abruptly intro-

Notes on Philippians

duced. He existed from all eternity in the form of God. It is a declaration of His true Deity. No *creature* could exist in the form of God. Lucifer aspired to this, and for his impiety was hurled down from the archangel's throne. Our Lord Jesus Christ was in the full enjoyment of this by right, because He was the eternal Son. He thought equality with God not a thing to be grasped or held on to. Equal with God He was, but He chose to take the place of subjection and lowliness. He chose to step down from that sublime height which belonged to Him, even "the glory which He had with the Father before the world was," and took the servant's form to do the Father's will.

The first man aspired to be as God, and fell. The second man, the Lord from heaven, came, as we sometimes sing,

> "From Godhead's fullest glory,
> Down to Calvary's depth of woe."

He would not retain the outward semblance of Deity. He relinquished His rightful position to become the Saviour of sinners. In order to do this He emptied Himself, or divested Himself, of His divine prerogatives.

Let there be no mistake as to this. While we reverently put off our shoes from our feet, and draw near to behold this great sight, let us not fear to accept the declaration of Holy Scripture in all its fulness. He divested Himself of something —but of what? Not of His Deity, for that could not be. He was ever the Son of the Father, and, as such, a divine person. He could take manhood into union with Deity, but He could not cease to be Divine. Of what, then, did He divest Himself? Surely of His rights as God the Son. He chose to come to earth to take a place of subjection. He took upon Him the form of a servant, and was made in the likeness of men.

Observe the distinction brought out in these two verses. He existed from all eternity in the form of God. He came here to take the form of a servant. Angels are servants, but "He took not hold of angels," we are told in the epistle to the Hebrews (chap. 2: 16, *N. Trans.*). He became in the likeness of men. It was all voluntary on His part. And, as a man on earth, He chose to be guided by the Holy Spirit. He daily received from the Father, through the Word of God, the instruction which it became Him, as a Man, to receive. His mighty works of power were not wrought by His own divine omnipotence alone. He chose that they should be wrought in the power of the Holy Spirit. This is the precious and important doctrine of the Kenosis as revealed in Scripture in contrast with the false teaching of men.

Men have added to this what Scripture does *not* say. They have declared that, when He came to earth, He ceased to be God; that He became but an ignorant Galilean peasant. Hence His knowledge of divine mysteries was no greater than what might have been expected of any other good man of His day and generation. Therefore His testimony as to the inspiration of Scripture has no real weight. He did not know more than others of His day knew. He was not competent to speak as to the authors of the Old Testament books. He thought Daniel wrote the book that bears his name, and that Moses penned the Pentateuch. But the wiseacres of to-day do not hesitate to declare that He was wrong, and they base their declaration on the position above taken. He emptied Himself of His divine knowledge they say, therefore He could not speak with authority.

The Exaltation of the Man Christ Jesus
(chap. 2: 9-11.)

"Wherefore God also hath highly exalted Him, and given Him a name which is above every name: that at the name of Jesus every knee should bow, of things in heaven, and things in earth, and things under the earth (or, of heavenly, earthly, and infernal beings), and that every tongue should confess that Jesus Christ is Lord, to the glory of God the Father."

THIS is the glorious fulfilment of the prophecy of the 110th psalm—a prophecy used by our Lord to confound the cavillers of His day, who professed to be waiting for the promised Messiah, but rejected His deity. "Jehovah said unto my Lord, Sit Thou at my right hand, until I make thine enemies thy footstool." He is David's Son— the Branch of David, yet David calls Him Lord, because He is likewise the Root of David. He descended from Jesse's son, yet the son of Jesse came into being through Him. His exaltation as man to the throne of God is not only Jehovah's attestation of perfect satisfaction in His work, but also the recognition of His equality with Himself. This Man, who had so humbled Himself as to go even to the death of the cross, is Jehovah's Fellow, as Zechariah 13:7 declares. Of none but a Divine person could such language be rightly used.

It is interesting to notice that God never permitted one indignity to be put upon the body of His Son after His work was finished, as the Roman soldier, having pierced His side, released the atoning blood. No enemies' hands thenceforth touched it. Loving disciples tenderly took it down from the cross, and reverently laid it away in Joseph's new tomb after wrapping it in the linen clothes.

Then, upon the expiration of the time appointed, He who had died came forth in resurrection-life, and God the Father received Him up into glory. He has highly exalted Him, and given Him a name which is above every Name. He is the preeminent one in every sphere. How suited it is that His glory should thus answer to His shame. "*As* many were astonished at Him...*so* shall He astonish many nations" (Isa. 52: 14, 15, *literal rendering*). God has ordained it, and so it must be. At the name of Jesus—His personal name, which means Jehovah-the-Saviour — the name borne upon the title placed above His head as He hung upon the cross — every knee shall bow: heavenly, earthly, and infernal beings—all must own Him Lord of all.

Observe that here, where it is a question of the recognition of His authority, three spheres are brought in, comprising all created intelligent beings—in heaven, earth and hell. There will be no exceptions. All must confess His Lordship to the glory of God the Father. All must bow in lowly submissiveness at the mention of the name of the Crucified.

Does this then imply universal salvation, even the final restoration of Satan and his hosts, as some have taught? Surely not. *Subjugation* is one thing; *reconciliation* is another. When the latter is in question, we have but two spheres mentioned, as in Col. 1: 20: "Having made peace by the blood of his cross, by Him to reconcile all things unto Himself; by Him, I say, whether they be things in earth or things in heaven." There is here no mention of the underworld. The lost will never be reconciled. Heaven and earth will eventually be filled with happy beings who have been redeemed to God by the precious blood of Christ. Then reconciliation will be complete.

But "under the earth" will be those who "have their part" in the outer darkness, the lake of fire. They flaunted Christ's authority on earth. They will have to own it in hell! They refused to heed the call of grace and be reconciled to God in the day when they might have been saved. In the pit of woe no gospel message will ever be proclaimed, but the authority of the Lord Jesus Christ will be supremely enforced there too. There will be no disorder in hell; no further rebellion will be permitted. All must bow at the name of Jesus, and every tongue confess Him Lord. Scripture depicts no wild pandemonium when describing the abode of the lost.

How blessed to own His Lordship now, according as it is written, "That if thou shalt confess with thy mouth Jesus as Lord, and shalt believe in thy heart that God hath raised Him from the dead, thou shalt be saved. For with the heart man believeth unto righteousness; and with the mouth confession is made unto salvation" (Rom.

10: 9, 10). How fitting it is that such, and such alone, should be eternally saved as a result of the work of the Cross.

"Working out Salvation"

(chap. 2: 12-16.)

"Wherefore, my beloved, as ye have always obeyed, not as in my presence only, but now much more in my absence, work out your own salvation with fear and trembling. For it is God which worketh in you both to will and to do of his good pleasure. Do all things without murmurings and disputings: that ye may be blameless and harmless, the sons of God, without rebuke, in the midst of a crooked and perverse nation, among whom ye shine as lights in the world; holding forth the word of life; that I may rejoice in the day of Christ, that I have not run in vain, neither labored in vain."

HAVING thus occupied the hearts of the saints at Philippi with the self-abnegation of our Lord Jesus Christ, the apostle, as guided by the Holy Spirit, goes on, in the balance of this chapter, to apply the truth in a practical way.

First, the verses now before us refer to assembly-life and responsibility. Then, from verse 17 to the end of this chapter, three men are brought before us who were seeking to manifest in their lives the devotedness and self-denying concern for others that was seen in Christ as a Man on earth.

Verse 12 has often perplexed those who thought they saw clearly from Scripture the simplicity of salvation by grace, apart from works. Here, in seeming contrast to this, the apostle tells the saints to work out their own salvation, and that with fear and trembling, as though possibly there were danger that salvation might be forfeited because of failure in properly working it out.

Notice first, however, that the apostle does not speak of working *for* salvation, but of working it *out*, which is a very different thing. One might instance the quaint saying of the little girl who listened to a legal sermon preached upon this text by a minister who was insisting that none could be saved by grace alone, but all must work out their own salvation. Innocently she asked at the close of the service, "Mother, how can you work it out if you haven't got it in?" If it were individual salvation that is here contemplated, it might be enough to say—it is your own; therefore manifest it — work it out. But there is really more than this. For, taken in its full connection, it will be seen the passage refers to assembly salvation, rather than to the individual: that is, direction is given to an assembly of Christians (exposed to difficulties from without and from within, passing through a world where all is in opposition to the testimony committed to them), showing them how to go on in fellowship together in spite of the fact that each individual has within him a corrupt nature, which will manifest itself to the detriment of the whole assembly, if given occasion.

We have already noticed that there was some difficulty in the Philippian assembly, between two sisters of prominence, Euodia and Syntyche. This might easily become the occasion for distressing quarrels, and even division, if not judged in the presence of the Lord. Similar things might arise from time to time, and would need to be carefully watched against. When the apostle himself was with them, they could refer all such matters to him, and he would, so to speak, work out their salvation from these perplexities. He would advise and guide as needed. Now he is far away, a prisoner for the gospel's sake, and cannot personally give the help he might desire. He, therefore, directs them in his absence, as obedient children, to work out their own salvation in godly fear, and with exercise of soul, lest they depart from the right path, or miss the mind of God.

Viewed from this standpoint, how salutary are his words for all future generations of Christians! There is no assembly of saints on earth but will probably, sooner or later, have its internal differences, and the advice or command here given applies in just such cases. It is God's way that assemblies should be put right from within, by self-judgment in His presence and submission to His word.

How often do saints take the very opposite method. Questions arise to trouble and perplex; differences of judgment occur, and bickerings and quarrels begin. Instead of coming together in the presence of God for humiliation and guidance, seeking His mind from His own Word and acting accordingly, they apply to this one or that one outside for help—often only to have things worse complicated. Those engaged in the ministry of the Word, traveling from place to place, are perhaps appealed to, and requested to adjudicate in matters which often only disturb their spirits, and, after all, cannot really effect the salvation of the assembly from the troubles that have arisen.

It is easy to see how the clerical system arose, from such experiences. We see in the early Church, men of the stamp of Diotrephes, who loved to have the pre-eminence, and Nicolaitanes, that is, rulers of the people, who sought to bring the saints into bondage. And, on the other hand, it was very early made manifest that believers generally found it much easier to apply to noted preachers or teachers for help, than to be cast directly upon God and His Word themselves. Thus gifted men became a court of appeal, and, eventually, were recognized as "the clergy." The same principle easily creeps in wherever saints look to men rather than to God and His Word. If it be said that they are too ignorant to know how to settle their differences, yet let it be remembered they have God, and the word of His grace; and if there be but humility and waiting upon Him, refusing to move until they find direction in the Book, He can be depended upon to help them work out their own salvation from whatever perplexing circumstances have arisen. He does not cast them upon their own resources, but on His Word, on Himself, who works in them the will to do His good pleasure. This does not mean that they should ignore or despise the advice and sound judgment of others—but they are not dependent upon it.

In verses 14 to 16 we see this working out of assembly salvation practically demonstrated. Murmurings and disputings must be judged in the presence of God. Instead of backbiting, and gossiping about matters, let the saints come together before the Lord, and deal with them in the light of His revealed Word. Thus they shall be blameless and harmless, the sons of God indeed, without rebuke; walking in a manner worthy of the Lord, in the midst of a crooked and perverse generation among whom they shine as lights in this dark world. Thus judging what would hinder fellowship within, they are in a suited condition to be a testimony to the power of grace to those without. And, as the apostle has already emphasized for us in chapter one, nothing so delivers believers from self-occupation as occupation with Christ and the presentation of Christ to those still in their sins. They who are busy holding forth the Word of Life have no time for selfish quarreling amongst themselves.

In so walking, the saints would give joy to the heart of the apostle, and he could rejoice in the day of Christ: that is, it would be manifest at His judgment-seat that his labors in Philippi had not been in vain. The godly order and devoted gospel testimony would together witness to the reality of the work of God in and among them.

Thus we see that "working out our own salvation" is simply submitting to the truth of God after we have been saved, in order that we may glorify Him, whether as individuals or assemblies of saints in the place of testimony. This will be "with fear and trembling" as we realize our liability to err, the faultiness of our understanding and the holiness of the One whom we are called to serve in this scene.

The Mind of Christ Exemplified in the Apostle Paul
(chap. 2: 17, 18.)

"Yea, and if I be offered upon the sacrifice and service of your faith, I joy, and rejoice with you all. For the same cause also do ye joy, and rejoice with me."

THE apostolic writer now goes on to cite, though in an apparently casual way, three examples of men of like passions with their fellow-believers, who have exemplified in their ways the spirit of Christ. The first of these is himself, and of his testimony we shall now speak. The other two are Timothy and Epaphroditus, whose lowly ways and devoted service will occupy us later.

Possibly no other mortal man ever drank into the spirit of Christ so deeply as the great apostle to the Gentiles. Once a proud, haughty Pharisee, glorying in his own righteousness, burning with indignant bigotry against any who pretended to a higher revelation than that given in Judaism, he had been transformed by a sight of the glorified Christ, when, religious persecutor as he was, he was hurrying to Damascus to apprehend any who confessed the name of Jesus. The sight of the once-crucified, but now enthroned Saviour, at God's right hand, was the means of a conversion so radical and so sudden, that probably no other since has been so intense.

From that moment it was the one desire of his soul, over-mastering all else, the inmost yearning of his being, to manifest Christ in all his ways. Yet he was not an absolutely sinless man, nor without the infirmities common to the human race. But he was one who ever sought to judge himself in the light of the Cross of Christ, with the power of Christ resting upon him. His whole philosophy of life is summed up in his fervent words to the Galatians, "But God forbid that I should glory, save in the cross of our Lord Jesus Christ, by whom the world is crucified unto me, and I unto the world" (Gal. 6: 14).

It was in this spirit that he could write to his beloved Philippians, "Yea, and if I be offered (literally "poured out") upon the sacrifice and service of your faith, I joy, and rejoice with you all." He had just told them that his joy in the day of Christ would be to find them approved, as having walked before God in this scene as unrebuked saints earnestly engaged in holding forth the word of life in a dark world: their abundant service and the reward meted out to them, he would look upon as reward to himself. He would thus feel that he had not run in vain, neither labored in vain. He was willing to count all his service as but an adjunct of theirs; to have their labors and devotedness looked upon as the completion of a work of which his was just the beginning.

In order properly to understand this 17th verse, it is necessary to observe carefully what the apostle has in mind. When he says, "If I be poured out upon the sacrifice of your faith," he alludes to the drink-offering. This was a cup of wine, which was poured out upon the burnt-offering, and was typical of the out-pouring of our Lord Jesus Christ's soul unto death; the voluntary surrender of everything that might naturally be expected to contribute to his joys as a man. Wine is the symbol of gladness. What man ever deserved to be happier than the Lord Jesus Christ? To whom was gladness a righteous due, if not to Him? Yet, in infinite grace, He became "a Man of sorrows and acquainted with grief." The burnt-offering spoke of Him in the highest sense as offering Himself without spot to God, but on our behalf. In the sacrificial service, the burnt-offering having been slain was cut in its pieces, was washed with water, then laid in order upon the fire of the altar and wholly consumed. The drink-offering was simply poured out upon it, and in a moment was lost to sight. Now, with this in mind, consider the beauty of the figure the apostle here employs. Whatever service the Philippians might be able to render to the Lord, would be in fellowship with Christ, and thus their devotedness could be viewed as an offering or a sacrifice of a sweet-smelling savor unto God. It was the result of lives surrendered to the Lord, and Paul was willing that his labor should be simply looked upon as the adjunct of theirs; as the drink-offering poured upon the burnt-offering.

What sublime self-abnegation was this! What delight in the labors of others! What absence of that which sometimes is so abhorrent in professed Christian service to-day! Laborers sometimes are jealous of the ministry of others, and envious of a success in which they think they have not shared. There was no such spirit in the apostle Paul. He rejoiced in everything that the Lord did through others, and his jealousy was only for the glory of God.

And so in this he followed Christ, and he could confidently appeal to them to follow him, as he walked in His steps. So he would have them joy and rejoice with him in the mutual devotedness of both.

It is significant that he speaks of himself and his service in this incidental way—in but one verse. When he turns to write of his fellow-laborer, Timothy, and of their messenger, Epaphroditus, how much more he has to say. He could dwell with delight on the labors and service

of others, but when writing of himself, as he tells
us elsewhere, he felt as though he were speaking
as a fool.

Timothy, the Unselfish Pastor
(chap. 2: 19-24.)

"But I trust in the Lord Jesus to send Timotheus shortly
unto you, that I also may be of good comfort, when I know
your state. For I have no man likeminded, who will naturally care for your state. For all seek their own, not
the things which are Jesus Christ's. But ye know the
proof of him, that, as a son with the father, he hath
served with me in the gospel. Him therefore I hope to
send presently, so soon as I shall see how it will go with
me. But I trust in the Lord that I also myself shall come
shortly."

PAUL was not only an ardent evangelist, but
he was also the prince of teachers, and, like his
fellow-apostle Peter, a true pastor, or shepherd,
of the flock of Christ. In this latter respect the
young preacher Timothy was his ardent imitator.
Whatever other gifts he may have had, that special gift which was given him in connection with
the laying on of the elder brethren's hands, when
he went out in the work of the Lord, was probably that of the pastor. This is perhaps one of the
rarest, and yet one of the most needed, of all the
gifts given by an ascended Christ for the edification of His Church. The evangelist ministers to
those without Christ; the teacher instructs those

already saved; the pastor is more concerned about the state of soul of the believer than as to his knowledge of abstract truth, though recognizing, of course, that saints are formed by the truth, and that a right state of soul and a walk in the truth go together.

Paul, therefore, was anxious to send Timothy to Philippi, that he might be a help and a means of blessing to the assembly there, trusting that he might be used of God to weld their hearts into one, and deliver them from the dissensions that had come in through the misunderstanding between Euodia and Synteche. He felt that he could depend on Timothy's judgment, and he counted on being himself comforted when he actually knew their state.

As often pointed out by others, and clearly developed in different parts of Scripture, our standing before God is one thing, our actual state is another. It was as to the latter that Paul was concerned. He did not know of anyone else with the same unselfish shepherd-heart as Timothy, who would whole-souledly care for their state. The word "naturally" does not adequately give the thought. Timothy's pastoral concern was not a gift of nature, but a spiritual one, the result of exercise of soul before God; and his whole soul was stirred with concern for the Lord's people.

Of others, however gifted in various ways, the apostle could only sadly say, "They seek their own, and not the things which are Jesus Christ's."

It is quite possible to be an admired teacher, upon whose words thousands hang, or an eloquent evangelist with eager multitudes flocking to listen with delight to his messages, and yet be a vain self-seeker, using the very gift that God has given, for personal aggrandizement, or to obtain wealth, even while professing to care little or nothing for money. But the more marked the pastoral gift, of very necessity the more unselfishly devoted must the servant be. It will be his great ambition to feed the flock and shield them from their dangers.

The patriarch Jacob is an apt illustration of the true shepherd. Despite all his failures, and the fact that he was largely under the discipline of God through the greater part of his life, he was, nevertheless, a lover of the flock, and ever considerate of their interests. Speaking to Laban, his father-in-law, he could honestly say, as he looked back over his years of caring for the sheep, "Thus I was; in the day the drought consumed me, and the frost by night; and my sleep departed from mine eyes" (Gen. 31:40). And in expostulating with his brother Esau, who would have him hurry on with all his host, he says, "My lord knoweth

that the children are tender, and the flocks and
herds with young are with me: and if men should
overdrive them one day, all the flock will die"
(Gen. 33:13). A Diotrephes might try to cajole
or coerce the flock into submission to his own im-
perious will, but a God-appointed shepherd will
seek to lead on safely, wearing himself out for the
blessing of others—not seeking to impress his own
will, but to serve the Lord, and to exalt Him.

As a son with a father, Timothy had commended himself to the aged apostle, serving with him
in the gospel in all lowliness and humility. Youth
is often exceedingly energetic, and impatient of
restraint. Age is inclined, perhaps, to be over-
cautious and slow in coming to conclusions, and it
often is a great difficulty for two, so wide apart in
years as Paul and Timothy, to labor together happily. But where the younger man manifests the
spirit that was in Timothy, and the elder seeks
only the glory of God and the blessing of His people, such fellowship in service becomes indeed
blessed.

Having thus proven himself, Paul could trust
Timothy on a mission such as that upon which he
was about to send him. He was waiting to learn
the outcome of his appeal to Cæsar, and then he
hoped to send him on to Philippi to be a healer of
dissensions, and thus a means of cheer and con-

solation to the assembly. Timothy followed **Paul** as he followed Christ; he thus became the second in this company of men who were worthy to be held up as examples of those who manifested the mind of Christ.

It was the apostle's desire and hope to follow later himself and again visit his beloved Philippians; but whether this yearning was ever fulfilled we perhaps shall never know, until all is manifested at the judgment-seat of Christ. Precious is the faith that can leave all with Him, assured that His ways are always perfect—always best!

Epaphroditus, the Devoted Messenger
(chap. 2: 25-30.)

"Yet I supposed it necessary to send to you Epaphroditus, my brother, and companion in labor, and fellow-soldier, but your messenger, and he that ministered to my wants. For he longed after you all, and was full of heaviness, because ye had heard that he had been sick. For indeed he was sick, nigh unto death: but God had mercy on him; and not on him only, but on me also, lest I should have sorrow upon sorrow. I sent him therefore the more carefully, that, when ye see him again, ye may rejoice, and that I may be the less sorrowful. Receive him therefore in the Lord with all gladness; and hold such in reputation; because for the work of Christ he was nigh unto death, not regarding his life, to supply your lack of service toward me."

IT was Epaphroditus who had brought the bounty of the Philippian saints to Paul, their father in Christ. Burning with love towards the Lord's dear servant who was shut up in prison for the gospel's sake, he took the long journey from Macedonia to Rome, the world's metropolis (whether by land or sea we have now no means of knowing), in order to assure him of the love and esteem of the assembly, and relieve his necessities by their gift.

Having accomplished his purpose, he fell sick, possibly overcome by the Roman fever, so dangerous to strangers unacclimated. That his illness was a protracted one is evident, for, ere he became convalescent, time enough had elapsed for word of his condition to reach the Philippians, and for a return message to get back to him, expressing their solicitude for his health and anxiety that he be restored to them again. It is touching to notice that Epaphroditus himself did not seem to be nearly so much concerned about his own illness as he was that it had been the cause of sorrow to them. He was one of those thoroughly self-denying men whose motto might well be expressed in the one word upon which we have already dwelt, "Others."

Now that he was well again he was anxious to be on his way, in order that he might comfort the assembly by his presence among them again, and by bringing to them this Philippian epistle, though it must have been hard for him to leave the apostle still a prisoner. It is evident from verse three of chapter four that he acted as amanuensis in the writing of this letter, which precious parchment he carried to Philippi, and thus preserved it for us and for all saints to the end of time—yea, and we may say forever!

Of Epaphroditus we know nothing save what is here recorded, unless, as some think, he is to be identified with the Epaphras mentioned in the epistle to the Colossions. Epaphroditus means "favored of Aphrodite"—the Greek goddess of love and beauty, answering to the Roman Venus. This makes it manifest that he was of heathen parentage, but he had been brought to know Christ. Epaphras is said to be a diminutive of the same word with the name of the heathen goddess omitted, and therefore simply meaning "graced" or "favored."

Having been won to Christ, he was characterized by a godly zeal to make Him known to others, and to build up and lead on those already saved. He was the exemplification of the mind of Christ as set forth in the beginning of this chapter. He may not have been physically strong; but, at any rate, he was a man who did not spare himself; and for the work of Christ he was sick, nigh unto death. It is evident that sickness is not always the result of sin, as some have taught. In the case of this devoted man of God, it was the result of his self-denying activity on behalf of those to whom he ministered. His illness was the cause of deep sorrow to Paul himself, and, no doubt, led to much prayer on his behalf, and God answered, showing mercy, and raised him up.

Let it be noted that the apostle did not consider he had any right to demand physical healing even for so faithful a laborer as Epaphroditus. Paul recognized it as simply the mercy of God, not as that to which saints have a right. This is true divine healing. And let it be remembered that sickness may be as really from God as health. It is clear that Paul never held or taught "healing in the atonement," and therefore the birth-right privilege of all Christians. Nor do we ever read of him or his fellow-laborers being miraculously healed. Paul himself, Trophimus, Timothy and Epaphroditus, all bear witness to the contrary. The apostle urges the saints to receive their messenger, when he should return to them, with all gladness, and commands them to hold such in reputation, because for the work of Christ he had been sick, nigh unto death, not regarding his life in order to serve Paul in their stead.

Such are the men whom God delights to honor. Like the Lord Jesus, Epaphroditus made himself of no reputation, and because of his very lowliness he is to be held in reputation. The man who holds himself as one worthy of honor and esteem is not the one whom God calls upon the saints thus to recognize; but he who is willing to take the lowly path, seeking not great things for himself, is the man whom the Lord will exalt in due time.

Salutary lessons are thus manifested in all these three devoted men of God, upon whose self-denying ways we have meditated. May we have grace to follow them as they followed Christ!

CHAPTER THREE

CHRIST, THE BELIEVER'S OBJECT, AND THE STEADFAST MIND

"Rejoice"

(vers. 1-3.)

"Finally, my brethren, rejoice in the Lord. To write the same things to you, to me indeed is not grievous, but for you it is safe. Beware of dogs, beware of evil workers, beware of the concision. For we are the circumcision, which worship God in the Spirit, and rejoice in Christ Jesus, and have no confidence in the flesh."

CAREFUL students of the epistles of Paul cannot but notice a peculiarity that frequently occurs in them. Having concluded the main part of his treatise, he seems about to come to an abrupt conclusion, then suddenly is moved by the Spirit of God to launch out into an altogether different line of things, which comes in as a kind of a parenthesis, ere he actually finishes his letter. An instance of this may be seen in the epistle to the Ephesians by comparing the first verses of chapters three and four. It is plain that all of chapter three, after verse one, comes in parenthetically, and in chapter four he concludes what he started to say. Here in Philippians we have a similar case: "Finally, my brethren," he

writes, "rejoice in the Lord;" and yet, when we
come to chapter 4:8, where he introduces his
closing remarks, we again have the same expression: "Finally, brethren." All of chapter 3 is a
new subject, which, as we might think, he had
no intention of discussing until pressed by the
Holy Spirit to bring in a message for which we
can truly thank God, as we would have lost much
precious ministry had it been omitted.

It has often been said that this letter is the
epistle of joy, and indeed it is. The apostle himself writes with his own heart filled with the joyful recollection of his past experiences in connection with those scenes so dear to him, and he desires them to fulfil his joy, to share with him in
the gladness that was his in Christ; and so we
have this brief exhortation, "Rejoice in the Lord."
Circumstances may at times be anything but con-
ducive to either peace or gladness, yet the trusting soul can always look above the fitful scenes of
earth to the throne where Christ sits exalted as
Lord at God's right hand. He is over all. There
are no second causes with Him. "Shall there be
evil in the city and the Lord hath not done it?"
asks the prophet. It is "evil," not in the sense of
sin, of course, but of *calamity*, even if that calamity be the result of sin; nevertheless, it cannot
come save as permitted by the Lord. And know-

ing that "All things work together for good to those who love God, who are the called according to His purpose," why should the believer either doubt or fear? Waves may roll high; stormy winds may beat tempestuously; all to which the heart had clung may seem to be swept away; but Christ abides unchanged and unchangeable, the everlasting portion of those who trust His grace.

We read on one occasion how David, when the people spoke of stoning him because of a calamitous event for which they held him largely responsible, "encouraged himself in the Lord his God." "The joy of the Lord is your strength," Nehemiah reminded the remnant of Israel; and ere returning to the Father's house from which He came, the Lord Jesus imparted His joy to the trembling company of His disciples. Therefore it is not only the Christian's privilege, but we may even say, his duty, to constantly rejoice in the Lord. Holiness and happiness are intimately linked together.

And yet how often we need to be reminded of this; as our apostle does here: "To write the same things to you to me indeed is not irksome, but for you it is safe." It is well that we should frequently be exhorted to "rejoice in the Lord." But now the mind of the Spirit refers to another line of things entirely. For our busy enemy has so many agencies through which he seeks to rob us of that joy in the Lord which is our rightful portion, that three times over in the second verse we have the significant word "beware."

"Beware of dogs." The Jew used this opprobrious title when speaking of the Gentiles who did not bear in their bodies the mark of the Abrahamic covenant. But in the prophet Isaiah, God uses the term to distinguish false pastors or shepherds in Israel: "His watchmen are blind: they are all ignorant, they are all dumb dogs, they cannot bark; sleeping, lying down, loving to slumber. Yea, they are greedy dogs which can never have enough, and they are shepherds that cannot understand: they all look to their own way, every one for his gain, from his quarter" (Isa. 56: 10, 11). And it is plain that when the apostle Peter says, " The dog has turned to his own vomit again," it symbolizes the false religious teacher going back to the things he once professed to abhor.

Now the Philippians, like the early Christians in general, were peculiarly exposed to the ravages of such "dogs." Evil teachers they were, from Judaism, among the flock of Christ, with the purpose of perverting the saints, and leading them back into bondage; and that for their own selfish ends; they are here, by the Holy Spirit, designated by this opprobrious term. They were introducing themselves among the assemblies of God to rend the flock of Christ, that they might have special recognition as leaders in the new company. Professing to be ministers of Christ, they were in reality servants of Satan, as their works proved. No heart have they for the afflicted sheep and lambs for whom Christ died. They would feed themselves, and not the flock, and their judgment is assured.

Consequently he adds, "Beware of evil workers." We need not necessarily distinguish the evil workers from the dogs, for false teachers, whatever their profession of righteousness, are, nevertheless, workers of iniquity. Another figure employed by the Lord in referring to the same general class, is that of "wolves in sheeps' clothing"—deceiving, misleading, destroying, working havoc among those who confess Christ's precious name. Legality, while professing to have in view greater righteousness than that produced by grace, yet proves to be, as the law itself is, simply "the strength of sin" (see 1 Cor. 15: 56).

"Beware of the concision," says the apostle — *i. e.,* mere mutilators of the body. It is a contemptuous term he uses to designate those who taught that the observance of circumcision was imperative to give one a full standing before God.

The apostle will not allow that the mere ordinance is really circumcision. The only true circumcision since the Cross is, not a carnal ordinance, but the putting off of the sins of the flesh—the heart-recognition of the fact that the flesh has been put to death in the cross of Christ. It is only as the soul enters into this, and uses the sharp knife of self-judgment upon the flesh, that one is delivered from its power.

The mere externalists, including legalists and ritualists of all descriptions, always make more of ordinances and outward forms than of the condition of the soul and the spiritual truths symbolized by those ordinances. In Israel we may see this in the fullest way. They boasted themselves of their connection with the temple of the Lord, and gloried in ordinances and legal observances, while actually far from God and under His disapproval. Nor should Christians forget that it is just as possible for believers now to be occupied with ordinances and church position, while forgetting the more important things of true piety and self-judgment. Nothing that God has commanded is unimportant; but our Lord said to the Jews of His times, concerning their intense regard for ordinances and neglect of justice and mercy, "These ought ye to have done, and not to have left the other undone."

In the third verse, we have four distinct statements made, which we do well to consider in detail.

First: "We are the circumcision," that is, we are those who have accepted by faith the end of all flesh in the cross of Christ. We recognize its utter corruption and its powerlessness for service to God, even though placed under the most careful training and supervision. We have, therefore, put it off in the cross of Christ, "Where there is neither Greek nor Jew, circumcision nor uncircision, Barbarian, Scythian, bond nor free; but Christ is all, and in all" (Col. 3:11). We began with God by accepting the mark of judgment upon the flesh; we do not now look for anything good in it, but triumph only in Christ.

Second: "We worship by the Spirit of God." The worship of the old dispensation was largely of a ritualistic character, but the Lord Jesus told the Samaritan woman, "The hour is coming, and now is, when the true worshipers shall worship the Father in spirit and in truth." Outward forms and services, music and genuflections, do not constitute worship. They may even be hindrances to it. Real worship is that of the heart, when the Spirit of God takes of the things of Christ and shows them unto us. As we are occupied with

Him, true praise and adoration ascend to the Father.

Third: "We glory in Christ Jesus." Our boast is in the Lord. We are, ourselves, utterly unprofitable, having nothing about us to commend us to Him who, in grace, has saved us. All our boast is in His loving-kindness and His mighty power exercised in mercy on our behalf.

Lastly he adds: "We have no confidence in the flesh." The flesh of the believer is no more to be trusted than the flesh of the vilest sinner. Regeneration is not a changing of flesh into spirit; nor is that sanctification in which we stand before God a gradual process of such a change within us. "That which is born of the flesh is flesh, and that which is born of the Spirit is spirit." The fleshly nature is never improved, and the new nature received in new birth does not require improvement. "The carnal mind is not subject to the law of God, neither indeed can be." And the spiritual mind is the mind of Christ. It is as we walk in the Spirit that we are delivered from the desires of the flesh. But even after years of godly living, the flesh itself is not one whit better than it was at the very beginning of our Christian life. Therefore, we dare not trust it, knowing that, however blessed the work of God is in our souls, "in our flesh dwells no good thing."

Self-confidence set aside for Christ

(chap. 3: 4-7.)

"Though I might also have confidence in the flesh. If any other man thinketh that he hath whereof he might trust in the flesh, I more: circumcised the eighth day, of the stock of Israel, of the tribe of Benjamin, a Hebrew of the Hebrews; as touching the law, a Pharisee; concerning zeal, persecuting the church; touching the righteousness which is in the law, blameless. But what things were gain to me, those I counted loss for Christ."

PAUL'S own experience comes in aptly to enforce the expression used in verse three, as to which we have been speaking. He had learned experimentally the utter unprofitableness of the flesh. Looked at from a human standpoint, he had far more to glory in before he was converted to Christ than any of the "concision" among the Philippians could possibly have even afterwards. If any had ground for confidence in the flesh, or thought he had, Paul could say, "I more." For they, to whom he wrote, were Gentiles according to natural birth, and, therefore, strangers to the covenants of promise, aliens, and without the true God in the world.

But it was otherwise with the apostle. He was born within the circle of the covenant. He bore upon his body the mark that he was within the sphere of the Abrahamic promise— he was circumcised on the eighth day, and thus marked off from the Gentile world. Nor were his parents "proselytes of the gate," as Gentiles were called who had forsaken idolatry, and, turning to the God of Abraham, Isaac and Jacob, had come within the blessings of the covenant through this rite. He, Paul, was of the stock of Israel; for generations back his family had belonged to the covenant people. Then, too, he was descended, not from a bond-woman but from the favorite wife of Jacob. Moreover, when the ten tribes revolted and turned away from the house of David, the particular tribe from which he sprung, that of Benjamin, had remained true to Jehovah's centre and loyal to the true kingly line. For though Benjamin had failed grievously in the days of the Judges, so that they were like to have been exterminated out of Israel, yet afterwards, through enabling grace, they remained steadfast in the face of grave departure, and thus won for themselves an immortal name. To be a Benjamite was something in which the flesh might well pride itself.

And as to positive religious conviction, Saul of Tarsus had been a Hebrew of the Hebrews. He was no mere Jew by birth, as some who are indifferent to their Hebrew faith. To the very core

of his being he was a follower of the first Hebrew, Abraham himself. As touching the law,
he was in practice, faith, and name, a Pharisee.
Of the various Jewish sects existing in his day,
the Pharisees were the most intensely orthodox,
and clung most tenaciously not only to the revealed word of God, but to a vast body of human
traditions which had been handed down from
their forefathers, and had become in their eyes
as sacred as the written Word itself. It is true that
our Lord describes many of them as hypocrites,
but on the other hand, when He wishes to emphasize the need of positive righteousness, He says,
"Except your righteousness exceeds that of the
scribes and Pharisees ye shall in no wise enter
into the kingdom of heaven." He would not have
thus spoken if it were not well known that the
Pharisees insisted on obedience to the law of
God; and Paul himself said, on another occasion,
"After the most straitest sect of our religion, I
lived a Pharisee." He lived what he professed,
and that was Judaism of the strictest kind.

His zeal for the traditions of the elders was
seen in the fact that he was a relentless persecutor of the newly-born assembly of God. "Exceedingly mad against them," as he himself confessed, he "persecuted them unto strange cities,"
and even "compelled them to blaspheme." Yet

there is no evidence that he was naturally a man of fierce and implacable disposition. In fact, the words of the glorified Lord, "It is hard for thee to kick against the goads," would seem to imply the contrary.* What he did, he did from a stern sense of duty, not as the fulfilment of his natural desires. Touching the righteousness which the law demanded, he was outwardly blameless. He tells us in the 7th of Romans that of all the commandments there was only one which really convicted him of sin, and the violation of that one commandment, there was no external way of detecting. Who that looked upon the stalwart champion of Jewish orthodoxy could see the covetousness that was in his heart? His outward life gave no evidence of it. Therefore he could speak of himself as blameless.

But when this religious bigot, this stern unyielding champion of what he believed to be the truth of God, was brought into contact with the glorified Christ—that never-to-be-forgotten day

---

*Does not the expression imply, however, that Saul had *fought* against the testimonies to his conscience?—such as Stephen's, whose face they saw "shining as an angel's" while testifying before the council of the Jews, yet to whose death Saul gave his vote, keeping the garments of those that stoned him. And how many other appeals to his conscience, if not to his heart, there must have been as he beat and dragged men and women to prison, compelling them to blaspheme Jesus, if possible!—[ED.

on the Damascus turn-pike—he realized in one moment the fact declared by the prophet that "all our righteousnesses are as *filthy rags.*" And these things which were gain to him—these things on which he had been building his hopes for eternity —these things which gave him a standing before the eyes of his fellows and caused them to look upon him with admiration, he now saw in their true light—as utterly worthless and polluted garments, unfit to cover him before the eyes of a holy God, and deserving only to be cast away. Therefore he exclaims, "What things were gain to me, those I counted loss for Christ."

Let it be carefully noted that he did not count them loss merely for Christianity. In other words, he was not simply exchanging one religion for another; it was not one system of rites and ceremonies giving place to a superior system; or one set of doctrines, rules and regulations making way for a better one. Often this has been all that conversion has meant. Many people have thought that "changing their religion" was all that God required of them. But it was otherwise with Saul. He had come into actual contact with a divine Person, the once crucified, but now glorified Christ of God. He had been won by that Person forever, and for His sake he counted all else but loss. If any fall short of this, they are missing entirely the point here emphasized. Christ, and Christ alone, meets every need of the soul. His work has satisfied God, and it satisfies the one who trusts in Him. By resting in Christ, confidence in the flesh is forever at an end. All confidence is in Him who died and rose again, and who ever liveth to make intercession for us.

Paul's Steadfast Purpose

(chap. 3: 8-11.)

"Yea, doubtless, and I count all things to be loss for the excellency of the knowledge of Christ Jesus my Lord: for whom I have suffered the loss of all things, and do count them but refuse that I may win Christ, and be found in Him, not having mine own righteousness which is of the law, but that which is through the faith of Christ, the righteousness which is of God by faith; that I may know Him and the power of his resurrection; and the fellowship of his sufferings, being made conformable unto his death; if by any means I might attain unto the out-resurrection from among the dead" (last part, literal rendering).

IT should be noted that many years of faithful witness-bearing intervene between verse 7, which closed our last section, and verse 8, which opens this. Not only had Paul counted all things but loss for Christ when first he saw His glory on the road to Damascus, but the long arduous years since had brought in no change as to this. He still counted all things to be of no worth as compared with that which had so dazzled the vision of his soul—the excellency of the knowledge of Christ Jesus the Lord. How different it is with many: fervent and self-sacrificing in their first love, how soon the fine gold of their devotedness becomes dimmed and their early freshness passes away! The world, which once seemed so worthless in view of the matchless glory shining in the face of the Saviour, begins again to exercise attractive power when the heart has "begun to wax wanton against Christ." It was blessedly otherwise with our apostle. Never for one moment did he go back on the great renunciation he had made when first won for that exalted Jesus whom he had ignorantly persecuted.

And so in this section of the epistle he reaffirms the faith with which he began. He still counted all that earth could offer as dross and refuse when placed alongside of Christ's surpassing glory, which was the one great object ever before him. And this was not with him mere mystical rhapsodizing, for already had he suffered the loss of all things, even of liberty itself, as we know (though in these verses he does not refer to it), and this was all in accord with the dominant purpose of his life, that he might win Christ and be found in Him in the great consummation.

It is not that he is putting the "being found in Christ" on the ground of attainment, or as something to be earned by self-abnegation, but he is letting us into the secret of the supreme emotion of his being. It is as though he were saying, "Ever since I saw Christ in the glory of God I have considered nothing else as worth living for. He has so won my heart that nothing now counts with me but the blessedness of knowing Him, of being completely identified with Him both in life and in death, yea, and beyond death. I would not stand before God in a righteousness of my own now if I could. I desire only to be found in Him. I long only to know Him more intimately, let the suffering involved be what it may; I would even die as He died at last, if need be—any way that He may choose, that at last, whatever way may lead me to it, I shall attain to the great rapture of all saints at His coming, the glorious out-resurrection from among the dead. This for me will be the goal attained which has been for so long before my soul; for then I shall be so completely identified with Him who has won my heart to Himself, that I shall be like Him forever, and with Him through all the ages to come."

I have sought thus to paraphrase his words in order that it may be clearly seen that there is here no element of uncertainty involved in them, as many have supposed, and some have taught. He did not fear that he might miss the first resurrection through unfaithfulness or lack of watchfulness. Nor was this out-resurrection from among the dead a matter of present experience (as the verses following show), but refers to .that one great event for which every instructed Christian should wait with eagerness—the coming of the Lord Jesus Christ and our gathering together unto Him.

To teach that the rapture is only for.certain devoted saints, and that even Paul himself was haunted with the fear that he would come short of it, would be to lose entirely the sense of the rich grace of God, which is to work in us that glorious change which will make us like Him for whom we wait. The uniform teaching of the apostle is that "they that are Christ's" shall rise "at His coming." And in this hope the aged prisoner of the Lord faced the prospect of martyrdom in its most cruel form. It would be but the appointed means by which he should attain unto the blessedness of the first resurrection.

Nor, it seems to me, can we with propriety say that what the apostle has in mind is the power of resurrection-life working in him here on earth so that he may live in the first-resurrection experience, as some have designated it. This would be dangerously near to the "death to nature" theories promulgated by earnest but misled men in the last century, and which resulted in grave departures from sobriety and scriptural order. None had more fully entered into that knowledge of "the power of His resurrection" in his human body than did the apostle, yet he puts the having part in the out-resurrection as the climax of all his years of devoted service. Everything would be incomplete without that. Nor do I know of any other place in the word of God where the expression is used as referring to a believer's experience. In fact there is added here a second preposition to intensify the thought of a selective resurrection; otherwise it is the regular expression which distinguishes the first resurrection from the second which brings up the remaining dead for judgment (Rev. 20: 4, 5).

That there are two resurrections*— not one general rising of saved and unsaved at one time— I take it for granted is clear to my readers, as so much has been written and orally taught upon this subject in recent years. The resurrection of the just; the resurrection of life; the first resurrection; the resurrection from, or out of, the dead

---

* If any are perplexed as to this, may I recommend "The Two Resurrections, and the Judgment," by C. H. M.

—these are all terms synonymous with the one the apostle uses here.

It is with the eye and heart set upon this that the apostle can cast aside as so much *impedimenta* all that would cause him to glory in the flesh, or give others an occasion to glory on his behalf. Like the racer stripped for the contest, he struggles ardently on with his eye upon the goal, which is for him this out-resurrection. In view of it, suffering cannot daunt him, nor death terrorize him. He sees in both but an opportunity for fuller, sweeter fellowship with his Lord. He would count it all joy to drink of His cup of suffering, and to share in His baptism of death—the last of course only as witness-bearer, as was promised to James and John before him.

How little do most of us enter into this holy "fellowship of His sufferings!" It is to be feared that some who make greatest pretension as to fellowship in things ecclesiastical, would be found sadly wanting when opportunity is given to enter into this fellowship of sorrow and of pain, in which, as in no other phase of fellowship, the soul enters into communion with Him who was on earth a Man of sorrows and acquainted with grief.

Perfection in Two Aspects

(chap. 3: 12-16.)

"Not as though I had already attained, either were already perfect: but I follow after, if that I may apprehend that for which also I am apprehended of Christ Jesus. Brethren, I count not myself to have apprehended; but this one thing I do, forgetting those things which are behind, and reaching forth unto those things which are before, I press toward the mark for the prize of the high calling of God in Christ Jesus. Let us therefore, as many as be perfect, be thus minded: and if in anything ye be otherwise minded, God shall reveal even this unto you. Nevertheless, whereto we have already attained, let us walk by the same rule, let us mind the same thing."

VERY early in the history of the Church men arose who confounded certain spiritual experiences, real or fancied, with the teaching of the Lord Himself and His apostles in regard to the first resurrection. We know of two by name, Hymenæus and Philetus, of whom Paul wrote to Timothy that they had erred concerning the truth, "saying that the resurrection is past already," and by this overthrew the faith of some. Nothing is more detrimental to Christian testimony than making high claims which cannot be substantiated by experience—as some who take the ground of sinlessness, or of the eradication of an evil nature, because their teachers instructed them that this is their privilege as Christians. If after-experience proves that it is impossible to maintain this practically, there is grave danger that they will become utterly disheartened, and possibly renounce the faith entirely, unless preserved by divine grace.

The apostle, therefore, is careful to make it clear that he did not claim to have reached a state of resurrection-perfectness while here upon earth. He uses a word, in this instance, which means completeness, that to which nothing can be added. This state, he declares, he had not already attained. But he had it in view, for he knew that, at the coming of the Lord Jesus Christ, he would be made like Himself, and thus forever free from all tendency to sin. Meantime, he could but follow after, seeking earnestly to lay hold of that for which Christ Jesus had laid hold of him, and in a devoted life to exemplify the power of Christ's resurrection, in which he shared. The 13th and 14th verses might, perhaps, better be rendered as follows: "Brethren, I count not myself to have apprehended; but this one thing, forgetting those things which are behind and reaching forth unto those things which are before, I press toward the mark for the prize of the calling of God on high in Christ Jesus." What he says is that there is only one thing he professes to have apprehended, or laid hold of, namely, that the

path of blessing is found in forgetting the things
that are past, and seeking to lay hold, practically,
of his portion in Christ from day to day while
ever keeping the goal in view.   To do this is to
"follow holiness, apart from which no man shall
see the Lord."   It is a great mistake to teach that
this verse means that unless one attains to certain
experiences in holy living he will be forever de-
barred from a sight of the Lord; it impresses the
fact upon us, rather, that he who will see the Lord
is one who follows that which characterized his
Master here—an inward and outward separation
from all that is contrary to the mind of God.

The calling of God on high, is that *heavenly*
calling which is characteristic of the present dispensation of grace.   Christ is no longer on earth,
His world-kingdom has not yet been set up, but
believers are linked with Him as the glorified Man
at God's right hand, and they are called to represent Him in this scene. The prize is the reward
conferred by His own hand at the end of the race,
and toward this Paul was pressing on, counting as
dross and refuse all that would hinder his progress.

To his fellow-believers he says, "Let us, therefore, as many as be perfect, be thus minded."
Are we then to understand that there is real or
implied contradiction here to what has gone be-

fore? He has told us that he was *not* perfect.
Here he speaks as though he were, and links
others with him in this perfection. The fact is,
a somewhat different word is here used from that
of verse 12. It implies perfection in *growth*—in
development. An apple in June may be a perfect
apple, so far, but it will have much greater completeness, or perfection in that sense, in August
or September. And so with the believer.

The perfection of verse 15 is that of full
growth, answering somewhat, if not altogether,
to the "fathers" of 1st John, chap. 2. Such have
eschewed the world and its follies. Christ has become to them the *one Object* before the soul. To
live for Him and seek His glory is the only thing
that counts in their estimation. And yet such
saints are still compassed with infirmity. They
are likely to err in judgment; they may make
grave mistakes, and come to wrong conclusions—
influenced as we are by early education, by environment, by mental capacity—and may even be
misled as to doctrinal questions. Nevertheless,
theirs is the mind of Christ, and they may be
comforted by the added words of the apostle that,
"If in anything ye be otherwise minded, God shall
reveal even this unto you."

Where there is a willingness to be taught of
God, the illuminating grace of the Holy Spirit can

be depended upon to open up His Word, and guide into all truth. But he would be a bold man indeed, who would dare to say, "I understand all truth, all mysteries are clear to me. I have a perfect apprehension of the divine revelation." Only the boldest egotism could lead anyone to take such ground. How patient, therefore, we need to be with one another; how ready to confess that we know but in part, and to recognize the fact that we are ever in need of further instruction. "Nevertheless, whereto we have already attained, let us walk by the same rule, let us mind the same thing." There are truths and principles so plainly put in God's Word, that any Spirit-taught believer may readily see them.

Where these truths are learned, it is our responsibility to walk in them—walk *together* in them, as far as possible, counting on God to reveal to us whatever may be lacking, as we patiently and prayerfully learn from Him through His Word. A wider recognition of these things would lead to more kindly consideration of one another, and tend to make us helpers of each other's faith, rather than judges of a brother's doubtful thoughts.

Enemies of the Cross of Christ

(ch. 3: 17-19.)

"Brethren, be followers together of me, and mark them which walk so as ye have us for an example. (For many walk, of whom I have told you often, and now tell you even weeping, that they are the enemies of the cross of Christ; whose end is destruction, whose God is their belly, and whose glory is in their shame, who mind earthly things)."

THE sentence is incomplete and needs the verses that follow to conclude it properly; but I have purposely left it so that we may consider this portion of it the more carefully, for the next part has to do with another and altogether happier theme. Here, the apostle is occupying us with the responsibilities and snares of the pilgrim path; there, he points us on to the goal when all danger will be forever past, and with it all opportunity to bear faithful testimony to a rejected Lord in a scene of contrariety. How it behoves us to consider the brevity of the time allotted us for witness-bearing! It will soon be forever too late to *suffer* for and with Christ, and this necessarily means too late to win an honored place in the everlasting kingdom of our Saviour-God. That which we call "time" is the training-school for the ages to come. What a mistake to fritter away its precious moments—so few at the most, as compared with the eternal ages—in things that are of no lasting profit.

Paul was an example both in life and doctrine for all who should come after him. It was not a prideful egotism that led him to plead with saints to follow him and his faithful companions as they followed Christ. He *lived* what he taught. His life was the practical exemplification of his teaching. He was not one man on the platform or in the meeting, and another in private or in business life. For we need to remember that Paul was no gentleman of leisure. He was not a clergyman afraid to soil his hands with honest labor. He wrought night and day tent-making, when funds were low or when he felt the need of setting an example of activity to any inclined to slothfulness; yet all the while preaching and teaching publicly and from house to house with a diligence that few if any have equalled, and none have surpassed. He was careful also as to his personal communion with the Lord, striving to keep a conscience ever void of offence toward both God and man. What an example for us all to follow!

That he could not please everybody, even his own brethren, at all times, goes without saying.

His work was belittled, his appearance ridiculed, his apostleship denied, and his integrity called in question. There were those who even intimated that he was a crafty deceiver who, by an appearance of frankness, caught with guile the unwary, and at times did evil that good might come! All these charges and insinuations he indignantly refutes in various parts of his writings, while never allowing calumnies to embitter him. He did not return railing for railing, or seek to injure those who would so willingly have injured him. He kept on the even tenor of his way, *living* Christ and *preaching* Christ with unchanged ardor to the very end; his wondrous life stood as an abiding answer to those who would malign him. Therefore he could say, "Be followers together of me," and he could consistently call upon the saints to mark his ways and to walk in the same paths.

And though centuries have rolled by since wicked men sought to dishonor him, and the executioner's axe severed his hoary head from his body by Cæsar's order, thus finishing his testimony in laying down his life for his Master's sake, he still remains the pre-eminent example of what the Christian should be, sustained by grace divine while passing through this valley of death's shadow. Let us examine our own ways and see how

they measure up to his—not excusing ourselves
for failure on the score that times and conditions
have changed from those that surrounded him.
The same One who wrought effectually in him so
long ago, will work in us to-day if there be but
a willing mind and a sanctified determination to
take his path of unworldliness and devotion to
Christ.

Of an altogether different class the next two
verses warn us. Many there were, then as now,
who, while professing to be in the pilgrim path,
walked in a vain show; by word proclaiming
themselves Christians, but by their actions proving that they were enemies of the cross of Christ.
Mark it well: they were not said to be enemies of
the *blood* or of the *death* of Christ; their opposition was directed against that which told of His
shame and rejection by the world—*His cross.* In
that cross Paul gloried. By it he saw himself
crucified unto the world and the world unto him.
But the world-lovers refused this. They desired
the benefits of His death while refusing to be
identified with His *shame.* They lived for self-
indulgence, yet made a pretence of piety. The expression, "Whose God is their belly," really means
that they worshiped themselves. "Belly" is self-
gratification; and, alas, how many live for self!
And yet it is out of this same self, or person, that,

when devoted to Christ, living waters shall flow for the refreshment and blessing of others, as our Lord says in the seventh of John. Until self is thus displaced as an object for which to live, and surrendered to God as an instrument to be used by and for Christ, there can be no true pilgrim character.

The apostle declares that for these enemies of the cross the end will be destruction. Consider for a moment the solemnity of this. They lived for self-gratification while in this scene; in the life to come they will be in a condition where the gratification of the smallest desire will be utterly impossible. Our Lord told of one who on earth was clothed in purple and fine linen, and fared sumptuously every day, but when suddenly snatched away from it all by the rude hand of death, he found himself in greatest torment, where not even his anguished prayer for a drop of water to cool his parched tongue could be granted. Such is the destruction awaiting those who live for self, ignoring the claims of the Christ of God. And yet, heedless of all this, they go on in their folly, indifferent alike to the admonitions of Scripture, of conscience, and of the Holy Spirit—indifferent also to the warnings and entreaties of men of God who, like Paul, have chosen the better part, and know whereof they speak.

Casting to the winds all godly counsel and sound advice, like flamboyant fools sporting on the edge of a moral precipice, displaying their heedlessness and folly before all, they glory in their shame, and exult in that which might well cause them to bow in penitent grief before redeeming mercy. Unlike Mary, who chose that good part never to be taken from her; or like Moses, who chose to suffer affliction with the people of God rather than enjoy the pleasures of sin for a season, they deliberately reject the good and choose the evil. They put away the hope of heaven for a brief season of sensual or sensuous pleasure here on earth. It is all summed up in the four little words — "Who mind earthly things." Despising the heavenly calling, they choose the earthly, and become indeed "dwellers upon the earth," only to be exposed to the fierce vials of the wrath of God in the day when He arises to shake terribly the earth. No wonder the apostle wept as he wrote of such, and warned them of their peril in pursuing their evil ways.

Heavenly Citizenship

(chap. 3: 20, 21.)

"For our conversation (or, citizenship) is in heaven; from whence also we look for the (or, a) Saviour, the Lord Jesus Christ: who shall change our vile body (or, this body of our humiliation) that it may be fashioned like unto his glorious body (or, the body of his glory) according to the working whereby He is able even to subdue all things unto Himself."

THE Greek word *politeuma* here rendered "conversation" means, as is now well-known, commonwealth, citizenship, or it might almost be transliterated "politics," for it involves all three thoughts. The apprehension of its scope, as here used by the apostle, should help the Christian to understand his true relationship and position regarding the affairs of this life and of the earth.

Philippi was, when Paul wrote, a Roman colony. That is, as a mark of special favor, Roman citizenship had been granted to all the free-born citizens of the former Macedonian capital. This was considered a great privilege. It enabled each Philippian, though dwelling in Macedonia, to say proudly, "My citizenship is in Rome." His responsibilities were directly to the Imperial Power. He had to do with the Emperor, not with the provincial government of Macedonia. Now, apply this to the Christian. Saved by matchless grace, though still living in the world, his commonwealth—the government to which he primarily owes allegiance — is in heaven. He is directly subject to the Lord Jesus Christ, and his conduct is to be regulated by His Word. The realization of this, while keeping him free from entangling alliances with the affairs of this world, will not, of course, tend to lawlessness or insubjection to world-rulers. A Philippian, subject to imperial authority, would not be a law-breaker in Macedonia, inasmuch as the same authority to which he owed allegiance had instituted the government of the country in which Philippi was the chief city. And so the apostle tells us elsewhere, "The powers that be are ordained of God," and he commands Christians to be subject in all things to magistrates, as recognizing the divine authority by which they rule.

But one will search in vain the distinctly Christian part of the Bible—namely, the New Testament Epistles—for any hint that Christians were to seek worldly power or dominion during this present age. Their place is that of subjection, not rule, until Christ Himself returns to reign.

The Emperor, to whom the Philippians owed allegiance, dwelt in Rome. Should he appear in

Heavenly Citizenship 99

Philippi, he would recognize with special honor those whose citizenship was directly linked with the capital of the empire. *Our* Lord is in heaven, and from there we look to see Him soon descend, when He shall openly confess all those whose citizenship is in heaven—confess them before an astonished and affrighted world. (See 2 Thess. 1: 3-12.)

It is now known, as a result of recent archeological discoveries, that the term *kurios* (the general word for "Lord" in the New Testament) was an imperial title. More than that, this imperial title was never used in reference to the emperors until, through a public ceremony, they were deified, according to pagan conceptions; therefore it was used as a divine title. At the very time that Paul wrote this letter, it was common to address the brutal man who occupied the imperial throne as "our Lord Nero," using the distinctive term just referred to. How marked the contrast, when the Christians, often writhing beneath the bitter persecutions of this unspeakably wicked tyrant, looked expectantly toward the heavens for the return of "our Lord Jesus Christ."

At His coming, the first resurrection will take place; the sleeping saints will be raised, and living saints will be changed. For "this corruptible must put on incorruption, and this mortal must

put on immortality" (1 Cor. 15 : 53), and our natural bodies will be changed to spiritual bodies.

It should be remembered that when our Bible
was translated in the 17th century, the word
"vile" did not necessarily have the thought of evil
connected with it.   That was "vile" which was
lowly or common : so here "our vile body" is really
"the body of our humiliation"—the body which
links us with the lower creation; a body common
to both saint and sinner.   At the Lord's return it
will be transformed, and made like unto the body
of His glory.   In that resurrection-body He came
forth from the tomb, was manifested to His disciples, ascended into heaven, appeared to Saul of
Tarsus, and in it He shall soon return with glory.
The natural body is really a *soulish* body, or soul-
ual, if we may coin the word; and a spiritual body
is a body suited to the spirit.   It is not that one
is material and the other immaterial: for both
are material, though the one is of finer substance
than "this mortal body," and no longer subject
to certain laws by which the natural body is now
controlled.   In *bodies* of glory, then, we shall
dwell forever in the city to which we even now
belong.   It is our own, our native country, as
children of God; and we shall never really be at
home until we are there with our glorified Lord
Himself.

The same divine energy that wrought in Him to raise Him from the dead, shall still work through Him until He subdues all things to Himself. Then as we learn from 1 Cor. 15: 24-28, He will deliver the kingdom to the Father, that God, in all His fulness—Father, Son, and Holy Spirit—may be all in all forever, and fully manifested in Christ Jesus, who remains eternally our Lord and our Head.

CHAPTER FOUR

CHRIST, THE BELIEVER'S STRENGTH, AND THE CONFIDENT MIND

Exhortation to Unity

(vers. 1-3.)

"Therefore, my brethren dearly beloved and longed for, my joy and crown, so stand fast in the Lord, my dearly beloved. I beseech Euodia, and beseech Syntyche, that they be of the same mind in the Lord. And I entreat thee also, true yokefellow, help those women which labored with me in the gospel, with Clement also, and with other my fellow-laborers, whose names are in the book of life."

THE long parenthesis of the third chapter concluded, the apostle again exhorts to steadfastness and unity. It is very evident that there was incipient division of some nature working in the Philippian assembly. It was in order to meet this, as we have already noticed, that the letter was written; but Paul did not immediately put his finger upon the difficulty. Through the three previous chapters he has been ministering that which should prepare the hearts of the offenders for a final word of exhortation. In this section, he calls them by name, and pleads with them not to let self-interest hinder the work of the Lord.

With expressions of deepest affection, he addresses the assembly as a whole. They are his brethren, dearly beloved, for whom he yearns, and who will be, at the judgment-seat of Christ, his joy and crown. It will be noticed that this expression is analogous to that of 1 Thess. 2: 19, 20. There, addressing the saints who had been won to Christ through his ministry, he could say, "For what is our hope, or joy, or crown of rejoicing? Are not even ye in the presence of our Lord Jesus Christ at his coming? For ye are our glory and joy." When, as a servant, he stands at the judgment-seat of Christ, that which will fill his heart with gladness will be the sight of those for whose eternal blessing he had been used while laboring in this scene. Rutherford beautifully expresses the same thought when, speaking of the town in which he had labored so long, he cries,

> "Oh, if one soul from Anwoth
>   Meet me at God's right hand,
> My heaven will be two heavens,
>   In Immanuel's land."

Then he that soweth and he that reapeth will rejoice together, as each servant shall come bringing in his sheaves, and, looking up into the face of the Lord, will be able to say, "Behold I and the children whom God hath given me."

The crown of rejoicing is the soul-winner's garland, composed of those he has won for Christ. Such must ever stand in a more precious relationship to the one who has been used to their conversion than they possibly can to any other. They are his children in the faith; his sons and daughters in Christ Jesus. Their happy progress in the things of God gladdens his heart, and is, in itself, rich reward for his service in their behalf; while, on the other hand, their failure or break-down by the way, as evidenced by loss of interest in divine things, dissension, worldly ways again taken up, must rend his heart with grief, and also fill him with a certain sense of shame. "Now we live," writes the apostle elsewhere, "if ye stand fast in the Lord." A brother-servant, the apostle John, writing to his converts, says, "And now, little children, abide in Him; that, when He shall appear, we may have confidence, and not be ashamed before Him at his coming" (1 John 2: 28). Notice, it is not that *they* may not be ashamed, but "we," that is, those who were instrumental in leading them to Christ.

So it is in view of all this that Paul earnestly exhorts his beloved Philippians to stand fast in the faith. It is always the effort of Satan to hinder the people of God from steadfastly clinging together, and presenting a united front to the enemy. Alas, that his efforts to introduce dissension so readily succeed because of the flesh in us.

And now, without further delay, and in perfect frankness, the apostle speaks directly to the two offenders against unity, whom he had in his mind from the beginning. And yet there is no sternness, no seeking to lord it over their consciences, but he pleads with them, as though Christ Himself were beseeching, and entreats Euodia and Syntyche. They had been earnest laborers in the gospel, but had fallen out with each other, as we say, and they are exhorted to be of the same mind in the Lord. He certainly does not mean by this that they must think alike in everything, or see all things from the same standpoint. This can never be while we are in this world. The very possession of mind, which differentiates man from the brutes, of necessity gives occasion for differences of judgment as to many things, and so calls for much patience toward one another. No two men ever saw the same rainbow. The slightest difference of position gives each a view at a different angle. The formation and contour of the eye itself has to be taken in consideration. One may discern clearly every distinct shade, while the other may be color-blind, and no amount of argument or persuasion will enable the second to see that which is so clear to the first. And so we may even say no two men have ever read the same Bible. Not that there is one book from God for one person and a different one for another, but the difference is in our apprehension of things. We are so influenced by our environment, by our education, or lack of it, that we are prejudiced when we least realize it; and, even when we try to be the most open-minded, we are often misled by our impressions and the limitations of our understanding. Therefore, the need of great patience one with the other.

But if what we have been saying is true, how then can we be of one mind? The verse does not end without making that very plain: "I beseech Euodia, and beseech Syntyche," he writes, "that they be of the same mind *in the Lord*." If both alike have the mind of Christ—which is the lowly mind—if both alike seek to be subject to the Lord, even though there may be differences of judgment as to many things, each will respect the other's view-point, and neither will try to force the other's conscience. Thus all occasion for dissension would be at an end. Alas, that we so little realize this, and are often so insistent on what seems to us exceedingly important truth, when nothing vital is at stake, while a brother or sister equally honest and earnest may fail to see things as we see them; and, at the judgment-seat of Christ, it may be manifested that, after all, they, and not we, were right, or perhaps that both were wrong.

I take it that the third verse was spoken by Paul to Epaphroditus personally, who was, I presume, his amanuensis in the writing of this letter. He was about to return to Philippi, having fulfilled his mission, and now, strengthened after his illness, was to be the bearer of this epistle. The apostle entreats him, as a true yokefellow, to help these women upon his return, to that unity of mind to which he had been exhorting them. He mentions that they had labored with him in the gospel, with Clement also, and with others of his fellow-laborers, whose names though not given here, are in the book of life. We are not to understand by this that they occupied the public platform or taught in the assembly of God, participating, with Paul and Clement and these other laborers, in public testimony: for this would contradict the words of the Holy Ghost through the same apostle, as preserved for us in 1 Cor. 14 and in 1 Tim. 2; but there were many ways in which devoted women could serve the Lord in the gospel. In fact, in oriental, as well as in occidental lands, work for women is of tremendous importance. There were many places where a man could not go, where godly women may have free access. And "laboring in the gospel" implies a great deal more than simply speaking from a platform. In fact, it is a question if this latter be not, in many instances at least, the lesser thing, and the individual heart-to-heart work the greater.

It seems clear that Epaphroditus caught the note of inspiration in these personal words to him, and so he embodied them in this letter; and we can be thankful to God that they have come down to us, for they give us deeper insight into the working of the spirit of grace in the mind of Paul, and will be valuable to all who seek to serve the Lord, until the Church's history on earth is ended.

Joy and Peace
(chap. 4: 4-7.)

"Rejoice in the Lord always: and again I say, Rejoice. Let your moderation be known unto all men. The Lord is at hand. Be careful for nothing: but in every thing by prayer and supplication with thanksgiving let your requests be made known unto God: and the peace of God, which passeth all understanding, shall keep your hearts and minds through Christ Jesus."

IN the opening verse of chapter 3 we have already had the exhortation, "Finally, my brethren, rejoice in the Lord." Undoubtedly, the apostle was, so far as his own mind was concerned, just ready to bring his letter to a close. But, as we have already seen, this was not the mind of the Spirit, and, like his brother-apostle, Jude, on another occasion, he was "borne along" to exhort the saints to "earnestly contend for the faith once delivered." Now he again refers to that which was so much upon his heart. He would have the saints always rejoicing in the Lord. Joy and holiness are inseparable. A holy Christian is able to rejoice even when passing through deepest afflictions; but a believer who, through unwatchfulness, has permitted himself to fall into unholy ways, loses immediately the joy of the Lord, which is the strength of those who walk in communion with Himself.

The second exhortation is one to which we may well give earnest heed. In the Authorized Version we read, "Let your moderation be known unto all men." Undoubtedly, "moderation" is a most commendable Christian virtue, but there is more to the original word than this. It has been rendered by some "yieldingness;" this, too, is an excellent translation, so far as it goes, and suggests that resilience of character which many of us sadly lack. Rotherham gives "considerateness," which adds to the thought, and helps us to a better understanding of the mind of the Spirit in this connection. The Revised Version has "forbearance," and "gentleness" in the margin. But if we take all these various terms we shall, I think, find them summed up in the very suggestive rendering given years ago by Matthew Arnold, the English critic, who translated the passage, "Let your *sweet reasonableness* be manifested to all men." He pointed out the interesting fact that the word here used is unknown in classical Greek and it was his impression that Paul coined it for the occasion. What a lovely trait is this sweet reasonableness in a Christian! It is the very opposite to that unyielding, harshly-dogmatic, self-determined spirit, that so often dominates in place of the meekness and gentleness of Christ. "I beseech you, my brethren," wrote Cromwell to the warring theologians of his day, "remember that it is possible you *may* be wrong." How apt we are to forget this when engaged in discussions as to either doctrines, methods of service, or church principles!

This does not mean that one need be lacking in intensity of conviction or assurance as to the correctness of doctrines, principles or practices which one believes he has learned from the word of God; but it does imply a kindly consideration for the judgment of others, who may be equally sincere, and equally devoted—and, possibly, even more enlightened. Nothing is ever lost by recognizing this, and remembering that we all know *in part.*

How aptly the brief sentence, "The Lord is at hand" comes in, in connection with the preceding exhortation! I take it that the thought is not exactly "The Lord is coming;" it is rather, "The Lord is standing by;" He is looking on; He hears every word spoken; He takes note of every action.

> "Closer is He than breathing,
> Nearer than hands or feet."

With the realization that He is thus, in the fullest sense, "at hand," though unseen, how quickly would strife and dissension cease, and the forbearance and grace ever manifested in Himself be seen in His followers!

And now we have a wonderful promise based on a third exhortation; this time in connection with prayer. Our Lord Himself has warned against anxious thought, and the Holy Spirit expands His teaching by saying, "In nothing be anxious." But how am I to obey an exhortation like this when troubles are surging around me, and my poor, restless mind will not be at peace? I feel I must tell somebody. My exercises are like those of the Psalmist perhaps, who wrote on one occasion, "I am so agitated that I cannot speak" (Ps. 77: 4, *F. W. Grant's Trans.*). What, then shall I do? To whom shall I turn? It is so natural to worry and fret under circumstances such as these; though I

tell myself over and over again that nothing is
gained thereby, and my trouble only seems to become exaggerated as I try to carry my own burdens.

But the Spirit of God points the way out. He
would have me bring everything, the great things
and the little things, perplexing conditions and
trying circumstances of every character, into the
presence of God, and *leave them there*. By prayer
and supplication, not forgetting thanksgiving for
past and present mercies, He would have me pour
out my requests unto God. I may feel that I do
not know the mind of the Lord in regard to them,
but that need not hinder. I am to make known
my "requests," counting on His wisdom to do for
me that which is best both for time and eternity.
Thus, casting my care upon Him, and leaving all
in His own blessed hands, the peace of God (that
peace which He, Himself, ever enjoys, though
storms and darkness may be round about), a
peace passing all understanding, shall guard, as
with a military garrison, my heart: and (blessed
truth, if I but enter into it) my *thoughts*, or
"mind," as it is here translated, through Christ
Jesus.

But this I cannot do for myself. I may tell myself over and over that I will not worry, will not
fret, but my thoughts, like untamed horses with

the bit in their teeth, if I may use such an illustration, seem to run away with me. Or, like an attacking army, they crowd into the citadel of my mind, and threaten to overwhelm me. But God, Himself, by the Holy Spirit, has engaged to so garrison my mind, and so protect my restless heart, that my thoughts shall neither run away with me, nor yet overwhelm me. Every thought will be brought into captivity to the obedience of Christ. Thus I shall enjoy the peace of God, a peace beyond all human comprehension, as I leave my burdens where faith delights to cast every care, at the feet of Him who, having not withheld His own Son, has now declared that through Him He will freely give me all things. In this I can rest, for He cannot deny Himself.

Exhortations

(chap. 4: 8, 9.)

"Finally, brethren, whatsoever things are true, whatsoever things are honest, whatsoever things are just, whatsoever things are pure, whatsoever things are lovely, whatsoever things are of good report; if there be any virtue, and if there be any praise, think on these things. Those things, which ye have both learned, and received, and heard, and seen in me, do; and the God of peace shall be with you."

THESE verses conclude the instructions of the apostle; all that follows being in the nature of a postscript—and, while of deep practical value, not directly addressed to saints as homiletical teaching.

Having throughout the epistle put Christ before his readers in so many different aspects, the apostle now sums all up in this brief exhortation to think on things holy, thus recognizing the Old Testament principle, "As a man thinketh in his heart, so is he." Many have missed the very point, however, which it seems clear he is pressing, by taking all these things in an abstract way. It will be found exceedingly difficult to think on things true, honest, just, pure, and lovely, if there be not some definite, concrete example before the mind. Mere occupation with beautiful sentiments and poetic ideals is not, I take it, what he would here inculcate. But all are found fully exemplified in our Lord Jesus Christ as the perfect Man here on earth; and, in measure, these qualities are reproduced by the Holy Spirit in all who have been made partakers of the divine nature. In a certain sense we may think of these words as linking with the exhortation already given to Euodia and Syntyche, who needed to see in each other what the Spirit had wrought.

Let Euodia look coldly and critically upon Syntyche, and occupy her mind with whatever she can find in her character or ways that is contrary to the virtues here mentioned, and the breach between them will be immeasurably widened. Let Syntyche retort by exaggerating every defect or short-coming in her sister in Christ, and she will soon become so alienated from her that reconciliation will be almost impossible.

But, on the other hand, if Euodia, realizing that Syntyche has been redeemed to God by the same precious blood as herself, and is indwelt by the same Holy Spirit, determines to think of the virtues or anything worthy of praise in her life and personality; to magnify her graces and minimize her faults, refusing to indulge in unkind criticism, she will be so attracted by what is of Christ in her that she will find herself linked in heart to the one from whom she had previously turned coldly away.

Is not this what we all greatly need in our dealings with each other? In every truly converted soul there are the manifest inwrought virtues of the Spirit of God ; things that are honest, just, pure, lovely and of good report—the activities of the new nature. If we think on these things, instead of dwelling upon the failures to which all are liable, our fellowship one with another will become increasingly precious as the days go by. And even when there is actual cause for blame, if we stop to consider the circumstances that may have led up to that which seems to us so blame-worthy, Christian pity and compassion will take the place of criticism and unkind judgment, which cannot help to restore, but only serves to drive farther into sin the erring one. "To err is human; to forgive divine." And even a poet of this world has taught us the folly of judging that which the eye cannot see, when, in his quaint Scottish way, he has written,

> "We only ken the wrang that's dune,
> We ken na' what's resisted."

We may severely blame the wrong-doer for things that have already deeply exercised his heart and conscience, and been long since cleansed away by the washing of water by the Word as applied by the Lord Jesus Himself.

And, of course, in all our ways it is important that we should never permit our minds to feed, like carrion vultures, on the wicked, filthy, and unholy things of the flesh. This is thoroughly natural to the carnal man, and the carnal mind is still in the believer, and will be until the day when our bodies of humiliation shall be changed and made like His body of glory. But we are not to permit it to dominate us, since the Holy Spirit dwells in us to control us for Christ. There is so much that is honest; so much that is just or righteous; so much that is pure; so much that is lovely and loveable; so much that is of good report; so much that is virtuous and trustworthy, that it were folly to be occupied with the opposites, when we might be taken up with positive good.

And, as we meditate on these things, we grow in grace and in the knowledge of our Lord Jesus Christ; for, as we have already noted, all these beautiful traits were fully exemplified in Him, and they have been imparted, in large measure, to each of His servants; probably to none more so than the writer of this epistle. Therefore, without pride, but as an example to the flock of Christ, he can add, "Those things, which ye have both learned, and received, and heard, and seen in me, do." And as thus practically walking, according to the power of the indwelling Spirit, we have the sweet assurance that "the God of peace shall be with you," thus connecting all this with the promise of verse 7 above, where we are assured that "the peace of God" shall garrison the minds and hearts of all who cast their every care on Him. Here we learn that the God of peace will walk with those who seek to walk before Him in piety and holiness of mind and ways.

Ministry in Temporal Things

(chap. 4: 10-23.)

"But I rejoiced in the Lord greatly, that now at the last your care of me hath flourished again; wherein ye were also careful, but ye lacked opportunity. Not that I speak in respect of want: for I have learned, in whatsoever state I am, therewith to be content. I know both how to be abased, and I know how to abound: everywhere and in all things I am instructed both to be full and to be hungry, both to abound and to suffer need. I can do all things through Christ which strengtheneth me. Notwithstanding ye have well done, that ye did communicate with my affliction. Now ye Philippians know also, that in the beginning of the gospel, when I departed from Macedonia, no church communicated with me as concerning giving and receiving, but ye only. For even in Thessalonica ye sent once and again unto my necessity. Not because I desire a gift: but I desire fruit that may abound to your account. But I have all, and abound: I am full, having received of Epaphroditus the things which were sent from you, an odour of a sweet smell, a sacrifice acceptable, well-pleasing to God. But my God shall supply all your need according to his riches in glory by Christ Jesus. Now unto God and our Father be glory for ever and ever. Amen. Salute every saint in Christ Jesus. The brethren which are with me greet you. All the saints salute you, chiefly they that are of Cæsar's household. The grace of our Lord Jesus Christ be with you all. Amen."

IN this, the closing section of the epistle, Paul thanks the assembly at Philippi for the practical way in which they had manifested their fellowship in the gospel. They were not of those who are willing to profit eternally through the gospel ministry, but have very little exercise as to the temporal welfare of the servants of Christ to whom they owe the knowledge of that truth which has made them free. From the beginning of their Christian lives, the Philippian saints had cared, as occasion offered, for the needs of the apostle, even sending to him of their substance when he was laboring in Thessalonica, where he and his companions had gone after being released from the Philippian jail. But years had elapsed since then, and Paul had travelled far, and passed through many varied experiences, often finding it quite impossible to keep in close touch with the different assemblies he had been used of God to establish. Consequently it was not strange that, at times, it should seem as if his dearest friends had forgotten him. Nevertheless, the love was there though they had lacked opportunity to display it. But now they had learned of his circumstances, as a prisoner in Rome for the truth's sake, and they had hastened to show their fellowship with him in his sufferings, by sending Epaphroditus with a gift of love, as we have already noticed.

In acknowledging this, Paul takes occasion to glorify God for His care of him, even when Chris-

tian assemblies forgot their indebtedness to him.
He had indeed known cold neglect and indifference, but it never soured his spirit nor led him to
complain. He noted the cold-heartedness, but he
did not find fault. He left it all with the Lord,
and committed his own circumstances to Him, assured that *He* never forgot, and was never an un-
concerned spectator of His servant's sufferings.
So, he accepted it all as a course in the school of
God, and he could say, "I have learned in whatsoever state I am to be content." The Lord was
his portion, and he could rest in the knowledge
of His unchanging love and care.

It was not in a moment that he entered into
this. He, like all disciples in God's school, had to
advance in the life of faith by learning practically
the things he could now teach to others. But he
had taken his degree, so to speak, and he could
now declare, "I know both how to be abased, and
to abound; everywhere, and in all things, I possess
the secret (or, I have been initiated) both to be
full, and to be hungry, to abound and to suffer
need." Blessed lessons these! And we may say
the soul is never really at rest in regard to the
trials and testings of the way until these precious
secrets have been apprehended.

John Wesley is reported to have said that he
did not know which dishonored God the most—to

worry, which is really to doubt His love and care, or to curse and swear. Yet every saint would shrink from the latter with abhorrence, while many of us have no sense of the wrong we do when we fret and worry. To rest in faith upon the knowledge that "all things work together for good to those who love God, who are the called according to His purpose," should ever be our attitude. And in a very special sense they who minister in word and doctrine (in entire dependence on the One who has sent them out as His ambassadors) are called upon to exemplify this in their calm dependence upon Him whom they serve.

This leads me to say something upon the New Testament principle for the support of those who labor entirely in spiritual things. And, first, let it be noted carefully, there is no such thing known in Scripture as putting the servant of God upon the low level of a salary basis. The only man mentioned in the Bible to be hired by the year as a "minister" was the recreant Levite who was engaged by Micah of Mount Ephraim, and later by the Danites to be their "father and priest" (Judges, chaps. 17 and 18). Even in the legal dispensation, Jehovah Himself was the portion of the Levites. They were prospered, and cared for, in accordance with the measure in which God blessed

His people and their hearts responded to His goodness. In the Christian economy we have no special clerical or extra-priestly class to be supported as professional men by their so-called lay-brethren. The distinction of clergy and laity is utterly unscriptural, and is but part of the Judaizing system that has so perverted the truth of the Church. But there are those who are specially gifted as evangelists, pastors, and teachers, and who, in many instances, though not in all, are called upon to separate themselves from secular pursuits in order to give their time unhinderedly to spiritual service. These of old "went forth for the Name's sake," we are told in 3rd John, "taking nothing of the Gentiles." They were cast entirely on the Lord, and He cared for them through His own grateful people, according to the word, "Let him that is taught in the Word communicate unto him that teacheth in all good things." And so John, by the Spirit, writes, "We therefore ought to receive such that we might be fellow-helpers to the truth." Such servants have a claim upon the people of God, not because they are official ministers, but because they are engaged in making known the truth, and in this service all believers are privileged to share.

But observe carefully:—the servant is never to look to the saints for his support, but to count directly on the Lord, and make his personal needs known only to Him. He need not fear to acquaint the assemblies with special opportunities for ministry to others as occasions arise. Paul did this frequently and earnestly. But rather than mention his personal needs, he would labor with his own hands; nor did he feel he was degrading his calling in so doing—that thus he might provide things honest in the sight of all men, and set an example to any who might be inclined to seek an easy path, and depend upon support by those in better circumstances than themselves.

And so the principle is clear: the servant of Christ is to go forth in absolute dependence upon the One who has commissioned him, and who makes Himself responsible to meet his needs. But the people of God are called upon to be exercised before Him as to what share they should have in the support of those who are thus engaged. No ministering brother has the right or authority to demand support from the saints. They, not he, must judge whether he is worthy of that support. But, on the other hand, if receiving from him in spiritual things, it is, we are told, a small matter that he should reap their carnal things. "They that preach the gospel should live of the gospel" (1 Cor. 9).

For a servant of the Lord to be finding fault be-

cause of the smallness of his support, is to make
manifest at once that his dependence is upon man
rather than on God; and for saints to be callously
indifferent to the temporal needs of those whom
they recognize as God-sent messengers, is to show
themselves out of touch with Him who has given
to them the privilege of being in this way fellow-
helpers to the truth. Thus should both those who
minister and those who are ministered to, be exercised before God as to their mutual responsibilities.

This had been the path in which Paul had
walked for many years, and as he looked back
over the journey and saw how he had been sustained of God, he knew he could count on Him
for the future, and so he faced the days to come
with the assurance that he could do all things
through Christ who was his strength. He who
was to him life, example, and object, was also his
unfailing source of supply for every emergency
that might arise, even to a martyr's death.

But while he did not look to man for his supplies, he shows himself truly grateful for the
ministry extended to him. He would not take the
gift of love sent by his dear Philippian children
in the faith as though it were a mere matter of
course. He expresses himself in most apprecia-
tive terms as he thanks them for their fellowship,

and in this he is an example to all Christ's servants, some of whom have been only too neglectful of the finer courtesies which often mean more to the saints than they realize.

Paul received the gift not because he desired to profit by means of their generosity, but because he saw in it an added evidence of the working of the Spirit of grace in their souls, and this was for their blessing, as well as relieving his need. And so he gladly accepted it all, seeing in it "an odor of a sweet savor, a sacrifice acceptable and well-pleasing to God."

Nor would He, for whose glory they ministered the gift to His imprisoned servant, allow them to put Him in their debt, but engaged Himself to supply all their need, according to *His* riches in glory, through Christ Jesus. The more blessed part must always be His, for when we have given to our utmost limit, we have only returned Him a little of His own, and even that He will abundantly repay.

The last three verses give the concluding salutation. Note again how "every saint" is affectionately greeted. He would refuse to the last to recognize any parties among them. And all with him joined in saluting them—particularly some, evidently newly come to the faith, and possibly as a result of coming in contact with him in his prison-cell, whom he mentions as "those of Cæsar's household," who belonged to the imperial guard.

And so we close our meditations on this instructive epistle with a message of "grace" ringing in our souls. H. A. I.

Colossians

PREFACE

Expositions of Colossians abound, many of them of great value, yet each generation seems to call for fresh and new applications of divine truth. Hence this volume.

These lectures have been delivered at many Bible Conferences throughout the United States and Canada, and are issued in book form in response to the earnest requests of many who heard them. If read with the open Bible beside them, and thus used not as a substitute for, but as an aid to, the study of the Word itself, it is hoped they may prove helpful to a wider circle of students of the Book of books.

The times are solemn. Old errors are being paraded in new terms, on all sides. Therefore the need of a new examination of this great Epistle which so effectively meets the philosophical, mystical, and legalistic speculations of carnal men. May God be pleased to bless these lectures to that end!

H. A. IRONSIDE

Oakland, California
December 12, 1928

Part One

DOCTRINAL

Colossians 1:1—3:4

LECTURE 1

GENERAL CONSIDERATIONS AND ANALYSIS

Colossians 1:1–3:4

No one familiar with the Pauline Letters can fail to see · how intimately linked are those to the Ephesians and the Colossians. It is very likely that the letter from Laodicea, referred to in the last chapter of the Epistle we are considering, is really our Epistle to the Ephesians, and therefore we can understand why the apostle was anxious that both should be read by the same people. My reasons for saying this will come out later. Some, in fact, who do not accept the inspiration of the New Testament have supposed that Colossians was a crude attempt to rewrite Ephesians from memory, but a careful examination of both letters shows that the one is the correlative of the other. Ephesians presents

7

the great truth revealed to Paul, and through him made known to all nations for the obedience of faith, and which he emphatically calls the mystery. It is the Church as the Body of Christ in its heavenly aspect, as 1 Corinthians reveals the Body in responsibility down here on the earth. Ephesians, of course, does not overlook the importance of our responsibility to walk according to the calling wherewith we are called, and to manifest the unity of the Spirit in our measure while still in this scene. Doctrinally, however, it is the Body as the aggregate of all believers from Pentecost to the Rapture, united to a risen Christ by the indwelling Holy Spirit, that seems the theme of that Epistle. Colossians, on the other hand, has to do with Christ as the Head of the Body, and seeks to fix the hearts of the saints upon Him as risen and glorified, known no longer after the flesh but, in resurrection, the Head of a new order; and believers as responsible to manifest Him, to hold the Head, here in this world. So we might say the Headship of Christ is the theme of this Epistle. We need not therefore be surprised to find great similarity in Ephesians and Colossians, for so intimate is the link between Christ and the members of His Body that what is said of the one may often be said of the other, and it is given to the members of the Body to manifest the risen life of the Head. He it is with whom the Holy Spirit occupies us, in order that we may

be separated practically from all that would dishonor Him, and delivered from anything that
would tend to keep Him at a distance.

At the beginning there was very real need for
such ministry. Christianity as a divine system
seemed likely to be overwhelmed (only that the
Lord Himself was watching over His own truth)
in the first centuries by a strange mixture of
Jewish legality, Grecian philosophy and Oriental
mysticism, so interwoven as to form several altogether new systems with which the name of
Christ was linked in a most cunning way. The
result was the "mystery of iniquity" referred to
in 2 Thessalonians 2. These various systems
were known under the general name of "Gnosticism." This, of course, in pretension, at least,
was the very opposite to what Huxley, some years
ago, designated "Agnosticism." The latter term
means "without knowledge." The Agnostic says
God is unknowable, the mystery of the universe
is unsolvable. He says, There may or may not
be a personal God back of this universe; matter
may or may not be eternal; man may or may not
survive death; I do not know; and he compla-
cently takes it for granted that because he does
not know, no one else does. He refuses the
divine revelation given us in the Holy Scriptures and so is content to be an ignoramus
(which is but the Latin equivalent for Agnostic),
when he might have assured knowledge as one

taught of God. The Gnostic, on the other hand, says, I do know. *Gnosis*, from which the term is derived, simply means knowledge. *Epignosis*, used by the apostle for Christianity, is really super-knowledge. The Gnostic professed to have fuller knowledge of the mysteries of life and death and heavenly beings than the Bible itself reveals. He added to, or perverted the scriptural revelation, linking with it weird Persian dreams and human reasonings. He was neither a Jew, a Christian, a Philosopher, nor a Zoroastrian. He considered himself superior to them all, very much as the Theosophists do to-day, having taken what he thought to be the best out of all these systems and made a new system therewith. This weird imitation of the divine mysteries pretended to great depth of spirituality, to remarkable fulness of knowledge, to great profundity of thought. It was therefore most attractive to the natural mind, ever delighting in speculation on sacred themes, but it was Satanic in origin, and deliberately planned by the enemy to hide the glory shining in the face of Christ Jesus, concerning whom the Gnostics indulged in the wildest speculations. I have neither time nor space here to go into the weird speculations of Gnosticism with its amazing conception of grades of spirit-beings mediating between the uncreated God and His creatures. Those who are interested can readily find access to full explanations con-

cerning the Demiurge and the host of Kabbalistic
Eons and inferior emanations supposedly coming
in between the soul and God. The place that
Christ Himself held in this system varied according to the vagaries of the respective teachers.
Some thought that Jesus was but a man, and the
Christ the divine Spirit which came to Him at
His baptism and which left Him at the cross; so
it could not be said Christ died, but simply Jesus
died. You will recognize this as the root error
of what is commonly called Christian Science and
of most phases of the so-called "New Thought"
of to-day. Others held that the body of Jesus
was only spiritual, not material. They linked
evil with matter and therefore refused to believe
that "the Word became flesh." The first of
these systems seems to be before the mind of
the Apostle Paul in the writing of Colossians.
The second is met by the Apostle John in his
three Epistles. Both systems would rob the saints
of the true Christ of God. They put Him afar off
with many angels intervening who must first be
invoked and placated before union with Christ can
be known. Paul shows that we come to Him immediately, He being the one Mediator between
God and men, the Man Christ Jesus. Again,
these Gnostics placed varied ranks of principalities and powers, glorious spirit-beings, above and
beyond Him, leading up to the invisible God,
whereas the Apostle Paul shows us that He is

the Creator of all principalities and powers, and that they must all be subject to Him who is Himself the image of the invisible God.

I would not think it necessary to occupy people with these old errors were it not that the danger of losing sight of the Head is as real to-day as it was then. Every modern erroneous cult is just some old Satanic heresy revived, and each is designed to misrepresent some aspect of revealed truth in regard to Christ and His redemptive work. The advocates of these systems may profess great humility and preach and practise great self-abnegation, even to the neglecting of the body and its physical needs, but they all put Christ Jesus—the true Christ of God—at a distance, and an imaginary Christ, a Christ who is not an atoning Saviour, in His place. Some degree of familiarity with the ancient theories might save honest souls from being entangled in the meshes of these newer systems. Therefore the need, in every age, of reading this Colossian letter afresh in order that we ever may hold the Head.

It has been observed by others, but will bear repeating, that so intent is the Spirit upon glorifying Christ in this wonderful Epistle that He ever hides Himself. In Ephesians, where it is the truth of the one Body that is being unfolded, the Holy Spirit is mentioned many times, and we have clear teaching as to His personality and

operations. In Colossians He is never mentioned
doctrinally, and only once incidentally, if I may
so say where I recognize divine design throughout, and that is in verse 8 of chapter 1,
where the writer speaks of having heard through
Epaphras of the Colossians' "love in the Spirit."
This is surely most significant; even the Holy
Spirit Himself, eternally co-equal with the Father
and Son, who all together constitute one God,
would nevertheless hide Himself if men belittle or
lose sight of the Lord Jesus as Head of the new
creation. The blessed Paraclete speaks not from
or of Himself but He takes of the things of
Christ and shows them unto us. He would not
even risk (to speak after the manner of men)
being put in as one coming between the believer
and Christ.

It may be well to point out that so far as we
have any record Paul had never been to Colosse
as a ministering servant, though Philemon, who
was of that assembly, had been converted through
him. But the saints in that city he had not seen
in the flesh. Many individuals may have heard
him during the time. he was in Ephesus when
"all in Asia" heard the Word, as related in
Acts 19. By Asia here we are not to understand either the continent nor yet Asia Minor,
but a much smaller district, ruled by a Roman
proconsul, and therefore known as the "proconsular province of Asia." Thither Paul was at

one time forbidden to go. There he later labored
with much blessing. There the seven Churches of
the Apocalypse were afterwards located. Though
Colosse was not one of these addressed by the
Lord when He appeared to John in Patmos, yet
it was situated very close to Laodicea, which
with Colosse and Hierapolis formed a trio of
cities in which were large Christian assemblies
in early days.

Epaphras was the chosen instrument for the
evangelization of Colosse. He evidently remained
among the saints and cared for them as a godly
pastor afterwards. But he found himself hard
beset by emissaries of Satan, who were bent
upon misleading these young believers, for their
own selfish advantage. He therefore sought the
help of Paul, the apostle, who was at this time a
prisoner in Rome. It was in response to his plea
that the letter was penned by divine inspiration,
which is now before us.

Another subject which is full of interest is
the fact that God in so many instances permitted
error in doctrine or corruption in life, in the
early churches, to be the means of adding to the
volume of divine revelation and instruction.

It is a signal mercy that in His wisdom God
allowed every possible form of error to arise in
the apostolic era of the Church's history, in order
that all might be exposed, and the truth declared
through inspired men, that thus the faith in its

simplicity might be preserved for the generations to come. As a result of this, Satan has nothing new to offer. Old heresies are re-dressed and brought forward as new conceptions of truth from age to age, but in this respect, "there is nothing new under the sun." Therefore, all the Christian needs to protect him from modern systems of an evil character is a better acquaintance with the Word of God, where the truth is taught in its purity and the lies of the adversary are brought out into the light and fully exposed. No one familiar with the teaching of Colossians, for instance, will ever be misled by the specious sophistries of the various occult systems now being foisted on a credulous public, such as Theosophy or Spiritualism, nor will he be deluded by the revived Gnostic religions of Eddyism, Unity School of Christianity, or other branches of the misnamed New Thought.

In studying any book of the Bible it is well to have its outline clearly in mind. I submit the following synoptic analysis as a suggestive outline of the Epistle to the Colossians:

PART ONE: DOCTRINAL. Colossians 1:1—3:4.

Salutation, 1:1-2.
Introduction, 1:3-8.
Paul's Prayer and Thanksgiving, 1:9-14.
Twofold Headship of Christ, 1:15-19.
Twofold Reconciliation, 1:20-22.

Twofold Ministry of the Present Dispensation,
   1:23-29.
Christ the True Wisdom—Revelation of the mystery
   of God, 2:1-7.
Christ the Antidote for Agnostic Philosophy,
   2:8-10.
Christ the Antidote for Jewish Legality, 2:11-17.
Christ the Antidote for Gnostic Mysticism, 2:18-19.
Christ the Antidote for Carnal Asceticism, 2:20-23.
Christ the Believer's Life and Object, 3:1-4.

PART TWO: PRACTICAL. Colossians 3:5—4:18.

Practical Holiness by Conformity to Christ, 3:5-17.
Natural Relationships Sanctified, 3:18-4:1.
Concluding Exhortations, 4:2-6.
Salutations, 4:7-18.

This is, of course, in no sense arbitrary. Many
other outlines have been suggested, and some of
these may be much better than that which I have
suggested. But it is along these lines that I purpose
examining afresh this precious portion of the Word
of God, which, like all Scripture, is written for our
learning, and seems to have increasing value as new
cults and false systems abound, all designed to
make us lose sight of the Head and forget our
union with Him in glory.

THE SALUTATION AND INTRODUCTION

Colossians 1:1-8

Paul, an apostle of Jesus Christ by the will of God, and Timotheus our brother, to the saints and faithful brethren in Christ which are at Colosse: Grace be unto you, and peace, from God our Father and the Lord Jesus Christ (Colossians 1:1-2).

Thirteen Epistles in the New Testament begin with the name Paul. A fourteenth letter, concerning the authorship of which there is considerable dispute, is nevertheless generally accepted as from the same pen, namely, the Epistle to the Hebrews. But the opening word of that Epistle is God. The thirteen beginning with the word Paul, are addressed either to churches among the Gentiles, or to individual believers, who were on full Church ground. Paul was the apostle to the Gentiles and as such he magnified his office. He was not the apostle to the Hebrews. If, therefore, he was the one chosen to write that wonderful opening up of the old and new covenants, as I firmly believe, it was quite in keeping with his Gentile apostleship that his name should be hidden. Christ alone was the Apostle and Prophet of the new covenant, as Moses and Aaron had been of the old, and so the opening word of Hebrews is simply *God,* but God speaking in His Son.

17

In this Colossian letter, as in the Philippian Epistle, Paul associated Timothy with him in the salutation. The bond between these two men of God, so far apart in age though they were, was a very real one. Timothy was converted during Paul's ministry at Lystra, and on his next visit to the same region the brethren took occasion heartily to commend this young man to him, as one in whom marked spiritual graces were manifest, and who gave evidence of considerable gift, and was therefore, in their judgment, suited to go out in the ministry of the Word. Acting on their advice, Paul took Timothy with him in the work after the elder brethren had solemnly laid their hands upon him, commending him to God for this special service. Throughout the years that followed, Timothy had proven himself in every respect reliable and devoted. His unselfish concern for the welfare of the people of God and his loyal attachment to his human leader endeared him very much to the venerable apostle. It would seem that Timothy had even accompanied Paul, or else followed him to Rome, and was either sharing his imprisonment, or within easy reach doing what he could to alleviate the suffering of the apostle, as well as ministering among the Roman believers. So he here connects the young preacher with himself when he sends his greetings to the saints at Colosse.

Paul attributed his own apostleship directly to

the will of God. It was He who had revealed
Christ both to and in him, and set him apart for
service, commissioning him to proclaim the un-
searchable riches of grace among the Gentiles. It
would be preposterous to suppose that the laying
on of hands of the Church at Antioch, as mentioned in Acts 13, conferred any authority whatever upon either Barnabas or Paul, inasmuch as
they had been approved laborers in the gospel
for some time. It simply expressed, as in Timothy's case, the fellowship of the local assembly.
It was the Holy Spirit who sent them forth and
ordained them. Writing to the Galatians also,
Paul uses similar expressions, and declares he is
an apostle not of men nor by men. This is a
principle of far-reaching importance in connection with the work of the ministry. Whenever
men presume to add anything to the divine call
or to confer authority on a servant of Christ,
they are usurping the place of the Holy Spirit.
The most that any "laying on of hands" can do
is to express fellowship in the work.

In the second verse the Christians at Colosse
are addressed as "the saints and faithful brethren." The first expression suggests the divine
call; the second, the human response. It is God
who designates His redeemed ones as saints,
yet Romanists and many Protestants are generally astray as to the meaning of the term.
With the first class, a saint is a particularly holy

person who displays great devotion or possesses miraculous powers, and is credited in the calendar of intermediaries with a superabundance of merit or goodness which may be appropriated by others. With many who profess greater enlightenment, a saint is one who has become victorious in the struggle with sin, and has been received triumphantly into Heaven. So they speak of the Christian dead as "sainted." But the scriptural conception is altogether different. The vilest sinner is constituted by God, a saint, the moment he puts his trust in the Lord Jesus Christ, "who was delivered for our offences and raised again for our justification." Thus we are saints by calling and not primarily by practice. However, we should be careful not to divorce the practical side of things from the doctrinal. Being saints, we are now responsible to live in a saintly way. In other words, we are to live out practically what God has already declared to be true of us doctrinally. We do not become saints by the display of saintly virtues; but because we are saints we are to cultivate saintly characters. This, of course, is done in communion with God, in obedience to His Word, as we walk in the power of the Holy Spirit.

The second expression, "faithful brethren," does not, I take it, imply any advance upon the first one, nor do the two terms indicate two classes of believers. "Faithful brethren" are really brethren who believe; even as we read elsewhere, "They that be of faith are blessed with faithful Abraham." It might be translated, either, "They that have faith are blessed with faithful Abraham," or, "They that believe are blessed with believing Abraham." There is an intentional connection between the two terms. All real Christians, therefore, are believing or faithful brethren. If any profess to be Christ's who do not believe His Word, they but show themselves to be unreal and false to their profession. For it is written, "He that cometh to God must believe that He is, and that He is the rewarder of them that diligently seek Him." And again we are told, "If ye continue in My word, then are ye My disciples indeed."

The usual apostolic salutation follows. "Grace be unto you and peace, from God our Father and the Lord Jesus Christ." Grace is God's free unmerited favor. It is even more than that. It is favor against merit. When we merit the very opposite God lavishes His loving-kindness upon us. That is grace; and what saint can but echo the words in the hymn,

> Since our souls have known His love,
> What mercies has He made us prove?

He who sits upon a throne of grace bids us come boldly to obtain grace and mercy as daily needs arise.

Peace is here, of course, the peace of God garrisoning His people's hearts in the day of evil. It is peace amid the most disquieting circumstances, because assured that "all things work together for good to them who love God, who are the called according to His purpose" (Rom. 8:28).

We pass on, then, to the introduction:

We give thanks to God and the Father of our Lord Jesus Christ, praying always for you, since we heard of your faith in Christ Jesus, and of the love which ye have to all the saints, for the hope which is laid up for you in heaven, whereof ye heard before in the word of the truth of the gospel; which is come unto you, as it is in all the world; and bringeth forth fruit, as it doth also in you, since the day ye heard (of it), and knew the grace of God in truth: as ye also learned of Epaphras, our dear fellowservant, who is for you a faithful minister of Christ; who also declared unto us your love in the Spirit (Colossians 1:3-8).

We are reminded of the introduction to the Epistle to the Ephesians as we read these words, which begin with an expression of thanksgiving to the God and Father of our Lord Jesus Christ. This presents God in a double character as Creator and as Saviour. It is through Jesus Christ that our salvation is mediated. Having heard of the conversion of the Colossians, the apostle's heart was stirred to prayer on their behalf. He writes, "Praying always for you since we heard." For him to learn of others coming to Christ invariably meant that his burden of prayer was increased. He felt, as few men ever have felt, the great need of intercession for the people of God, for he knew well the fearful opposition of Satan, the prince and god of this world, toward those who trust in the Lord Jesus Christ; and he realized the prevailing power of prayer to defeat the adversary. Therefore he bows in the presence of God in earnest supplication on behalf of those whom grace has saved, and he tells us farther on what it was for which he prayed; so we do not now linger on that.

It is interesting to notice how faith, love and hope are linked together here as in so many other places in Scripture. The order is different in 1 Corinthians 13. There, where he is exalting love, he puts faith first, hope second, and love last, as that which will abide when the other two have passed away. But here it is hope that closes that life which begins with faith, and the two are linked together by love. Faith lays hold of the cross. Hope looks on to the glory. Love is the power that constrains the saint in view of both.

It was a Divine Person to whom they had trusted their souls. People are troubled sometimes for fear their faith should not be of the right quality, or might prove of insufficient quantity to save them. But it is important to observe that it is not the character nor the amount of faith that saves. It is the Person in whom faith rests. The strongest faith in self-effort, or in the Church, or religious observances, would leave the soul forever lost. But the feeblest faith in the Christ who died and rose again saves eternally. Some people try to make a Saviour of their faith, but Christ alone is the Saviour; and faith is but the hand that reaches out to Him.

Then he speaks of the love which they had to all the saints. This is precious indeed, and is the evidence both of the divine nature imparted in new birth and of the indwelling of the Holy Spirit. It is the very nature of the new-born soul to love not only God, but those who are begotten of Him. This love knows no sectarian limitation, but embraces all the people of God.

Hope looks on to the future; so he speaks of the hope which is laid up in Heaven, and of this they had learned in the word of the truth of the gospel. No one fully appreciates the gospel who leaves out the blessed hope of the Lord's return to receive His people to be with Himself in the Father's house. This is the glad consummation of the believer's life of faith and love and hope. Death is never set before the believer as his hope —but always it is the Lord's return for which he is to wait.

The gospel is God's good news about His Son, and therefore, when fully preached, necessarily includes the proclamation of His true sinless humanity, His Deity, His virgin birth, His vicarious sacrifice, His glorious resurrection, His present session as Advocate and High Priest at God's right hand in Heaven, and His coming again to reign in power and righteousness when all His redeemed will be associated with Him. All these precious truths are included in the word of the truth of the gospel.

In verse six we learn that this gospel, even in Paul's day, had been carried to the very ends of the earth. The same message that had reached Colosse had been preached in all the world, as verse twenty-three also declares. And, wherever this great evangel of the cross had gone, it had produced fruit to the praise and glory of God in those who believed it. It is the height of folly to look for fruit before the soul has settled peace, or to expect evidence of salvation in the life before the gospel has been believed. Salvation is altogether of grace. Human effort has no place in it at all. Neither are we saved by the work of the Spirit within us producing that ninefold fruit mentioned in Galatians 5. We are saved by the work of Christ for us, a work done altogether outside of ourselves, and in which we had no part excepting to commit the sins that put the Saviour on the cross. The old colored man expressed it correctly when he said, "I did my part and God did His—I did the sinning, and God did the saving; I took to running away from Him as fast as my sins could carry me, and He took after me until He run me down!" Others might express it more elegantly, but no one could tell it more clearly.

The gospel is a message to be believed, not a collection of precepts or a code of laws to be obeyed. It is of faith that it might be by grace —"Not of works lest any man should boast." But the moment the message is believed it produces new life in the soul, and the Spirit seals the believer by coming to dwell within him. This invariably results in precious fruit for God. And this the Colossian believers had exemplified in their own experiences since they heard and knew the grace of God in truth. Observe that the italicized words, "of it," are better omitted.

It was not through the Apostle Paul that the message had been carried to Colosse, as we have already noticed. So far as we know he had never visited that city as a messenger of the cross. He speaks in this letter of those whose faces he had not seen in the flesh. It was another devoted man of God, Epaphras by name, who had proclaimed the gospel to them. Paul speaks of him affectionately as "our dear fellowservant," and he declares that he was a faithful minister of Christ. His outstanding characteristic, as gathered from Colossians 4:12, was that of fervency in prayer. How blessed when faithful preaching and fervent prayer go together! Alas, that they are so often divorced!

In verse 8, as we have seen, we get the only reference to the Holy Spirit that is found in this Epistle. It has already been remarked that when the truth as to Christ, the Head of the Church, is being called in question, or when Satan is seeking to interpose anything between the soul and Christ, God will not even occupy the saints with the person or work of the Spirit, lest by occupation with subjective truth they lose sight of the great objective verities. So here the reference to the Spirit is only incidental. He simply mentions the fact that Epaphras had told them of their love in the Spirit. It was a precious testimony to the happy state of these dear young Christians, so recently brought out of Paganism with all its abominations. Now as a company set apart to the name of the Lord Jesus Christ, they were characterized by that love which the Spirit sheds abroad in the hearts of those who are born of God. This is all-important.

To pretend to great zeal for the truth of the one Body, while failing to manifest the love of the Spirit, is to put the emphasis in the wrong place. Doctrinal correctness will never atone for lack of brotherly love. It is far more to God who is Himself love, in His very nature, that His people walk in love one toward another, than that they contend valiantly for set forms of truth, however scriptural. "Truthing in love" (which would correctly convey the thought of Ephesians 4:15) is more than contending for formulas. It is the manifestation of the truth in a life of love to God and to those who are His, as well as for poor lost sinners for whom Christ died.

LECTURE 3

PAUL'S PRAYER AND THANKSGIVING

Colossians 1:9-14

For this cause we also, since the day we heard it, do not cease to pray for you, and to desire that ye might be filled with the knowledge of His will in all wisdom and spiritual understanding; that ye might walk worthy of the Lord unto all pleasing, being fruitful in every good work, and increasing in the knowledge of God; strengthened with all might according to His glorious power, unto all patience and longsuffering with joyfulness; giving thanks unto the Father, which hath made us meet to be partakers of the inheritance of the saints in light; who hath delivered us from the power of darkness, and hath translated us into the kingdom of His dear Son: in whom we have redemption through His blood, even the forgiveness of sins.

This section reminds us of the prayers of the apostle for the Ephesians, as recorded in chapters 1 and 3 of that Epistle. There is something very precious and exceedingly instructive in being thus permitted to share the thoughts of, and notice the petitions offered up by the Apostle Paul for the Lord's people in various circumstances. His deep concern for their growth in grace, their enlightenment in divine things, their apprehension of the purpose of God, and the manifestation of spiritual power in the life—all these come out very strikingly as he bows his knees before the God and Father of our Lord Jesus Christ. He was not content to know people were justified and hence safe for eternity.

28

He was controlled by the earnest desire that each one should understand the hope of his calling, in order that the life and walk might be in harmony with it, and that they might remember they were here to represent Christ, their risen Head. These are what formed the burden of his prayers. It is questionable if any merely human writer has ever been able to give as helpful suggestions for our own prayer life as will come to us in our meditation upon these various petitions.

In verses 9-11 we have set forth certain blessings for which he prays. In verses 12-14 there are others for which he gives thanks. It is very important to distinguish these things; that is, to have clearly in mind the privileges and blessings which are non-forfeitable, because confirmed to us by God in Christ from the moment we believe on Him who died to make them good to us; and the additional blessings for which we need to pray daily, and concerning which there should be constant soul-exercise lest we fail to enter into and enjoy them. Many believers fail in not distinguishing the two classes of blessings. In certain circles almost every public prayer will be concluded somewhat as follows: "We pray Thee, forgive us our sins, and wash us in the blood of Jesus; receive us into Thy kingdom, give us Thy Holy Spirit, and save us at last for Christ's sake, Amen." Yet every petition in this prayer has already been granted to the believer

in Christ! God has forgiven us all trespasses.
We are cleansed by the blood of Jesus. He has
already translated us out of the kingdom of darkness into that of the Son of His love. He has
sealed us with His Holy Spirit, for "if any man
have not the Spirit of Christ, he is none of His."
And we are saved eternally from the moment we
believe the gospel. Therefore we might far rather
cry exultantly in faith: "We thank Thee that
Thou hast forgiven all our sins, and washed us
from every stain in the blood of the Lamb. Thou
hast brought us into Thy kingdom, given us Thy
Holy Spirit, and saved us for eternity." Faith
says "Amen" to what God has declared in His
Word to be true. To go on praying for blessings
that He tells us are already ours is the most subtle
kind of unbelief, and robs us of the enjoyment
that should be our portion if we but had faith to
lay hold of the exceeding great and precious
promises which are ours in Christ.

      Let us then follow carefully the apostle's
prayer, weighing every phrase and clause. He
says, "I pray for you that you might be filled
with the knowledge of His will." Those who were
troubling the Colossian saints boasted of their
superior knowledge. They had evolved a complex
system of mystical and wholly imaginative teaching in regard to the soul's approach to God
through an interminable number of intermediaries, coupled with ascetic regulations and legal

observances. In their eyes the gospel as preached by Paul was simplicity indeed; so much so that they looked upon it as a child's conception of the philosophy of the universe, which was puerile for men of mature minds. But he who knew this gospel in all its grandeur, as few other men have ever known it, speaks here of being "filled with the *knowledge* of God's will"; and he uses a superlative in the place of a word which the Gnostics were very fond of. They boasted of *"Gnosis"*–"knowledge." He says, *"Epignosis,"* meaning, literally, "super-knowledge." It is in the divine revelation alone that this is found. By this term, "the knowledge of His will," I do not understand him to be referring merely to God's will for the individual believer's life from day to day (though, indeed, that would be involved in the fuller thought of the will of God, as the drop of water is included in the ocean), but by His will, I take it, he means the wondrous plan or programme of the Father known from eternity and now being carried out in time to have its consummation in the ages to come–"The eternal purpose of God." Here is super-knowledge indeed! Here is that which the cleverest human intellect could never fathom, apart from divine revelation. And this revelation we have in our Bibles. It runs throughout the Scriptures from Genesis to the Apocalypse; furnishing a theme for devout contemplation, and demanding enthusiastic study and careful examination by men of the most erudite minds and brilliant intellects, and the deepest investigation of the most spiritual believers: but in which also the unlearned and the ignorant Christians will find constant enjoyment if they but allow themselves to be guided by the Spirit in searching the Scriptures to see whether these things are so.

So the words that follow stress the important fact that truth is not learned through the intellect alone. He prays that they may comprehend these things "in all wisdom and spiritual understanding." Wisdom is the ability to use knowledge aright, and is imparted by the Spirit, and He alone gives true understanding. Therefore, if we would learn the mind of God as revealed in His Word, there must be subjection of heart to the divine Teacher, and that self-judgment and self-distrust which leads one to walk softly before God; not in self-will or egotism, but in humility and lowly dependence on the One who inspired the Holy Scriptures, which alone can make wise the simple.

Then we learn in verse ten that if God opens up His truth to us it is not merely that we may delight in the wondrous things He has revealed, but it is His desire that we walk in the power of that which He makes known to us. So the prayer goes on, "That ye might walk worthy of the Lord unto all pleasing." We can only walk worthy of the Lord as we know His mind. The study of His Word and a godly walk should ever go together.

It is noteworthy that in Ephesians 4:1 we are exhorted to "walk worthy of our vocation," or calling, as members of the Body of Christ, while in Philippians 1:27 we are told to "walk worthy of the gospel," which we are left in the world to proclaim. Then in 1 Thessalonians 2:12 we are bidden to "walk worthy of God," Himself, who has called us to His kingdom and glory. Our walk is ever to be in accordance with the truth revealed to our souls. So here we are to walk worthy of the Lord, He who is the Head of the New Creation to which we now belong.

Dr. Griffith Thomas points out that the word here rendered *"pleasing"* is not found in any other passage in the New Testament, but is used in Greek elsewhere to mean "a preference of the will of others before our own." Bishop Handley Moule translated the phrase, "Unto every anticipation of His will."

This is blessed indeed, when the will of God is sweeter far than our own will, and we delight in doing as He would have us, not in order to propitiate His favor, but to give joy to His heart. Yet most of us learn so slowly that the only true happiness in life is to be found in doing the will of God. In vain we seek for satisfaction by trying to have our own way, until at last like a bird, wearied out with flying against the bars of its cage, we fall back upon the will of God and learn that in it the mind and heart find perfect rest.

> Oh, the peace my Saviour gives;
>   Peace I never knew before;
> And the way has brighter grown
>   Since I've learned to trust Him more.

It is the subject believer who becomes fruitful, so he adds, "being fruitful in every good work." Or it might be better rendered, "bearing fruit in every good work." When we speak of every good work, we are not to think simply of preaching the gospel, teaching the Holy Scriptures, or engaging in what is sometimes called Christian activity or church work. We are very prone to do this and to distinguish between secular employment and sacred. But we need to be reminded over and over again that everything in a believer's life is sacred. The Church of Rome distinguishes seven sacraments. But every act of a Christian should have a sacramental character, using the word as generally understood. Whatever is right and proper for me to do in any circumstance, I should do with an eye single to the glory of God, and by so doing I shall be bearing fruit unto Him. The testimony of the little maid who said, "I know I am converted, and my mistress knows I am converted too, because I sweep under the mats now," has gone around the world, and wherever this gospel is preached it is told for a memorial of her. She was right, for even in the most commonplace duties she was bearing fruit for God, and she sought to glorify Him by the faithful performance of her responsibilities, done not with eyeservice as a man-pleaser, but as pleasing "God which trieth the heart."

Then we have, "Increasing in the knowledge of God." This is more than the knowledge of the Word of God, though undoubtedly the one leads to the other, for God has made Himself known through His Word. But we increase in the knowledge of God as we walk with Him from day to day, learning more of His love and grace, His tender compassion, His care for those who trust Him; and proving, too, how solemn a thing it is to deviate from the path of obedience and thus be exposed to the rod of correction. We know God as we walk with Him. We walk with Him as we obey His Word.

> We know Him as we could not know
> Through Heaven's golden years;
> We there shall see His glorious face,
> On earth they saw His tears;
>
> The touch that heals the broken heart
> Is never felt above;
> His angels know His blessedness,
> His way-worn saints His love.

We shall thank Him for all eternity for every trial along our pilgrim path that gave Him a new opportunity to display His grace and to manifest His heart to us, His needy people, so dependent upon His power and grace.

As we thus go on with Him, we will be strengthened with all might according to His glorious power, and this "unto all patience and long-suffering with joyfulness." How much have we here upon which our souls may well meditate! It is He who supplies strength, giving all needed power in order that we may overcome in every adverse circumstance, according to the might of His glory. What room is there for discouragement, as temptations and trials surround me and seem about to overwhelm me, if I realize that the very same spiritual dynamic, that wondrous energy which raised Christ from the dead, operates in me by the Spirit, that I may be even more than victorious through Him who loves me!

But we might have supposed that all this manifestation of divine energy would result in producing some great outward display that would astonish and amaze an unbelieving world. But no, it is "unto all patience." I need this dynamic force so to keep the flesh in subjection that I can patiently endure whatever God in His wisdom sees fit to let me go through while in this wilderness world. Neither will I simply endure with stoical resignation, such as even a pagan philosopher might exhibit, but God would have me patiently wait upon Him and rest in His love

even amid circumstances that press hard upon
my soul, with long-suffering, that is uncomplain-
ing endurance. But there is even more than
this. In the hour of trial a song of gladness
will well up in the heart where the will of
God is supreme. And so he adds, "With joyfulness." Here is something that the natural
man knows nothing of—joy in the time of trial;
gladness in the time of hardship; songs in the
night, though the darkness be overwhelming;
praises to the God of my salvation when nature
shrinks and trembles. It was thus the martyrs
could rejoice in the arena when thrown to the
lions; or exult in the Lord when the flames
leaped up around them as they suffered at the
stake. And myriads of sufferers all through the
Christian era have been able to testify to the sus-
taining grace of God, when the spirit seemed
about to be overwhelmed. "The joy of the Lord
is your strength."

The three verses that follow are in marked
contrast to those we have just been considering.
We have now thanksgiving instead of prayer.
Here all is positive and eternally settled. The
blessings enumerated are ours from the moment
we believe in the Lord Jesus Christ, and are absolutely non-forfeitable. To pray for these is to
dishonor God by casting doubt upon His Word.
Notice the three "haths" and the one "have" of
the Authorized Version; words that speak of

present possession. Faith lays hold of such testimonies and rejoices in the assurance that these wondrous blessings are to be enjoyed even now.

First we read, "Giving thanks unto the Father, which hath made us meet to be partakers of the inheritance of the saints in light." This is true of every Christian, and there are no degrees in this divine fitness. We are made meet to be partakers of our glorious inheritance the instant we are cleansed from our sins and receive the new nature, which is imparted by a divine operation when we are born of God. How different are the thoughts of even some of the best of men! How often we hear it said of some devoted and aged believer, "He is fit for Heaven at last." But he was just as truly fit for Heaven the moment he received Christ as he is at the end of a long life of devoted service. Fitness does not depend upon experience. But in this connection it is well to remember that there is something more than the Father's house, the inheritance of the saints in light, before us. It is important that we should also have in mind the coming glorious kingdom. In 2 Peter 1:10 and 11 we are told, "Wherefore the rather, brethren, give diligence to make your calling and election sure: for if ye do these things, ye shall never fall: for so an entrance shall be ministered unto you abundantly into the everlasting kingdom of our Lord and Saviour Jesus Christ." The expression, "these things," refers to the various Christian virtues enumerated in verses 5-7. It is through these things we are fitted for a place in the coming kingdom, but it is the justifying, regenerating grace of God that alone makes us meet for our heavenly inheritance. In other words, it is important that we distinguish between salvation by grace and reward for service.

We next read, "Who hath delivered us from the power [or, authority] of darkness, and hath translated us into the kingdom of the Son of His love." This is a different kingdom to that of which we have been reading in 2 Peter. It is the present sphere where Christ's authority is owned, the kingdom which we see and enter by new birth. This kingdom consists not of "meat and drink, but of righteousness, peace and joy in the Holy Ghost." As born of God we have lost our old standing as sons of fallen Adam in the Satanic kingdom of darkness. We have been brought out of the darkness into the marvelous light of children of God, and it is here, of course, that responsibility comes in to walk as children of light. J. N. Darby was once asked, "But suppose a Christian turned his back on the light; what then?" He replied, "Then the light will shine upon his back!" Most blessed it is to see this. We are in the light in all the value of the precious atoning blood of our Lord Jesus Christ sprinkled upon the mercy-seat, the very throne of

God from which the light shines.

Lastly we read, "In Him we have redemption through His blood, even the forgiveness of sins." There is some question as to the MS. authority of the expression, "through His blood." The best editors generally omit it. It seems to have been inserted from Ephesians 1:7. But that does not for a moment touch the truth of which we have been speaking. It would only suggest the fuller character of redemption which is both by blood and by power. The blood having been shed, the omnipotent power of God makes redemption real to the believer, whose sins have all been forgiven and who has been lifted completely out of those circumstances in which he was once exposed to the judgment of God. As the soul meditates on the wonderful truths so succinctly presented in these three verses the heart will surely go out to God in worship and the life be yielded for devoted service!

Let me recapitulate, as I close:

He hath made us meet for the inheritance of the saints in light.

He hath delivered us from the authority of darkness.

He hath translated us into the kingdom of the Son of His love.

We have redemption through His blood.

Blessed certainties these that tell in unmistakable terms of our eternal security if once in Christ!

LECTURE 4

CHRIST THE FIRSTBORN

Twofold Headship of Christ and Twofold Reconciliation

Colossians 1:15-22

Who is the image of the invisible God, the firstborn of every creature: for by Him were all things created, that are in heaven, and that are in earth, visible and invisible, whether they be thrones, or dominions, or principalities, or powers: all things were created by Him, and for Him: and He is the Head of the Body, the Church: who is the beginning, the firstborn from the dead; that in all things He might have the preeminence. For it pleased the Father that in Him should all fulness dwell (Colossians 1:15-19).

We have had our Lord Jesus before us as the Son of God's love in whom we have redemption. Our attention is now directed to Him as the One who has made God known to us. Coming into the world as man He is the image of the invisible God—that God who to the Gnostic could never be known or understood. We are told in John 1:18, "No man hath seen God at any time; the Only Begotten Son, which is in the bosom of the Father, He hath declared Him." Five times in the New Testament He is called the Only Begotten, and this endearing term always refers to what He is from eternity, with no thought of generation connected with it. It implies unity in

41

life and nature. Isaac is called, in Hebrews 11: 17, Abraham's only begotten son—yet Ishmael was also his son. But the link between Abraham and Isaac was of a unique character. And so, as the Only Begotten, our Lord is the unique Son, eternally that, for if He be not the Eternal Son then we lose the Eternal Father too. God existed from all eternity as three Persons, Father, Son, and Holy Spirit, but never became visible to created eyes whether of angels or men until the Holy Babe was born in Bethlehem. The Son was as truly the invisible God as the Father or the Spirit until the incarnation. Then He was seen of angels, and later on by men. As thus begotten of God of a virgin mother without any human father, He is Son of God in a new sense. And it is as such He is owned of the Father as the firstborn of every creature, or perhaps the expression would be better rendered, the firstborn of all creation. It is not that He is Himself created, but He is the Head of all that has been created.

It will be seen from what has been said above that the title "Firstborn" is not to be taken solely as a divine title, though He is divine who bears this name. But it is as Man He is owned of God the Father as the Firstborn. And how right it is that such a title should be conferred upon Him, for "by Him were all things created." Coming into the world as Man, He takes that place in virtue of the dignity of His person. His is the glory of the Firstborn because He is the Creator. The firstborn is the heir and pre-eminent one. It is important to remember that in Scripture the firstborn is not necessarily the one born first. Many instances might be cited where the one born first was set to one side and the right of the firstborn given to another. One only needs to mention the cases of Ishmael and Isaac, Esau and Jacob, Reuben and Joseph, Manasseh and Ephraim, to which many more might be added. The first man is set aside and the second man is acknowledged as the firstborn. And so Adam and all his race are set to one side as unfit to retain authority over the world in order that Christ, the Second Man, the Lord from Heaven, may be acknowledged as the Firstborn.

It will be seen how tremendously all this would weigh against the Gnostic conception of a created Jesus to whom the Christ, a divine emanation, came, upon His enlightenment following His baptism, and who left Him again at the cross. It was the Eternal Son who stooped in grace to become the Son of God as born of a virgin. It should never be lost sight of that His Sonship is spoken of in these two distinct ways in Scripture. As the Eternal Son, pre-incarnate, He is called "the Son," "the Son of the Father," and also the "Son of God," but the latter term generally refers to what He became when He took humanity into relation with Deity and became God and Man in one Person with two natures, in accordance with the word of the angel, addressed to His virgin mother, "That Holy One, who shall be born of thee, shall be called the Son of God." It is necessary to be very accurate in our thinking when considering this great mystery, and not to let our thoughts run beyond Holy Scripture. It was of the virgin-born Saviour that Micah prophesied, saying, "But thou, Bethlehem-Ephratah, though thou be little among the thousands of Judah, yet out of thee shall He come forth unto Me that is to be ruler in Israel; whose goings forth have been from of old, from everlasting," or, as the margin puts it, "from the days of eternity" (Micah 5:2).

The five passages in which He is called the Only Begotten, if carefully weighed, will make this clear.

The Word became flesh, and tabernacled among us, and we beheld His glory (the glory as of the only begotten of the Father), full of grace and truth (Lit. Rend., John 1:14).

No man hath seen God at any time; the only begotten Son, subsisting in the bosom of the Father, He hath told Him out (Lit. Rend., John 1:18).

For God so loved the world, that He gave His only begotten Son, that whosoever believeth in Him should not perish, but have everlasting life (John 3:15).

He that believeth on Him is not condemned: but he that believeth not is condemned already, because he hath not believed in the name of the only begotten Son of God (John 3:18).

In this was manifested the love of God toward us, because that God sent His only begotten Son into the world, that we might live through Him (1 John 4:9).

The five other passages referred to in which He is called the Firstborn, or First Begotten, are as follows:—

Who is the image of the invisible God, the firstborn of every creature [or, of all creation] (Col. 1:15).

And He is the Head of the Body, the Church; who is the beginning, the firstborn from the dead; that in all things He might have the preeminence (Col. 1:18).

For whom He did foreknow, He also did predestinate, to be conformed to the image of His Son, that He might be the firstborn among many brethren (Rom. 8:29).

Jesus Christ, who is the faithful witness, and the first begotten of [or, from among] the dead, and the prince of the kings of the earth (Rev. 1:5).

And when He bringeth the firstborn into the habitable earth, again He saith, And let all the angels of God worship Him (Lit. Rend., Heb. 1:6).

It was He who brought all things into being. "Without Him was not anything made that was made." All the inhabitants of Heaven and of earth owe their life to Him. Beings visible or invisible are all the creatures of His hand. Angels, no matter how great their dignity, whether thrones, or dominions, or principalities, or powers, all were created by Him and for His glory. The Gnostics placed these varied ranks of exalted beings between Him and God; but He is shown to be superior to them all, for He brought them into being. He is Himself the

uncreated Son who became Man to accomplish
the work of redemption. Higher than all angels,
He was made a little lower than they for the
suffering of death.

In verse 17 His priority is insisted on in another way. "He is before all things." By the
term "all things" we understand all that has
been created, whether *personal* or *impersonal*. He
Himself existed as the eternal Word before them
all. "In the beginning was the Word, and the
Word was with God, and the Word was God."
Full Deity is ascribed to Him, yet distinct personality. Moreover, it is He who sustains the
universe, for "by Him all things consist," or,
"hold together." It is His hand that holds the
stars in their courses, directs the planets in their
orbits, and controls the laws of the universe.
How great is His dignity, and yet how low did
He stoop for our salvation!

But He is firstborn in another sense in verse
18. Man rejected Him saying, "This is the heir;
come, let us kill Him that the inheritance may
be ours." So they slew Him, hanging Him on
a tree. But it was then that God made His
soul an offering for sin, and He accomplished the
great work of redemption for which He came.
"He died, the Just for the unjust, that He might
bring us to God." But having been delivered on
account of our offences, He was raised again
on account of our justification. As brought

again from the dead He became the Firstborn in
a new sense, the Head of the new creation. As
Man on earth in incarnation there was no union
with Him. Union is in resurrection. He was
alone as the Incarnate Son here in the world; as
He Himself says: "Except a corn of wheat fall
into the ground and die, it abideth alone; but if
it die, it shall bring forth much fruit." It is
in resurrection that He is hailed as the Firstborn
from among the dead. As such He becomes the
Head of the Body, the Church; the Beginning of
the creation of God; Firstborn among many
brethren; the Resurrection King-Priest; the One
who is yet to rule the world in manifested glory;
the Melchizedek of the age to come, as Hebrews
shows us.

Verse 19 is admittedly difficult to translate
euphoniously, and in our English version the
words "the Father" have been supplied in order
to complete what seems like an incomplete sentence. But it should be carefully noted that there
is nothing in the original to answer to the term
"the Father." It is rather "the fulness" that was
pleased to dwell in Jesus. And if this verse is
connected with verse 9 of chapter 2 we shall
understand at once what is in view. "In Him
all the fulness (of the Godhead) was pleased to
dwell." Deity has been fully manifested in Jesus
our adorable Lord. This is the mystery of godliness of 1 Timothy 3:16. The Gnostics used this

term, "the fulness," or *"pleroma,"* for the divine
essence, dwelling in unapproachable light; and
in a lesser sense for the illumination that comes
when one reaches the higher plane of knowledge.
But all the divine *pleroma* dwelt in Jesus. All
that God is, He is, so that we may now say, "We
know God in knowing Him." He has fully manifested Him.

As we ponder the wondrous truths brought before us in these verses the spiritual mind will
feel more and more that we have here mysteries
of a character beyond the ability of the human
mind to grasp. Here is truth for pious meditation, to stir the soul to worship and thanksgiving;
not at all for the exercise of the intellect in
theological speculations. As we read we would
bow our hearts in lowly adoration and thus gaze
upon the face of Him who has come forth from
the glory that He had with the Father in all the
past eternity in order to bring us into the knowledge of God.

In the next section we are told of a *Twofold
Reconciliation.*

And having made peace through the blood of His cross,
by Him to reconcile all things unto Himself; by Him, I
say, whether they be things in earth, or things in heaven.
And you, that were sometime alienated and enemies in
your mind by wicked works, yet now hath He reconciled
in the body of His flesh through death, to present you
holy and unblameable and unreproveable in His sight
(Colossians 1:20-22).

In the portion we have just considered Christ
has been presented as the Firstborn in two distinct ways. We have had His twofold Headship;
first over all creation and then as Head of the
Body, the Church. In the verses now before us
we have reconciliation presented in a double
aspect. First, we have the future reconciliation
of all things, and then present individual reconciliation. He in whom all the fulness dwells has
made peace through the blood of His cross. Man
is never called upon in Scripture to make his own
peace with God. He is viewed as alienated and
an enemy; manifestly so, through wicked works.
Sin has come in between God and man, requir-
ing expiation ere the guilty rebel could be received by God in peace. Not only on earth, but
in Heaven has sin lifted up its serpent-head. In
fact it was in Heaven that sin began, when
Lucifer apostatized, leading with him a vast number of the angelic hosts. Therefore the heavens
themselves were unclean in the sight of God and
had to be purified by a better sacrifice than those
offered under the law. On the cross Christ tasted
death, and so far-reaching are the results of His
work that eventually all things in earth and in
Heaven will be reconciled to God upon the basis
of what He there accomplished. Whether for the
universe or for the individual sinner, He made
peace through the blood of His cross. Yet rebels remain in spite of the fact that peace has been made.

We may understand it if we remember that two nations which have been at war with one another may through their plenipotentiaries have agreed on terms of peace, and yet guerilla bands may insist on fighting, ignoring the peace that has been made. So men and demons still persist in refusing to own the divine authority, notwithstanding the fact that,

> Jesus' blood, through earth and skies,
> Mercy, free boundless mercy, cries.

For angels the terms of peace offer no pardon, but to the sinful sons of Adam clemency is extended, and he who will may trust in Christ and thus be reconciled to God. "Being justified by faith we have peace with God through our Lord Jesus Christ" (Rom. 5:1).

The reconciliation of all things includes two spheres, and two only. The time will come when all in earth and all in Heaven will be happily reconciled to God. When it is a question of subjugation, as in Phil. 2:10, there are three spheres. Heavenly, earthly, and infernal beings are at last to own the authority of our Lord Jesus Christ. But there is no hope held out in Scripture that the sad inhabitants of the infernal regions will ever be reconciled to God.

The reconciliation of verse 20 carries us on to the new Heaven and the new earth where righteousness will dwell, and the tabernacle of God shall be with men, and all the redeemed with the elect angels abide with Him in holy harmony. Sin has ruptured the state of peace and harmony that once existed between God and His creatures. Christ in death has wrought reconciliation, and so made it possible for that lost concord to be re-established, but in new creation.

This reconciliation is already accomplished for individual sinners who "were sometime alienated and enemies in their mind by wicked works," but who through infinite grace have been reconciled to God by the death of His Son. It is the soul's apprehension by faith of the infinite love of the offended Deity manifested in the death of the cross, that destroys the enmity and draws out the affections of the renewed man to God revealed in Christ. Well may the apostle exclaim elsewhere, "And all things are of God, who hath reconciled us to Himself by Jesus Christ, and hath given to us the ministry of reconciliation; to wit, that God was in Christ, reconciling the world unto Himself, not imputing their trespasses unto them, and hath committed unto us the word of reconciliation. Now then we are ambassadors for Christ, as though God did beseech you by us: we pray you in Christ's stead, be ye reconciled to God" (2 Cor. 5:18-20).

It is not the holy, wondrous life of Christ that has thus reconciled us. It is His sacrificial death. And as a result of that death we shall eventually be presented before God the Father unblameable in holiness and unreproveable in His sight. The sentence is not concluded in the 22nd verse, but the passage that follows introduces a new subject and therefore must be considered in a different connection.

In leaving the verses which we have been considering let us bear in mind the great outstanding truths that they would teach us. He who is the image of the invisible God has made peace for us by the blood of His cross. Now in resurrection He is our exalted Head, and we are the members of His Body. As Head, He is concerned about every redeemed one here on earth, who has thus, through grace, been united to Him. To own Him as Head is our first responsibility. We are to let nothing put Him at a distance or hinder our loyal subjection to Him through whom we have been reconciled to God.

LECTURE 5

PAUL'S TWOFOLD MINISTRY

Colossians 1:23-29

If ye continue in the faith grounded and settled, and be not moved away from the hope of the gospel, which ye have heard, and which was preached to every creature which is under heaven; whereof I Paul am made a minister; who now rejoice in my sufferings for you, and fill up that which is behind of the afflictions of Christ in my flesh for His Body's sake, which is the Church: whereof I am made a minister, according to the dispensation of God which is given to me for you, to fulfil the word of God (Colossians 1:23-25).

The "if" with which the 23rd verse begins has been the occasion of much perplexity to timid souls who hardly dare to accept the truth of the believer's eternal security, so conscious are they of their own weakness and insufficiency. But, rightly understood, there is nothing here to disturb any sincere believer in the Lord Jesus Christ. There are a number of similar "ifs" in the New Testament, and all with precisely the same object in view—the testing of profession. In 1 Cor. 15:1-2 we read, "Moreover, brethren, I declare unto you the gospel which I preached unto you, which also ye have received, and wherein ye stand; by which also ye are saved, *if* ye keep in memory what I preached unto you, unless

ye have believed in vain." Here the "if" is inserted in order to exercise the consciences of any
who, having professed to believe the gospel, are
in danger of forgetting the message, so proving
that they have never really received the truth
into their hearts. He would have them carefully
examine their foundations. Many there are
who readily profess to adopt Christianity and
unite themselves outwardly with the people of
God, who have never truly turned to the Lord
in repentance and rested their souls upon His
finished work. Such endure for a time, but soon
forget the claims of the gospel when Satanic
allurements would draw them away.

In Hebrews 3:6 we have another such "if."
"But Christ as a Son over His own house; whose
house are we, if we hold fast the confidence and
the rejoicing of the hope firm unto the end." The
meaning is plain. It is not enough to profess to
have the Christian hope. Those who are real will
hold fast unto the end, as we also read in chapter 10:38-39 of the same Epistle. Endurance is
the proof of reality. What God implants in the
soul is lasting, and we may be assured that He
who hath begun a good work in any one will perform it until the day of Jesus Christ, the time
when He shall come for His ransomed people, to
complete in glory what His grace began on earth.

Paul did not pretend to say who of the Colossians were really born of God. While he had

confidence that most of them were, he wrote in such a way as to stir up the consciences of any who were becoming slack. A readiness to adopt new and fanciful systems was a cause for grave concern. Those who are really children of God, grounded and strengthened in the truth, are not of the number who will be moved away from the hope of the gospel. They know too well what it has already done for them, to lightly turn away from it to some new and untried theory.

This gospel they had heard, as in the providence of God it had been preached in all the creation under Heaven. This is probably a better translation than that of the Authorized Version. It is hardly thinkable that the apostle meant that every creature in the habitable earth had heard the gospel. But it is a wonderful testimony to the devotion of the early believers that even within one generation after our Lord's ascension the evangel had been carried throughout the known world. Of this gospel Paul was made "minister." The indefinite article does not really help; it only lends color to the idea which came in later, that the ministry is a special class to which all believers do not belong. The apostle is not claiming that he is a minister in the sense in which that term has been used in later years. He was one addicted to the work of the ministry. That is, the gospel had been committed to him by God whom he served, as he says elsewhere, with his spirit in the gospel of His Son. This gospel ministry has been committed to all believers, and Paul is a sharer with others in making the testimony known. But in a preeminent way it was given to him to reveal it. As preached by Paul it bears the distinctive character of "the gospel of the glory."

Another ministry had also been given to him, even that of the assembly, the Body of Christ. So he goes on to say that he rejoices in whatever he might be called upon to suffer on behalf of the people of God, as in doing this he was filling up what was lacking of the afflictions of Christ in his own flesh. That is true of every real servant of God. To such an one the people of the Lord will ever be precious. And he will realize that in serving them and enduring trial on their behalf he is ministering in place of his absent Lord. Christ suffered once for all on the cross to put away sin. His faithful servants suffer in fellowship with Him for the perfecting of the saints, "for His Body's sake, which is the Church." The more devoted one is to Christ's interests down here, during His absence in Heaven, the more one will enter into this phase of suffering. It is godly shepherd-care that he has in mind; enduring affliction for the blessing of Christ's beautiful flock.

Of the Church Paul was made minister according to the dispensation of God given to him on our behalf to complete the divine testimony, or to fill up the Word of God. The whole counsel of God was not made known until Paul received this revelation of the mystery. This dispensation, or stewardship (for the two words are exactly the same in Greek), he unfolds more fully elsewhere; noticeably in the Epistle to the Ephesians which, as previously intimated, is the correlative to that to the Colossians. It was a special revelation given not to the twelve, but to him as the apostle of the new dispensation. He goes on with this theme in the verses that follow.

Even the mystery which hath been hid from ages and generations, but now is made manifest to His saints: to whom God would make known what is the riches of the glory of this mystery among the Gentiles; which is Christ in you, the hope of glory: whom we preach, warning every man, and teaching every man in all wisdom; that we may present every man perfect in Christ Jesus: whereunto I also labor, striving according to His working, which worketh in me mightily (Colossians 1:26-29).

It is important to remember that the mysteries of the New Testament are not necessarily things mysterious or abtruse. They are rather sacred secrets made known to the initiated.*

*A fuller discussion of this interesting subject appears in the author's handbook entitled, "The Mysteries of God," now out of print.

These divine secrets could never have been discovered by human reason, nor even by the child of God unless a special revelation had been given. The Gnostics made much of the mysteries of their systems. The Christian mysteries are in vivid contrast to these dreams of insubject men.

The mystery of the Church as the Body of Christ was never made known in Old Testament times, nor yet in the days when our Lord was on the earth. We are told distinctly it had been "hid from ages and generations, but now is made manifest to the saints." The divine method of making it known was by a special revelation to the Apostle Paul, as he tells us in Ephesians 3. But this revelation was not for him only. It was a ministry committed to him to pass on to the saints, "To whom God did make known the wealth of the splendor of this sacred secret among the nations, which is Christ among the Gentiles, the hope of glory." The Old Testament Scriptures clearly predicted the calling of the Gentiles, but always in subjection to Israel. During the present dispensation Israel, as we read in Romans 11, is set aside because of unbelief, and Christ is working among the nations, attracting weary hearts to Himself altogether apart from any thought of Jewish priority. Believing Jews and Gentiles are united by the Holy Spirit's baptism into the one Body, and thus all fleshly distinctions are done away. The middle wall of partition is broken down. This *is* the mystery.

Christ Himself, the Head of this Body, is the apostle's theme. Note his words, "whom we preach." To substitute *what* for *whom* we preach is a serious mistake. Christianity is centered in a Person, and no one preaches the gospel who does not preach Christ. When there is faith in Him the Spirit unites the believer to Him.

How earnest was the apostle in seeking to lead Christians into the knowledge of this precious truth, "warning every man, and teaching every man in all wisdom." His was the true pastor's heart, and he combined in a marvelous way the teacher's gift with this. The subject of his ministry was the perfecting of the saints, as he says elsewhere. He would present every man complete or full grown in Christ Jesus. To this end he earnestly labored according to that divine energy which wrought so powerfully in him for the salvation of souls and the upbuilding of the people of God.

False teachers would turn the eyes of the saints away from Christ, the glorified Head of the Body, in order that they might occupy them with specious systems of Satanic origin, and thus draw away disciples after themselves, as Paul had warned the Ephesian elders. But all true Spirit-given ministry is Christo-centric. Every faithful minister of the new dispensation would lift up the Lord Jesus before the admiring gaze of His people so that, occupied with Him, they might be transfigured into His likeness. Like John the Baptist he will say, "He must increase, but I must decrease."

No man really preaches the whole truth to-day who does not enter into the twofold ministry of this section of Colossians—the gospel and the Church. The former is proclaimed to sinners and is the power of God unto salvation to every one who believes. The latter is taught to saints and builds them up in the faith as to their present privileges, and corresponding responsibilities. I am called upon, not only to win sinners to Christ that they may be saved from impending wrath, but I am to seek to make "good churchmen" out of those already saved. This is not to insist on what is called denominational loyalty, nor to endeavor to sectionalize the saints and bring them into bondage to legal principles and practices for which there is no biblical warrant, but it is to show them their position as in the new creation, linked with their risen, glorified Head, and to lead them into the recognition of the unity of the Body, in which all believers have a part; that thus they may endeavor to keep the unity formed by the Holy Spirit, as they walk together in the uniting bond of peace.

Sad indeed is it when this very truth becomes a means of dividing those of like precious faith, when perverted by men of sectarian spirit and narrow cramped sympathies who are more concerned about building up local "causes" than edifying the Body of Christ!

That saints are not to neglect local responsibilities, out of which grows the relationship of church to church, is perfectly true. But it is not a unity or confederacy of assemblies that is denominated "the unity of the Spirit." It is rather that abiding unity which the Holy Ghost has formed by baptizing believers into one Body. If I set at nought any fellow-believer I am to that extent failing to keep this unity. As members one of another, having the same care one for the other, we show in a practical way the truth that we are one in Christ.

LECTURE 6

CHRIST THE TRUE WISDOM

THE REVELATION OF THE MYSTERY OF GOD

Colossians 2:1-7

For I would that ye knew what great conflict I have for you, and for them at Laodicea, and for as many as have not seen my face in the flesh; that their hearts might be comforted, being knit together in love, and unto all riches of the full assurance of understanding, to the acknowledgment of the mystery of God, and of the Father, and of Christ: in whom are hid all the treasures of wisdom and knowledge. And this I say, lest any man should beguile you with enticing words. For though I be absent in the flesh, yet am I with you in the spirit, joying and beholding your order, and the steadfastness of your faith in Christ. As ye have therefore received Christ Jesus the Lord, so walk ye in Him: rooted and built up in Him, and stablished in the faith, as ye have been taught, abounding therein with thanksgiving.

Men who know little of the deep convictions that stirred the heart of the Apostle Paul will have difficulty in realizing the intensity of his feelings when the truth of God was called in question, and the people of the Lord were in danger of being corrupted by false doctrine and turned aside from the simplicity that is in Christ. He says, "For I would have you know what intense agony I have for you." He was not one who could play fast and loose with revealed truth.

His very soul was tortured when Christ was dishonored by those who professed His Name. He
was not a self-complacent liberal in theology care-
lessly tolerant of any teaching, no matter how
pernicious, so long as outward unity is maintained. To-know that both at Colosse and Laodicea
designing men were seeking to seduce the saints
from their first love, who was Christ Himself,
caused him intense concern. That the enemy was
largely successful at Laodicea we know; for
John, as the amanuensis of the glorified Son of
Man, writing to them later from Patmos, charges
them with being neither cold nor hot. Proud of
their culture and wealth they were indifferent to
Christ. It is from this Paul sought to save them,
and it is to be hoped he succeeded at Colosse.

The truth unites. Error divides. He desires
"that their hearts might be comforted, being knit
together in love, and unto all riches of the full
assurance of understanding, to the acknowledgment of the mystery of God, even Christ" (verse
2). There is some MS. diversity in regard to
the last part of this sentence. The Authorized
Version reads, "The mystery of God, and of the
Father, and of Christ," which is admittedly
peculiar. One could understand, "The mystery
of God, even of the Father, and of Christ," and
it might be so translated; but the reading of
some MSS., "The mystery of God, even Christ,"
seems clearer, and is probably correct. It is the

great divine mystery of the new man, as we read in
1 Corinthians 12:12-13: "For as the body is one,
and hath many members, and all the members of
that one body, being many, are one body: so also
is Christ. For by one Spirit are we all baptized
into one Body, whether we be Jews or Gentiles,
whether we be bond or free; and have been all
made to drink into one Spirit." The definite
article before "Christ" does not appear in the
Authorized Version, but probably should be
there. It is the mystical Christ that is in view,
and I take it that we have a similar idea in
Colossians 2:2. The mystery of God is that which
He has now revealed regarding Christ as Head
of the Body, and consequently of the entire new
creation. As believers enter into the truth of
this they are delivered not only from vain speculations but from fleshly strivings, for all perfection is found in Christ. So the apostle would
have them understand the wealth of this great
mystery as they enjoy the full assurance of
understanding in their hearts' acknowledgment. In
Hebrews 6:11 we read of the full assurance of
hope, and in 10:22 of the same Epistle we
get the full assurance of faith. These together
establish the soul and set it free from doubt
and fear.

In Christ, or if you prefer, in this mystery of
God now revealed, are hid all the treasures of
wisdom and knowledge. It is not necessary to

go elsewhere, investigating human systems and philosophies, for an explanation of the mystery of the universe and the relations of the Creator to His creatures. All these are fully told out in Christ. As we learn to know Him better and apprehend the truth concerning Him, every question is answered, every perplexity made clear, and every doubt dissolved. Why turn aside to idle speculations, no matter how pretentious, when God has spoken in His Son and given His Holy Word to lead us by the Spirit into all truth? Paul says all this in order to protect the saints from being led astray by persuasive talk, or with enticing words. Advocates of error delight to clothe their evil systems in most attractive phraseology, to entrap the souls of the unwary. Only the truth of God can preserve from such. It is important to remember that no amount of intellectual culture or human learning can take the place of divine revelation. If God has not spoken we may speculate and reason as we please. But if He has given the truth in His Word there is an end to all our theorizings.

In this chapter he shows us how Christ is the antidote for human philosophy, Jewish legality, Oriental mysticism, and carnal asceticism. These have no place in Christianity. Christ supersedes them all. And Paul knew through the testimony of Epaphras what Christ had meant to these Colossian saints from the time of their conver-

sion, and he was very jealous lest they should
now be turned aside. Though not with them in
the flesh, he was one with them in spirit, and
rejoiced in all he had heard of their godly order
and their steadfast confidence in Christ. This was
how they began; moreover they had continued in
the same paths and he would have them continue
so. Having received Christ Jesus the Lord, that
is, having trusted Him as Saviour and owned Him
as Master, he would now have them walk in Him,
not turning aside to any new system or per-
version of the truth. He desired to see them
rooted and built up in Him; rooted like a tree,
sending its roots deep down into the soil; he
would have all their hidden sources of supply
so centered in Christ. Built up like a building
founded on a rock and firmly established; he
would so have them recognize Christ as their only
foundation. He uses the same double figure in
Ephesians 3:7, "That Christ may dwell in your
hearts by faith, that ye being rooted and grounded
in love." God is love, and God has been revealed in
Christ; so to be rooted and established in love
is to be rooted in and founded upon God, and it
is God revealed in Christ. Why then should any
go after speculative theories that cannot give
the soul peace and which make light of Christ the
Head? As thus walking in Him the man would
be established in the faith, in accordance with
the instruction already received, "abounding

therein with thanksgiving." Nothing so causes the soul to overflow with worship and gratitude to God as a deep knowledge of Christ. It is noteworthy that true joy is only found in acquaintance with Him.

It is hardly necessary to make the application to present-day systems. Each one who really knows Christ will readily do that for himself or herself. An illustration may help to make clear what I believe the apostle is here indicating: A follower of Mrs. Eddy, the now-deceased head of the so-called Christian Science cult, labored long to unfold the professed benefits and beauties of that system to a simple Christian woman who, after listening for several hours, found herself utterly unable to follow the specious sophistries and vapid theorizings of her visitor. Finally she exclaimed, "I do not understand what you are getting at. Can you not put it all in simpler terms so that I may know what it is you want me to believe?" "Well," replied the other, "in the first place you must get hold of this: God is principle not a person. You see, my dear, we worship a principle—" "Enough," exclaimed the other with a relieved expression on her countenance; "that would never do for me! I worship a personal God revealed in Christ, my blessed, adorable Saviour." And at once her soul was delivered from the net spread before her by the soft-voiced emissary of Satan who had been endeavoring to ensnare her. And this is ever the test. Every system that makes light of Christ or His atoning blood is from the pit, and to be shunned as a viper by all who know Him.

John Newton has well written:

> "What think ye of Christ?" is the test,
>   To try both your state and your scheme;
> You cannot be right in the rest,
>   Unless you think rightly of Him:
> As Jesus appears in your view—
>   As He is beloved or not,
> So God is disposed to you,
>   And mercy or wrath is your lot.
>
> Some take Him a creature to be—
>   A man, or an angel at most;
> But they have not feelings like me,
>   Nor know themselves wretched and lost.
> So guilty, so helpless am I,
>   I durst not confide in His blood,
> Nor on His protection rely,
>   Unless I were sure He is God.
>
> Some call Him a Saviour, in word,
>   But mix their own works with His plan;
> And hope He His help will afford,
>   When they have done all that they can:
> If doings prove rather too light
>   (A little they own they may fail),
> They purpose to make up full weight,
>   By casting His name in the scale.
>
> Some style Him "the Pearl of great price,"
>   And say, He's the fountain of joys;

Yet feed upon folly and vice,
    And cleave to the world and its toys.

Like Judas, the Saviour they kiss,
    And while they salute Him, betray:
Oh! what will profession like this
    Avail in His terrible day?

If asked what of Jesus *I* think,
    Though still my best thoughts are but poor,
I say, He's my meat and my drink,
    My life, and my strength, and my store;
My Shepherd, my trust, and my Friend,
    My Saviour from sin and from thrall;
My Hope from beginning to end,
    My Portion, my Lord and my All.

The natural man cannot understand why Christians should insist upon a clear-cut confession of the truth as to Christ. What matters it, he will ask, whether Jesus be a mere man, spiritual beyond most, or be in very deed the Divine Eternal Son become flesh? If a man only, He is still the great Exemplar and the Master-Teacher. If more than man He is but the manifestation of the Father, and by His life of love and purity has shown us God's attitude toward all mankind and so leads us into a better understanding of God and our relationship to Him.

But this is not the truth of Holy Scripture concerning Him. His holy life—whether He be only human or divinely-human—can never put away our sins or fit us to stand uncondemned before the eternal throne. He had to be both God and Man in order that He might make atonement for sin, meeting as Man—yet Man in all perfection —every claim that the throne of outraged Deity had against man. Touch the Person of Christ and you touch His work. If that work was not divinely perfect there remains no other sacrifice for sins and so we are left without a Saviour.

But, blessed be God, He who came forth from the Father has glorified Him on the earth, and having finished the work given Him to do, has gone back to that glory that He had with the Father before the world was. There He sits, the exalted Man who made purification for sins, on the right hand of the Majesty in the heavens, ever living to make intercession for those His grace has saved. Happy in this knowledge we may well sing, with chastened joy,

> Head of the Church! Thou sittest there,
> Thy members all the blessings share—
> Thy blessing, Lord, is ours:
> Our life Thou art—Thy grace sustains,
> Thy strength in us each vict'ry gains
> O'er sin and Satan's pow'rs.

May we prove our loyalty to Him, not only by confessing a true Christ with our lips, but by giving Him the supreme place in our lives!

CHRIST THE ANTIDOTE
TO HUMAN PHILOSOPHY

Colossians 2:8-10

Beware lest any man spoil you through philosophy and vain deceit, after the tradition of men, after the rudiments of the world, and not after Christ. For in Him dwelleth all the fulness of the Godhead bodily. And ye are complete in Him, which is the Head of all principality and power.

Scripture nowhere condemns the acquisition of knowledge. It is the wisdom of this world, not its knowledge, that is foolishness with God. Philosophy is but worldly wisdom. It is the effort of the human mind to solve the mystery of the universe. It is not an exact science, for the philosophers have never been able to come to any satisfactory conclusion as to either the "why" or the "wherefore" of things. "The Greeks seek after wisdom," we are told; and it was they who led the way for all future generations in philosophical theorizing. Before a divine revelation came it was quite natural and proper that man should seek by wisdom to solve the riddles that nature was constantly propounding, but now that God has spoken this is no longer necessary, and it may become grave infidelity. From Plato to Kant, and from Kant to the last of the moderns,

71

one system has overturned another, so that the
history of philosophy is a story of contradictory,
discarded hypotheses. This is not to say that the
philosophers were or are dishonest men, but it is
to say that many of them have failed to avail
themselves of that which would unravel every
knot and solve every problem, namely, the revelation of God in Christ as given in the Holy Scriptures.

Plato yearned for a divine Word—"logos"—
which would come with authority and make
everything plain. That Word is Christ of whom
John writes, "In the beginning was the Word,
and the Word was with God, and the Word was
God." And again, "The Word became flesh, and
tabernacled among us, and we beheld His glory,
the glory as of the only begotten of the Father,
full of grace and truth." The Word is no longer
hidden. We do not need to search for it. "The word
is nigh thee, even in thy mouth, and in thy heart:
that if thou shalt confess with thy mouth the
Lord Jesus, and shalt believe in thine heart that
God hath raised Him from the dead, thou shalt
be saved." Socrates pondering the, to him, unsolvable problems relating to possible future rewards and punishments, said, "It may be, Plato,
that the Deity can forgive sins, but I do not see
how." No such perplexities need trouble any
honest mind now, for what philosophy could not
explain, the gospel has made clear, that gospel in

which is revealed the righteousness of God for sinful men. Apart from this divine revelation the wisest philosopher of the Twentieth Century knows no more in regard to the origin and destiny of man than the Attic philosophers of so long ago.

Two great systems were still contending for the mastery over the minds of men in the Western world when Paul wrote this letter to the Colossians—Stoicism and Epicureanism. The one said: Live nobly and death cannot matter. Hold appetite in check. Become indifferent to changing conditions. Be not uplifted by good fortune nor cast down by adversity. The man is more than circumstances, the soul is greater than the universe. Epicureanism said: All is uncertain. We know not whence we came; we know not whither we go; we only know that after a brief life we disappear from this scene, and it is vain to deny ourselves any present joy in view of possible future ill. "Let us eat and drink, for to-morrow we die." To many of the former class the Christian message appealed, and one has only to read 1 Corinthians 9:24-29 or Philippians 4:11-13 to see how readily Paul's message would lay hold of an honest Stoic. With Epicureanism Christianity had nothing in common. But while the Stoic might find in Christianity the fulfilment of his heart's yearning, there was not in his philosophy anything the Christian needed, for everything that was best in that system he already had in Christ. Besides these two great outstanding philosophical schools there were many lesser systems among both the Greeks and Romans, all of them seeking to draw away disciples to themselves. The Gnostics embodied parts of all the different schools of thought in their new system. From the weird guesses embodied in the Pythagorean fables down to the evolutionary theories of the present time the Church of God is still in conflict with these vagrant philosophies.

Against all such the Christian is warned. "Beware lest any man spoil you" (that is, lest any make a prey of you) "through philosophy and vain deceit." These may make a great show of learning and their adherents may look down with contempt from their heights of fancied superiority upon people simple enough to believe the gospel and to accept the Holy Scriptures as the inspired Word of the living God. But with all their pretentiousness they are simply the traditions of man, the rudiments or elements of the world. The apostle thus expresses his contempt for mere reasoning in comparison with divine revelation. These systems that claim so much were after all but elementary; it was the ABC of the world offered to those who were in the school of Christ and had left the kindergarten of human tradition far behind. "Can a man by searching find out God?" Impossible. But God is already known in His Son.

It is most important that Christians should see this, particularly the young men who are called of God to be ministers of His Word. It is a sad commentary on conditions in Christendom that in the average theological seminary far more time is given to the study of philosophy than to searching the Scriptures. A minister of an orthodox church said recently, "I could have graduated with honors from my seminary without ever opening the English Bible." Thank God, this is not true of all such training schools; but it is true of perhaps the majority; and the result is we have to-day thousands of professed ministers of Christ, many of them unconverted, and others who, though children of God, have been so stunted and hindered by their philosophical education that they are utterly unable to open up the Scriptures to others, for they are so ignorant of the Word themselves. Christianity owes no debt to Greek, Roman, Medieval, or Modern philosophy. It is like the Bible itself in this—

> A glory gilds the sacred page;
> Majestic, like the sun,
> It sheds a light on every age,
> It gives, but borrows none.

A man can be a well furnished minister of Jesus Christ who has never heard the names of the great philosophers, whether pagan or Christian, and who is utterly ignorant of their systems and hypotheses, providing he will "study to show himself approved unto God, a workman that needeth not to be ashamed, rightly dividing the word of truth." The truest culture, intellectual or spiritual, is that which is drawn from the constant study of the Bible. How often as one comes in contact with men of most gracious personality, gentlemanly appearance, high spirituality, and well-trained intellect he finds upon inquiry that they are like John Wesley, "men of one book," and in some instances, hardly conversant with the literature of earth. And in saying this I do not mean to put a premium on ignorance, for as mentioned in the beginning of this address, the knowledge of this world is not under the ban. The Christian may well avail himself of any legitimate means of becoming better acquainted with the great facts of history, the findings of science, and the beauties of general literature; but let him never put human philosophy in the place of divine revelation. If he studies it at all, and there is no reason why he should not do so, let him begin with this—God has spoken in His Son and in the Holy Scriptures He has given us the last words upon every question that philosophy raises. Browning was right when he wrote:

> I say, the acknowledgment of God in Christ,
> Accepted by the reason, solves for thee
> All questions in the earth and out of it,
> And has so far advanced thee to be wise.

When the Saviour revealed Himself to the Samaritan woman she found her every question answered as she gazed upon His face.

"In Him dwelleth all the fulness of the Godhead bodily." We have already seen in a previous lecture that this word fulness, *pleroma,* was a favorite term of the Gnostics. It represented to them the sum of the qualities of Deity, and with them Christ was but one of many stepping-stones or intermediaries leading up to the *pleroma,* but here we learn that not only are all the attributes of God seen in Christ, as Arius afterwards thought, and as Theistic philosophers everywhere admit, but the very essence of the nature of God in all its entirety dwells in Him.

All that God is, is fully told out in Christ. He could say, "He that hath seen Me hath seen the Father." So that we may say without hesitation, if any ask as to the character of God, that *God is exactly like Jesus.* Jesus is the Christ, and in Christ all the fulness of Deity dwells in a body, so that when at last we come into the presence of the Father we shall find in Him one known and loved before, not a stranger still unknown and possibly unknowable. J. N. Darby was thinking of this when he wrote:

> There no stranger-God shall meet thee!
>   Stranger thou in courts above:
> He who to His rest shall greet thee,
>   Greets thee with a well-known love.

"Confessedly great is the mystery of piety, He who hath been manifested in flesh, justified in the Spirit, seen of angels, proclaimed unto the Gentiles, believed on in the world, received up into glory" (1 Tim. 3:16). God is revealed, He is no longer hidden. All His glory shines in the face of Christ Jesus. This solves at once for me as a believer the mystery of the universe.

> And that which seemed to me before
>   One wild, confused Babel,
> Is now a fire-tongued Pentecost
>   Proclaiming Christ is able;
> And all creation its evangel
>   Utters forth abroad
> Into mine ears since once I know
>   My Saviour Christ is God.

In the 10th verse we are told, "And ye are complete in Him which is the Head of all principality and power." The word "complete" is literally "filled full." In Christ dwells all the *pleroma* of Deity, and we have our *pleroma* in Him. We do not need to go elsewhere for illumination or information. "And of His fulness have all we received, and grace for grace. For the law was given by Moses, but grace and truth came by Jesus Christ. No man hath seen God at any time; the only begotten Son, which is in the bosom of the Father, He hath declared Him" (John 1:16-18). This revelation floods our being with rapture, fills our cup of joy, and satisfies every demand of the intellect. We are filled full in Him. I would suggest that it is not the believers' standing exactly that is in view here. We have that in Ephesians 1:6. There we are told we are "accepted in the Beloved." In that sense we may be said, of course, to be complete in Him; but Colossians 2:10 is rather our state; it is the state of those who have found every need met in Christ, who is the Head of all principality and power.

It has already been pointed out that "principalities" and "powers" are terms relating to different ranks of spiritual beings. In a pretended knowledge of the nature and office of these glorious intelligences, the Gnostics reveled, and placed them high above Christ Himself who was, according to them, but one who introduced the initiate into the fellowship of this great serried host leading on up to the invisible God. But the truth is the very opposite, for all the principalities and powers (and these may be good or evil, fallen or unfallen) were created by Him and for Him in whom all the fulness dwells, and He is the Head of all angelic companies as well as human beings.

> No place too high for Him is found,
> No place too high in Heaven.

God would have His people ever realize that He who stooped to the depths of shame and suffering of the cross for their salvation is as to the mystery of His wondrous Person, God over all, blessed for ever.

It will be observed that the 10th verse does not complete the sentence, which is carried right on in verses 11 and 12, but as what follows is intimately linked with the next subject for our consideration, I leave them now to take them up in the next address, only observing that it is immediately after the declaration of Christ's Headship over all angels that we are told of the depths of His humiliation; for God would never separate the Person and work of our Lord Jesus Christ. But He would have us remember that it was because of His transcendent character and His true Deity that He could undertake the work of purging our sins when He gave Himself a sacrifice on our behalf. He had to be who He was in order to do what He did. The settlement of the sin question could never be effected by a created being. The issues were too great. Of all men it is written, "None of them can by any means redeem his brother or give to God a ransom for him, for the redemption of the soul costs too much. Therefore, let it alone for ever." This is a somewhat free translation, but authorized by the best Hebrew scholars. It emphasizes what is here brought before us. Low thoughts of Christ result from low thoughts of sin. When I realize the enormity of my iniquity I know that only the Daysman for whom Job yearned can

save me from such a load of guilt. He, because
He is God and Man, can "lay His hand upon us
both," and thus by making atonement for sin
bring God and man together in holy, happy harmony.

> .... Can a mere man do this?
> Yet Christ saith, this He lived and died to do.
> Call Christ, then, the illimitable God,
> Or lost!
>   —Browning

And so we may conclude with this tremendous
truth: God has no other answer to all the ques-
tionings of the mind of man as to spiritual
verities than Christ; and no other is needed, for
Christ is the answer to them all. He who refuses Christ refuses God's last word to mankind. He has said everything He has to say in
sending Him into the world as the Giver of life
and the propitiation for our sins. To turn from
Him is to refuse the living incarnation of the
Truth and to shut oneself up to error and delusion.

LECTURE 8

CHRIST THE ANTIDOTE TO JEWISH LEGALITY

Colossians 2:11-17

In whom also ye are circumcised with the circumcision made without hands, in putting off the body of [the sins of] the flesh by the circumcision of Christ: buried with Him in baptism, wherein also ye are risen with Him through the faith of the operation of God, who hath raised Him from the dead. And you, being dead in your sins and the uncircumcision of your flesh, hath He quickened together with Him, having forgiven you all trespasses; blotting out the handwriting of ordinances that was against us, which was contrary to us, and took it out of the way, nailing it to His cross; and having spoiled principalities and powers, He made a show of them openly, triumphing over them in it. Let no man therefore judge you in meat, or in drink, or in respect of an holyday, or of the new moon, or of the sabbath days: which are a shadow of things to come; but the body is of Christ.

This somewhat lengthy section, beginning (as previously mentioned) in the middle of a sentence, might be more easily expounded if divided into two parts, but it is so intimately linked together that I am taking it up as a whole. Philosophy, as we have observed, is the working of the human mind independently of divine revelation. Legality is the endeavor to use a divinely given code, to which may be added precepts of men, as a means either of salvation in the first instance or of growth in grace afterwards. Neither of these conceptions is in accordance with Scripture. "By the works of the law there shall no flesh be justified in His sight;" this forever bars out legal works as a procuring cause of salvation. "Ye are not under law but under grace;" this, as effectually, forbids the thought that holiness of life for the Christian is found in subjecting himself to legal principles. "The law is the strength of sin," we are told in 1 Corinthians 15:56. It is not, as multitudes have supposed, the strength of holiness or the power for righteousness. It is the indwelling Holy Spirit, who occupies us with Christ crucified, raised, and glorified, that is the dynamic of spirituality.

Gnosticism was as much indebted to Judaism, which it perverted to its own ends, and to a weird Jewish Kabbalism, as it was to the vapid reasonings of Gentile philosophers and, as we shall see later, to Mithraic and Zoroastrian mysticism. Here the apostle specifically deals with Jewish legality, and shows how Christians have been forever delivered from the law and the legal principle in its entirety, but are now linked with the risen Christ. For the believer to go back to the law for his perfecting in holiness is, as he shows in the Epistle to the Galatians, to fall from grace. That is, it is the virtual setting aside of the gospel of grace; forgetting that having begun in the Spirit we are not to be made perfect by the flesh. There were those ever dogging the footsteps of the great apostle to the Gentiles who sought to pervert his converts by teaching them, "Except ye be circumcised and keep the law of Moses, ye cannot be saved." While the council at Jerusalem gave forth no uncertain sound in opposition to this it is evident that its decisions were by no means everywhere accepted. It was hard for converts from Judaism to realize their complete deliverance both from the law of Moses as a rule of life, and from the ceremonies and ritual of that law as a means of growth in grace. Here the question at issue is handled in a remarkable manner through the inspiration of the Holy Spirit. Having declared that we have our completeness in Christ, our exalted Head, he continues: "In whom also ye are circumcised with the circumcision made without hands, in putting off the body of the flesh by the circumcision of Christ." I omit the words "of the sins" as being without sufficient MS. authority. It is not merely a question of sins here, but the flesh itself that is in view. Circumcision was the cutting off of the flesh physically, and it was given by God to picture the judgment of the carnal nature and its complete setting aside. This is what God has done in the cross of Christ. In His cutting off by death when He stood vicariously in our place, we see the end of the flesh as viewed from the divine standpoint. It is cut off, put to one side, as absolutely worthless. "The flesh," we read, "profiteth nothing." "It is not subject to the law of God, neither indeed can be." Therefore God is making no attempt to improve it; consequently, there is no place for merit so far as man is concerned. He has none, and, blessed be God, he needs none. All merit is in Another!

The same truth is set forth in Christian baptism. Personally, I have no sympathy with those who in our day would seek to do away altogether with water baptism on the plea that there is now, since the full truth of the Church is revealed, only one baptism, and that the baptism of the Holy Spirit. Ephesians 4:4-6 was just as true from Pentecost to Acts 28 as it has ever been since. Paul did not receive the revelation of the mystery after he went to prison. The rapture, which is part of that great mystery, is taught in his earliest Epistle—First Thessalonians. In his postscript to the Roman letter he tells how he has been making known the mystery throughout his ministry, "Made known to all nations for the obedience of faith." To the Ephesian elders he said (as recorded in Acts 20) that he had "not shunned to declare unto them the whole counsel of God." That counsel in its entirety had already been made known to him and was proclaimed among the Gentiles. The baptism of the Holy Spirit whereby believers were brought into the Body of

Christ took place on the day of Pentecost. It
was thus that the Body, the Church, was formed.
There is no hint of any such supernatural work
in a wide-spread manner after Paul's imprisonment. The Body had been formed for years, and
each believer was added to it when he received
the Spirit. The one baptism of Ephesians 4:5, in
my judgment, cannot refer to this event because
this is already mentioned in the previous verse. In
verse 4 we read, "There is one Body, and one
Spirit, and one hope of your calling." This is the
full revelation of the mystery, the Body formed
by the Spirit's baptism, waiting for the coming
of the Lord. In verse 5 we have "one Lord, one
faith, one baptism." This is responsibility here
on earth—Christ owned as Lord, the Church
called upon to contend for the faith once for all
delivered to the saints, and water baptism in the
name of the Father, Son, and Holy Spirit in recognition of our subjection to the one Lord. It is
not a question of form, formula, or subjects. It
is simply the broad fact declared, that Christianity knows only one baptism, and that, of course,
is baptism unto the death of Jesus Christ. To
speak of the Holy Spirit's baptism as a burial
with Christ unto death is nonsense. It is after
my identification by faith in death, burial, and
resurrection that the Holy Spirit baptizes me into
the Body.

Nor is this to say that persons who for various

reasons, valid or otherwise, may not have been scripturally baptized are not in Christ. In drawing an illustration from what is scripturally correct one does not unchristianize those who fall short either because of ignorance or wilfulness. The argument of verse 12, as I see it, is this: the Christian confesses his identification with a rejected Christ in his baptism; he has owned that the man after the flesh deserved to die; he *has* died in Christ's death. This therefore is the end of the responsible man before God. Necessarily then, it is the end of all self-effort, of every attempt to improve the flesh by subjecting it to ordinances, that is, regulations, whether divinely given as in the Old Testament, or humanly devised as in so many unscriptural systems. God is not attempting to improve the old man, He has judged him as too evil for any improvement and has therefore set him to one side in death. Baptism is the recognition of this. It is burial unto death.

Some translators read, "Wherein also ye are risen with Him," but the preponderance of evidence is, I believe, in favor of the reading, "In whom also ye are risen with Him through the faith of the operation of God who hath raised Him from the dead." It is through faith in the risen Christ that we become the recipients of the new life, and are henceforth accounted by God as those who, having gone down into death with Him, are now one with Him in resurrection. What place does legality have here? None whatever. To put the new man, the man in Christ, under rules and regulations is contrary to the entire principle of new creation.

This is further emphasized in verse 13. We who once were dead in our trespasses and as Gentiles in the uncircumcision of our flesh have now been made to live together with Him, God having forgiven us all trespasses. The word is the same in each case, and if translated "sins" in the first part of the verse should be "sins" in the last, otherwise "trespasses" in each instance. Moreover, the bond that was against us ("the handwriting," a term which could only be properly used of the Ten Commandments, which we are distinctly told were the handwriting of God, embraced in ten ordinances, or divinely-given rules) because of the sinfulness of our natures, making our disobedience to the law, when once it came to our knowledge, a foregone conclusion, and which therefore made it to us a ministration of death and condemnation, has now been taken out of the way and no longer hangs over us as an unfulfilled obligation. Christ nailed it to His cross.

What are we to understand by this expression, "Nailing it to His cross"? It may help us if we remember that it was customary under Roman law, when criminals were executed by crucifixion,

hanging, or impalement, to write out a copy of
the law they had broken, or to indicate the nature
of their offence on a placard, and nail it above the
victim's head, that all might know how Rome
executed vengeance upon those who violated her
criminal code. Pilate wrote out the inscription
to be placed over the head of Christ Jesus,
and that in three languages, Hebrew, Greek, and
Latin, that all might know why the patient Suf-
ferer from Galilee was being publicly executed.
"This is Jesus of Nazareth the King of the Jews."
As the people read this they understood that he
was being crucified because He made Himself a
king and was thus disloyal to Caesar. But as
God looked upon that cross His holy eye saw,
as it were, another inscription altogether. Nailed
upon the rood above the head of His blessed Son
was the handwriting of ten ordinances given at
Sinai. It was because this law had been broken
in every point that Jesus poured out His blood,
thus giving His life to redeem us from the curse
of the law. And so all of our sins have been
settled for. There the law, which we had so
dishonored, has been magnified to the full in the
satisfaction which He made to the divine justice.
Thus Christ has become the end of the law to
every one that believeth. It is of course the Jewish believers Paul has in mind when he says "us,"
for Gentiles were not under the law. But it is
true now in principle for us all, to whom the

knowledge of the law has come. Christ has, by
His death, met every claim against us and can-
celled the bond we could not pay.

And now as a victorious leader He has come
forth from the tomb, having made a prey of
the evil principalities and powers who gloated
over His apparent defeat when He was crucified
through weakness, but who are now themselves
defeated in His resurrection. He has ascended
to heaven in a glorious triumph, having made a
spectacle of them, openly triumphing over them
in His cross.

> His be the Victor's name
>   Who fought the fight alone,
> Triumphant saints no honor claim
>   His conquest was their own.
>
> By weakness and defeat
>   He won the meed and crown,
> Trod all our foes beneath His feet
>   By being trodden down.
>
> Bless, bless the Conqueror slain,
>   Slain in His victory;
> Who lived, who died, who lives again,
>   For thee, His Church, for thee.

He took our place upon the cross and now we
share in all the results of that work. We are
one with Him in the new creation. The law and
all its ritual was given to man in the flesh.
Christians are not in the flesh but in the Spirit,

and the law, as such, has nothing to say to the man in this new sphere beyond the reach of death. And so he concludes this marvelous section with a solemn admonition not to permit ourselves to be disturbed by any who would put us back under the law in any shape or form. "Let no man therefore judge you in meat or in drink, or in respect of an holyday, or of the new moon, or of the sabbaths." All these once had their place and he who would be an obedient child of the old covenant was called upon to observe the regulations regarding them scrupulously. All these, however, were but a shadow of things to come—things which have now come—"For the body is of Christ." In the Old Testament dispensation the light of God was shining upon Christ, and all the forms and ceremonies, including even the weekly sabbaths, were but shadows cast by Him. Since He Himself has come and fulfilled all the redemptive types the believer has "Everything in Jesus, and Jesus everything." The very fact that He links the sabbath with the other ceremonies shows clearly that the rule of life for the believer is not the ten words given at Sinai. While confessing this law to be holy, just and good, the new creation man is not under it. He is, as Paul expresses it elsewhere, "under law to Christ," or more properly "enlawed to Christ" (1 Cor. 9:22). That is, his responsibility now is to walk in fellowship with the risen Christ, the Head of the Body of which he is but a feeble member, in whom dwells the Holy Spirit to be the power of the new life— manifested in subjection to the exalted Lord. None need fear that this will make for a lower standard of piety than if one were under the law as a rule of life. It is a far higher standard. He whose one thought and desire is to manifest the risen life of Christ in all his ways will lead a holier life than he who is seeking to subject the flesh to rules and regulations, even though given from heaven in a dispensation now past. This comes out very strongly in the contrast between the sabbath of the law and the Lord's day of the new creation. There is no commandment in the New Testament inculcating the sacredness of the first day of the week and demanding that Christians observe it scrupulously for holy purposes, yet the consensus of judgment of spiritually minded believers all through the centuries has led to the honoring of this day as a time of worship, meditation and Christian testimony, which has given it a preeminence from a spiritual standpoint that the Jewish sabbath never had.

Nor are we called upon to substitute a Christian ritual service for the Jewish ritual which we have discarded. We worship now by the Spirit of God whose delight it is to occupy the hearts of the redeemed with Him to whom they owe all their blessing. Thus all that is fleshly or carnal must give way, as but prefatory and evanescent, and that which is spiritual and abiding takes its place.

CHRIST THE ANTIDOTE
TO ORIENTAL MYSTICISM

Colossians 2:18-19

Let no man beguile you of your reward in a voluntary humility and worshipping of angels, intruding into those things which he hath not seen, vainly puffed up by his fleshly mind, and not holding the Head, from which all the Body by joints and bands having nourishment ministered, and knit together, increaseth with the increase of God.

The natural man is distinctly religious. He does not need to be regenerated in order to *feel* after God. While it is true of all the unsaved that "there is none that seeketh after God" in the sense of seeking Him for His own sake, yet it has been well said that man is incurably religious; he must have something to worship. And so Satan has supplied him with cults of all descriptions to suit every type of mind. One of the oldest systems that has come down even to our own day is that of Parseeism, based upon the Zend Avesta, supposed to have originated with the Persian hero and prophet, Zoroaster, or Zarathustra, as he is called in the Persian scriptures. This system teaches a mystical dualism. Ahura Mazda, or Ormuzd, is the infinite God, the Eternal Light; a lesser deity, Ahriman, the Prince of Darkness, sometimes looked upon as the creator of matter, is in constant conflict with the supreme deity. For twelve thousand years he is destined to wage war against the light and then his kingdom of darkness will be destroyed. This system permeated various schools of thought, and in apostolic days had been widely accepted throughout the Greek and Roman world under the name Mithraism. Its votaries went everywhere proclaiming it as the great unifying world religion. It was a vast secret society, its initiates going from one mystical degree to another until they became adepts. This Satanic system trembled before the advancing hosts of Christianity, and finally sought to combine certain of its views with a part of the Christian revelation; and, as we have already seen, by an eclectic combination of Judaism, Greek philosophy, and oriental mysticism a new religion was formed, divided, however, into many different sects all alike unsound as to Christ, and all rejecting the inspiration of the Holy Scriptures and substituting the vain speculations of the human mind. Yet imitations of almost every Christian doctrine were found in some one or other of these systems, but with certain accretions and contradictions which made them most dangerous. Justin Martyr wrote some years after the apostle John passed from this scene, "Many spirits are abroad in the world and the credentials they display are splendid gifts of mind, eloquence and logic. Christian, look carefully, and ask for the print of the nails." All these systems denied the true Christ of God who gave Himself for our sins upon the cross of shame. Some, like the Docetists, taught that the humanity of Jesus was simply an appearance, unreal and immaterial. The first Epistle of John meets this in a very wonderful way. Another sect, afterwards headed up in Cerinthus, the great arch-heretic of the second century, called by Polycarp, "the firstborn of Satan," taught that Jesus was the natural son of Joseph and Mary, who died on the cross finally to separate himself from his own sin, but to whom the Christ (identified with the eternal Spirit) came at his baptism and illumination, but left him at the cross. This system seems to be particularly before the mind of the Apostle Paul and he combats it in a masterly manner. In all of these systems knowledge was given the preeminence over faith. The latter, which is confidence in revealed testimony, was repudiated by these theorists who assumed acquaintance with divine mysteries far beyond that of ordinary people and quite in advance of the Biblical revelation. In their pride and folly they put a great number of spirit-beings, known as eons, between the soul and the unknowable God. These were all classified and named, as for instance, Reason, Wisdom, Power, and similar divine attributes. All this appeals to the natural man. It sounds like humility to say, "In myself I am so utterly ignorant and unworthy, it is not for me to go directly to God the Father or to Christ the Son. I will therefore avail myself of mediating angels and spirits who can present my cause in a more suitable manner than I can myself." But it is really pride of intellect, and is the grossest unbelief, when God has declared that "there is one Mediator between God and men, the Man Christ Jesus, who gave Himself a ransom for all to be testified in due time." The lowly man will receive what He has made known in His Word.

Through the infinite mercy of God the early Church triumphed largely over these Satanic efforts to ally these dying cults and systems with Christianity. The Holy Ghost so clearly exposed that the Church repudiated in one council after another these vile theories which would have made man his own Saviour. But all down the centuries since there have been those who from time to time have taken up certain elements of these discarded schools of thought and sought to foist them upon Christians as though they were new and wonderful truths. Romanism, with its doctrine of justification by works, purgatorial purification after death, and mediating saints and angels, has simply adopted much that the apostles refused, and palms it off on its credulous dupes as traditional Christianity. Imagine anyone praying to saints and angels, or adoring their images, with the solemn words before him of this eighteenth verse, "Let no man beguile you of your reward in a voluntary humility and worshipping of angels, intruding into those things which he hath not seen, vainly puffed up by his fleshly mind." How striking the contrast between the expressions "voluntary humility" and "vainly puffed up." I recall a friend of my youth, a very gracious and kindly man, who had been brought up from childhood in the Roman communion, with whom I often sought to reason out of the Scriptures, in order to show him the simplicity of the gospel of Christ. I remember, when I asked why he prayed to the blessed Virgin Mary instead of directly to our Lord Jesus, how with an air of the greatest humility he answered, "Oh, I am too sinful, too utterly unworthy, to go directly to our blessed Lord. He is infinitely above me, so pure and holy, His majesty is so great that I would not dare to prostrate myself before Him. But I know that no one has such influence with a son as his mother, and I know, too, that a pure woman's tender heart feels for sinners in their sorrows and failures, therefore I go to the blessed Virgin Mary and pour out my heart to her as to my own mother, and I plead with her to speak for me to her holy, spotless Son, and I feel sure that she will influence Him as no other could."

This sounds like lowliness of mind and humility of spirit. It is really the most subtle kind of pride, for it involves proposing to be wiser than the revealed Word of God. There, as we have seen, we read of only the "one Mediator"; and we learn that "the Father sent the Son to be the Saviour of the world"; that "He bore our sins in His own body on the tree"; that His tender heart was filled with compassion for sinners here on earth. None were too vile or degraded but that they were invited to come to Him. The worst His enemies could say of Him was, "This Man receiveth sinners and eateth with them." And up there in yonder glory He is the same Jesus that He was when here on earth. We may rest assured that "we have not an High Priest which cannot be touched with the feeling of our infirmities, but One who was tempted in all points like as we are, apart from sin," and who is "able to succor those who are tempted." In His name we are bidden to "come boldly to the throne of grace, that we may obtain mercy and find grace for seasonable help." Why turn aside to angels or saints, however devoted, or even to His blessed mother herself, when we can go directly to Him, assured of His deep interest in all that concerns us? He made intercession for transgressors on the cross; up there at God's right hand He ever lives to make intercession for those who trust in Him. And so it is not an evidence of humility to say, I am too unworthy to go to Christ; it is only unbelief that would lead one thus to speak. He stands with arms outstretched, pleading with all who are in trouble or distress, "Come unto Me all ye that labor and are heavy laden, and I will give you rest." What base ingratitude to turn from Him to any other! What amazing folly to think it necessary to have anyone speak for me to Him, when He stands there showing His wounded hands and saying, "Peace be unto you." It is only pride and unbelief that would put Him off at a distance and bring angels in between.

This voluntary humility and worshipping of angels is in itself a complete denial of the new creation. It fails to recognize the wondrous truth that all believers are one Body with their exalted Head. And so the apostle goes on to say, "And not holding the Head, from which all the Body by joints and bands having nourishment ministered, and knit together, increaseth with the increase of God." "Holding the Head" is recognizing our link with Him, both in life and by the Spirit. He, the exalted One at God's right hand, is the source of blessing for all His people in this scene. As of old the holy oil poured upon Aaron's head went down to the skirts of his garment (Ps. 133:2), so now from the Head in heaven blessing in the Spirit's power comes down to every member of His Body on the earth. It will be observed that the figure of a body is not merely that of a society or, as we would say, an organization. It is far more wonderful than that. It is a divine organism. Just as truly as all the members of a human body form the complete man, so do all believers in Christ, through the Spirit's baptism, form the one new man. See in this connection 1 Corinthians 12:12-13 and Ephesians 2:15. If out of touch with the Head through failure to apprehend the intimacy of our relation to Him we put anything or any creature between ourselves and Him, we are not holding the Head. Satan knows, as one has well put it, that if he could get but the thickness of a sheet of paper between the Head and the Body, all life would be destroyed. This, of course, can never be, but it is sadly possible so utterly to misunderstand our relation to the Head, and so fail to avail ourselves of the supplies of grace that might be ours did we but walk in fellowship with Him, that we would be out of communion with Him and therefore not consciously guided by Him.

We are told that from the Head all the Body is nourished, and this through the ministry of joints and bands placed in the Body for this very purpose by the Holy Spirit, so that all being knit together grows, or increases, with the increase of God. This is most blessedly expanded and elaborated in Ephesians 4:11-16. There we see how the risen Lord has given various gifts to His Church for the perfecting of the saints, with a view to the work of the ministry for the edifying of the Body of Christ. Note specially verses 15 and 16, where we are told that He would have us "grow up into Him in all things, which is the Head, even Christ: from whom the whole Body fitly joined together and compacted by that which every joint supplieth, according to the effectual working in the measure of every part, maketh increase of the Body unto the edifying of itself in love." What a marvelous picture is this, and how strikingly does the one passage complement the other, and what responsibility does it put upon each one of us as members of Christ and members one of another! There are no useless members in this Body. Just as in the human body every joint, every ligament, every hidden part, has some service to perform for the good of the whole, even though as yet physicians and surgeons may not fully understand the need of every gland and organ, and may speak, as some do, of certain useless parts, or discarded vestiges of earlier forms, yet we may be very sure that God in His infinite wisdom has a use for every member of the body; so in the mystical Body of Christ let no believer think of himself as useless, as without any special gift, and therefore as having no part in the building up of the whole. There is one term used in 1 Corinthians 12:28 that is most suggestive; it is the little word "helps." Notice how it is sandwiched in between gifts of healings and governments. We may not all have spectacular gifts, but we can all be helps. The apostle writing to one Church says, "Ye all being helpers together by prayer." Here is a service the feeblest saint may perform for the benefit of the whole Body.

If in spiritual health each member will function aright for the edification of all; but just as in the natural order diseased members become a menace to the entire body, so Christians out of fellowship with God, in a low or carnal state, are hindrances where they should be helpers. May each one of us be concerned about our responsibility here. May we be so occupied with our blessed, glorified Head, so careful to see that there is nothing interfering with our communion with Him, that He may be able to use us as joints or bands to minister nourishment and blessing to His people that all may be the more knit together because of our faithfulness in seeking to be helpers of one another's faith, that thus the Body may indeed increase with the increase of God.

And now in closing let me say a word to my younger brethren in Christ who seek to preach the gospel, or to minister for the edification of believers. Bear in mind that if you would be true ministers of Jesus Christ you are to preach the Word and seek to occupy your hearers with the truth of God. Do not, I beg of you, give way to a very common vanity of preachers, speculation in regard to things not revealed. You are not sent forth to acquaint men with unsubstantiated theories, nor to occupy their minds with speculative systems. God has entrusted you with His own holy Word, and He holds you responsible to give that out in all its clearness and simplicity. One "Thus saith the Lord" is worth a ton of human thoughts and ideas. Unreliable theological disquisitions and philosophical discussions never saved one poor sinner or comforted a discouraged saint. It is the truth of God, ministered in the power of the Holy Spirit, that alone can accomplish this. All else is but wasting precious time, and is dishonoring to the Lord who sent you out to proclaim His truth. This divinely given message ministered in the power of the Holy Ghost sent down from Heaven, will awaken the careless, quicken the dead in trespasses and sins, give peace to the anxious, comfort the distressed, and sanctify believers. To substitute the empty dreams of carnal, or unregenerate men for this, is the utmost folly. Of old, God said, through Jeremiah, "The prophet that hath a dream, let him tell a dream, and he that hath My Word, let him speak My Word faithfully. What is the chaff to the wheat? said the Lord" (Jer. 23:28).

To add to His Word is but to pervert it. Neither tradition, nor the voice of the Church, nor yet fancied superior intellectual illumination, can complete that which is already perfect—the revelation of the mind of God in His holy Word. "The Bible and the Bible alone" is the foundation of our faith.

CHRIST THE ANTIDOTE
TO CARNAL ASCETICISM

Colossians 2:20-23

Wherefore if ye be dead with Christ from the rudiments of the world, why, as though living in the world, are ye subject to ordinances (Touch not; taste not; handle not; which all are to perish with the using) after the commandments and doctrines of men? Which things have indeed a show of wisdom in will worship, and humility, and neglecting of the body; not in any honor to the satisfying of the flesh.

It is a great mistake and a fatal blunder into which the best of people readily fall, to fail to distinguish the two very different senses in which the term "the flesh" is used in the Bible. Sometimes it refers solely to our bodies, "this mortal flesh," but in the doctrinal parts of the New Testament it generally means the nature which fallen man has inherited from his first father. God created man, we are told, "in His own image, after His own likeness, male and female created He them, and called their name Adam in the day when they were created" (Gen. 5:2). Physically perfect, they were morally innocent, and spiritually like unto God, who is a Spirit and the Father of spirits. But in the

106

very next verse we read, "Adam begat a son in his own likeness after his image" (Gen. 5:3). This was after sin had defiled his nature and poisoned the springs of life; and all his children now bear this fallen image and likeness.

Hence the need of regeneration, and so our Lord said to Nicodemus, "That which is born of the flesh is flesh, and that which is born of the Spirit is spirit." He is not merely saying that that which is born of the physical body is a physical body, but that personality which comes into the world through natural generation and birth is one with the fallen nature which Adam acquired when he fell. This is called distinctively, "the flesh," "the body of the flesh," "sin in the flesh," "sin that dwelleth in us," "the carnal mind which is not subject to the law of God, neither indeed can be"; and is the nature of the old man—the unregenerate natural man. We are told that we all were by nature children of wrath, even as others. When converted, or regenerated, this carnal nature is not altered in the slightest degree; it is never improved nor sanctified, either in whole or in part. In the cross of Christ God has condemned it utterly as too vile for improvement. The believer has received a new nature which is spiritual, the nature of the new man; and he is now responsible to walk in obedience to the Word of God, which appeals only to this new nature. The old and the new natures are in the believer and will be until the redemption of the body.

It is true that the flesh, or the old nature, acts through the members of the body, but the body itself is not evil. Every natural instinct or physical appetite, no matter how perfectly right and proper it may be, and used as God intended, may be perverted to selfish and dishonorable purposes. But we are called upon to mortify, or put to death, the deeds of the body and no longer to yield our members as instruments of unrighteousness unto sin, but to present the body with all its ransomed powers unto God, to be used for His service under the controlling power of His Holy Spirit. Hence the Christian is called to a life of self-abnegation and so the Apostle Paul could say, "I keep under my body and bring it into subjection." But by that he does not mean that he visits needless punishment upon his physical flesh in order to purify his spirit, but rather that he does not permit unlawful or inordinate physical appetites to dominate him, and so lead him into excesses which would bring dishonor upon the ministry committed to him and upon the name of the Lord whose servant he is. This subjection of the body will ever be necessary as long as we are in this scene of testing. So the Apostle Peter tells us, "He that hath suffered in the flesh hath ceased from sin." It is not that we obtain deliverance from the power of sin by ascetic practices such as flagellation, fasting, or ignoring physical comfort, but rather by refusing obedience to carnal impulses the gratification of which may give physical pleasure while they war against the soul.

And in this we may see the contrast between our Lord's temptation and our own. Of Him we read that "He suffered being tempted." Of us, that we cease from sin if we suffer in the flesh. In other words, to Him, the Holy One, temptation caused the keenest suffering. His holy nature shrank from the slightest contact with evil even in Satanic suggestion. But with us, fallen as we are, the suggestion of evil may be seductively pleasing, and we must resolutely refuse the thought of sensual pleasure in order that we may walk in purity before God. "He was tempted in all things like as we are, apart from sin." That is, He was never tempted by inward desire for sin. He could say, "The prince of this world cometh and hath nothing in Me." With us it is far otherwise; when temptation is presented from without we are sadly conscious of the fact that we have a traitor within who would open the door of the fortress to the enemy if he were not carefully watched. And right here is where purpose of heart is needed in order that we may cleave to the Lord and give no ground to the suggestions of the flesh or the promptings of the Adversary.

An Indian, in explaining the conflict of the two natures, said, "It seems to me as though two dogs are fighting within me: one is a black dog, and he is very savage and very bad; the other is a white dog, and he is very gentle and very good; but the black dog fights with him all the time." "And which dog wins?" someone asked. Laconically the Indian replied, "Which ever one I say 'sic him' to." And it was well put, for if the will is on the side of the evil, the flesh will triumph; but if the will is subdued by grace and subject to the Holy Spirit the new nature will control.

It is for lack of understanding this important truth that many have supposed they could perfect themselves in holiness by imposing penances and suffering of various kinds upon the body. At a very early day such views came into the Church. The Jewish Essenes and the Stoic philosophers had accustomed both Jews and Gentiles to the thought that the body in itself is evil, and must be subdued if one would advance in holiness. These views were taken up by certain sects of Gnostics, while others went to the opposite extreme and taught that the spiritual alone was important, and that the body might be used in any way without polluting the soul.

But in these last four verses of our present chapter the apostle warns against the folly of seeking holiness through asceticism. He describes these practices as being part of that philosophy of which he has already spoken in verse 8, which he designated the rudiments, or elements of the world. Challenging the believer, as a new man in Christ, who died with Him to his old place and condition in the world, he asks: "Wherefore if ye died with Christ from the elements of the world, why, as though living in the world, are ye subject to ordinances after the commandments and doctrines of men?" I have purposely left out certain parenthetical expressions which we will look at in a moment. The great thing now to see is that all these rules and regulations for the subduing of the body are according to the principles of the world. They all take for granted that God is still trying in some way to improve the flesh, and this we know is not His purpose. Through John the Baptist He said, "The axe is laid to the *root* of the tree."

Not only in modern times, but in those early days of Christianity which we are considering, men have laid the axe, or the pruning-knife, if you will, to the *fruit* of the tree, as though the tree might be improved if the bad fruit were cut off. Get men to reform, to sign pledges, to put themselves under rules and regulations, to starve the body, to inflict physical suffering upon it, and surely its vile propensities will be at least annulled if not eliminated, and little by little men will become spiritual and godlike. The formula which thousands have taken up within the last few years,

> Every day, in every way,
> I am getting better and better,

expresses the mind of many. But no amount of self-control, no physical suffering whatever can change the carnal mind, called emphatically, "the flesh."

Saint Jerome tells how, having lived a lecherous life in his youth, after he became a Christian he fled from all contact with the gross and vulgar world in which he had once sought to gratify every fleshly desire. He left Rome and wandered to Palestine, and there lived in a cave near Bethlehem, where he sought to subdue his carnal nature by fasting almost to starvation. And then he tells us how disappointed he was when, exhausted and weary, he fell asleep and dreamed he was still rioting among the dissolute companions of his godless days. The flesh cannot be starved into subjection. It cannot be improved by subjecting it to ordinances whether human or divine. But as we walk in the Spirit, and are occupied thus with the risen Christ, we are delivered from the power of fleshly lusts which war against the soul.

In the parenthetical portion of verses 21 and 22 the apostle gives us a sample, if we may so say, of the carnal ordinances or doctrines of men to which he refers, "Touch not; taste not; handle not." He is not saying, Do not touch, taste, or handle these ascetic regulations—that would be nonsense—but these are the human rules, through obedience to which the ascetic hoped to attain to a higher degree of spirituality. How often we have heard this 21st verse quoted as though for the guidance of Christians to-day, exactly the opposite of that which the apostle intended. All such regulations are to perish with the using.

These things have, indeed, an appearance of wisdom in will worship and humility and neglecting of the body, or punishing the body by making it suffer. It is natural to suppose that such things would have a tendency to free one from carnal desires, but untold thousands of monks, hermits, and ascetics of all descriptions, have proved that they are useless against the indulgence of the flesh. One may shut himself up in a monastery in order to escape the world, only to find he has taken the world in with him. One may dwell in a cave in the desert in order to subdue the flesh, only to find that the more the body is weakened and neglected, the more powerful the flesh becomes.

Dr. A. T. Robertson translates the last part of verse 20: "Why, as though living in the world, do you dogmatize; such as, Touch not; taste not; handle not?" These rules may be elevated to the importance of dogmas but they will never enable one to achieve the object he has in view. You have heard of the man who, anxious to fit himself for the presence of God, and awakened to a sense of the emptiness of a life of worldly pleasure, fled from the city to the desert and made his home in a cave in the rocks, there practising the greatest austerities, and hoping through prayer and penance to reach the place where he would be acceptable to God. Hearing of another hermit who was reputed to be a very holy and devout man, he made a long, wearisome journey across the desert, supported only by his staff, in order to interview him and learn from him how he might find peace with God. In answer to his agonized questions the aged anchorite said to him, "Take that staff, that dry rod which is in your hand, plant it in the desert soil, water it daily, offering fervent prayers as you do so, and when it bursts into leaf and bloom you may know that you have made your peace with God."

Rejoicing that at last he had what seemed like authoritative instruction in regard to this greatest of all ventures, he hastened back to his cell and planted his rod as he had been told to do. For long, weary days, weeks, and months, he faithfully watered the dry stick and prayed for the hour when the token of his acceptance would be manifest; until at last one day, in utter despair and brokenness of spirit, weakened by fasting

and sick with longing for the apparently un-
attainable, he exclaimed bitterly, "It is all no use;
I am no better to-day than I was when I first
came to the desert. The fact is, I am just like
this dry stick myself. It needs life ere there can
be leaves and fruit; and I need life, for I am
dead in my sins and cannot produce fruit for
God." And then it seemed as though a voice
within said, "At last you have learned the lesson that the old hermit meant to teach you. It is
because you are dead and have no strength or
power in yourself that you must turn to Christ
alone and find life and peace in Him." And leaving his desert cave he went back to the city to
find the Word of God and in its sacred pages
learn the way of peace.

And let us remember it is as impossible to obtain holiness by ascetic practices as it is to buy
salvation by physical suffering. We are saved in
the first place, not through anything we undergo,
but through that which our blessed Lord Jesus
Christ underwent for us on Calvary's cross, and,
blessed be God, He who died for us upon that
cross now lives for us at God's right hand, and
He is the power for holiness as well as for justification. By the Holy Spirit He dwells within us,
and as we yield ourselves unto God as those who
are alive from the dead, He is enabled to live
out His wondrous life in us. Does your heart
sometimes cry:

> Tell me what to do to be pure
>   In the sight of all-seeing eyes;
> Tell me is there no thorough cure,
>   No escape from the sins I despise?
> Will my Saviour only pass by,
>   Only show how faulty I've been?
> Will He not attend to my cry?
>   May I not this moment be clean?

Oh, believe me, dear, anxious, seeking Christian, you will find holiness in the same Christ in whom you found salvation. As you cease from self-occupation and look up in faith to Him you will be transformed into His own glorious image; you will become like Him as you gaze on His wonderful face. There is no other way by which the flesh may be subdued and your life become one of triumph over the power of sin. Asceticism is but a vain will-o'-the-wisp which, while it promises you victory, will plunge you into the morass of disappointment and defeat. But occupation with Christ risen at God's right hand is the sure way to overcome the lusts of the flesh and to become like Him who has said, "For their sakes I sanctify Myself, that they also may be sanctified through the truth."

Of Him they said He was a glutton and a wine-bibber, because He came, not as an ascetic but as a Man among men, entering with them into every sinless experience of human life. He has "left us an example that we should follow

His steps." He has come to sanctify every natural relationship, not to do violence to those affections and feelings which He Himself implanted in the hearts of mankind.

LECTURE 11

CHRIST THE BELIEVER'S LIFE AND OBJECT

Colossians 3:1-4

If ye then be risen with Christ, seek those things which are above, where Christ sitteth on the right hand of God. Set your affection on things above, not on things on the earth. For ye are dead, and your life is hid with Christ in God. When Christ, who is our life, shall appear, then shall ye also appear with Him in glory.

After the somewhat lengthy digression of verses 13 to 23 in the previous chapter, the apostle comes back to apply the truth taught in verse 12. I think we shall get the connection better if we read these two passages without anything intervening: "Buried with Him in baptism, wherein also ye are risen with Him through the faith of the operation of God, who hath raised Him from the dead. If ye then be risen with Christ, seek those things which are above, where Christ sitteth on the right hand of God." All that has come in between these two verses was in the nature of warning against false systems that would have robbed the believer of this great truth of unity with Christ in death and

118

resurrection. It is of all importance that we realize that we do not stand before God on the ground of responsibility. The responsible man failed utterly to keep his obligations. There was nothing for him, therefore, but condemnation, but our Lord Jesus Christ has borne that condemnation; He voluntarily, in infinite grace, took the place of the sinner and bore his judgment upon the cross. Now in resurrection, as we have seen, all who believe are not only given a perfect representation by Him before the throne of God, but we are in Him in virtue of being partakers of His life. "In Adam" meant that we were born of his race; "in Christ," in contrast clearly indicates that we have received a new life from Him and, therefore, we are not to think of ourselves as in any sense on probation. All that was ended on the cross of Christ.

> Jesus died and we died with Him,
>   Buried in His grave we lay,
> One in Him in resurrection,
>   Soon with Him in Heaven's bright day.
>
> Death and judgment are behind us,
>   Grace and glory are before;
> All the billows rolled o'er Jesus,
>   There exhausted all their power.

It is when the soul enters into this experimentally, realizing that the death of Christ, in which faith has given him part, has severed the

link that bound him to the world and all its purposes and has freed him from all necessity to be
subject to sin in the flesh, that he will be free to
glorify God as he walks in newness of life. Most
theological systems fail to apprehend this great
truth of the new man in Christ, hence so few
believers have settled peace and realize their
union with Him who sits at God's right hand,
not only as the Head of the Church, but as the
Head of every man who has found life through
Him.

Occupation, then, with Christ risen in the
energy of the Holy Spirit, is the power for holiness. We are called upon to seek those things
which are above, where Christ sitteth on the right
hand of God. Our real life is there, our truest,
best interests are all identified with Him. Heav-
enly-mindedness is the natural, or I should say,
spiritual outcome of this realization. As the
heart is taken up with Him we will be concerned
about representing Him aright in this world
where He is still rejected and His claims refused.

The marginal reading of verse 2 is better than
the text of the Authorized Version—"Set your
mind on things above, not on things on the
earth." That is, as a watch is set to the sun, in
order to mark the time correctly, so let your mind
be set to Christ risen, in order that His life may
be seen in you. This is in contrast to the things

spoken of in Philippians 3:19—"who mind earthly things." The time for this is past for those who are now one with Christ risen. This will not make us impractical and visionary, but we shall live all the more consistently, thus fulfilling our varied responsibilities in the home, in business, in the State and, of course, in the Church, as our minds are fixed on heavenly things. This is indeed the "ribbon of blue" to which reference was made in an earlier address. We will manifest the heavenly character, just where we come closest into contact with the things of the earth. I think we may see in Christ during the forty days between resurrection and ascension something of what this involves. He was still here upon the earth but He was altogether heavenly. "Though we have known Christ after the flesh, yet now henceforth know we Him so no more," and we are called into association with Him to manifest the heavenly character as we walk the desert sands. Men of the world will not understand this, and we need not expect them to; but nevertheless they can and will recognize and appreciate true piety and Christian character even though they hate those who possess it, as Cain hated Abel because his own works were evil and his brother's righteous. But it should be true of us, as of our blessed Lord Himself, that this hatred is undeserved, according as it was written of Him, "They hated Me without a cause."

The third verse epitomizes this in a very wonderful way, "For ye have died, and your life is hid with Christ in God." We have died to all that we once were as children of Adam, and now we do not have independent life as Christians, but Christ Himself is our life and, while it is true we have this eternal life abiding in us, He who is the source and sustainer of it is hidden yonder in the heavens "in God," and so our life is safe in His keeping. One can understand and appreciate the rather crude expression of the simple brother who, after his conversion, had been greatly concerned lest by some sinful act or lack of faith he might in some way forfeit his salvation and lose the new life given in grace. But as he listened to an address upon these wonderful words of this third verse, his anxiety disappeared and he exclaimed with rapture, "Glory to God! Whoever heard of a man drowning with his head that high above water!" Admitting all their crudity, his words nevertheless expressed a great truth. Our Head is in heaven, our life is in Him, hidden in God, therefore we are eternally one with Him and nothing can ever separate the Christian from the risen Christ.

Outwardly, believers in the Lord Jesus are like other men, they are still in dying bodies, and often distressed by the flesh within and in conflict with Satan and the world without, yet each believer is to walk through this scene in the power of resurrection life, manifesting his union with his glorified Head. He is called to be a man of God, though in the humblest condition of life.

> There is no glory halo
>   Round his devoted head,
> No luster marks the sacred path
>   In which his footsteps tread.
>
> But holiness is graven
>   Upon his thoughtful brow,
> And all his steps are ordered
>   In the light of Heaven e'en now.
>
> He often is peculiar,
>   And oft misunderstood,
> And yet his power is felt by all—
>   The evil and the good.
>
> For he doth live in touch with Heaven
>   A life of faith and prayer;
> His hope, his purpose, and his all,
>   His life is centered there.

This is indeed to be a consistent member of the Body of Christ, manifestly displaying the character of the new man whose Head is in Heaven. And, though like his Lord despised and rejected of men, the Christian is called to run with patience the race set before him, knowing that the day of manifestation is nearing when he, too, according to his measure, shall see of the travail of his soul and be satisfied. Christ will find His satisfaction in us, we will find ours in Him.

> He and I in that bright glory
>   One deep joy will share;
> Mine to be forever with Him,
>   His that I am there.

And when the day of the Lord dawns after earth's long, dark night—or, to put it in another way, after man's garish day is ended—then those who are content to be strangers and pilgrims here during His rejection, shall shine forth with Him when He comes to reign as King of kings and Lord of lords. And so we read in verse four, "When Christ who is our life shall appear, then shall we also appear with Him in glory." We might read, "be manifested," for "appear"—it would perhaps make the thought even clearer. When He with whom we have died and in whom we are risen shall return from Heaven and be manifested before His earthly people who will be waiting for Him in that day, and before His foes as well, then we also shall be manifested with Him in glory.

As we think of His coming we know it is presented to us in two aspects in the New Testament, and perhaps that which appeals most to every real lover of Christ is what we commonly call "the Rapture." Our hearts long for the hour when "the Lord Himself shall descend from

heaven with a shout, with the voice of the archangel, and with the trump of God: and the dead
in Christ shall rise first, and we which are alive
and remain shall be caught up together with
them in the clouds, to meet the Lord in the air."
We think of this as the end of the race, and as
the time, too, when "He will change these bodies
of our humiliation and make them like unto the
body of His glory," when "this mortal shall put
on immortality and this corruptible shall put on
incorruption," and we shall be fully "conformed
to the image of God's Son." This will be the fulfilment of our Lord's promise given before He
went away: "I go to prepare a place for you, and
if I go and prepare a place for you I will come
again and receive you unto Myself, that where I
am there ye may be also." This will be the occasion of our reception into the Father's house: but
all of this, blessed as it is, and calculated to stir
the souls of His waiting ones to their deepest
depths, is but an introduction to the glories yet to
be revealed in the everlasting kingdom of our
Lord and Saviour Jesus Christ. He is coming back
to the earth that rejected Him, and all His saints
are coming with Him, not, of course, to take up
human conditions here in the world again; but
in resurrection bodies to appear with Him
before the astonished eyes of those who still reject Him, and to the delight of those who will be
waiting for Him as the delivering King in that

day when the word will be fulfilled, "Behold, He cometh with clouds, and every eye shall see Him, and they also which pierced Him, and all the tribes of the land shall wail because of Him." That will be the time when we shall appear with Him in glory, and to this the apostle refers again in 2 Thessalonians 1:5-11, where he comforts the suffering saints with the assurance that tribulation will be recompensed to those that trouble them, and rest will be the portion of the redeemed, "when the Lord Jesus shall be revealed from heaven with His mighty angels, in flaming fire taking vengeance on them that know not God, and that obey not the gospel of our Lord Jesus Christ, who shall be punished with everlasting destruction from the presence of the Lord and from the glory of His power, when He shall come to be glorified in His saints and to be admired in all them that believe, in that day." I have purposely omitted the parenthetical words, "because our testimony among you was believed." They explain why any from among earth's inhabitants will be associated with Christ in the glory of that revelation.

> Lamb of God, Thou soon in glory
>   Wilt to this sad earth return;
> All Thy foes shall quake before Thee,
>   All that now despise Thee, mourn.
>
> Then shall we, at Thine appearing,
>   With Thee in Thy kingdom reign;

> Thine the praise and Thine the glory,
>   Lamb of God for sinners slain!

This is the consummation to which the Christian dispensation is tending; when the kingdoms of this world shall become the kingdoms of our God and of His Christ, and His one-time pilgrim people shall reign with Him in righteousness throughout Messiah's glorious years.

And with this the apostle completes the doctrinal teaching of the Epistle to the Colossians. In these first two chapters with which the three opening verses of chapter three are linked, he has unfolded in a marvelous way the truth of the new creation and our link with the risen Man, God's firstborn Son, the Heir of all things. We have seen that in Him we have deliverance from the power of darkness and we are even now translated into His spiritual kingdom; in Him we have redemption, the forgiveness of sins, and have been made meet to be partakers of the inheritance of the saints in light. He has made peace by the blood of His cross, and we have been reconciled to God through His death. We are now members of His mystical Body and thus members one of another, called upon to hold the Head and in all things to be subject to Him as we pursue our way in faith through the wilderness of this world. Christ Himself is to be our heart's blessed object. He is the Antidote for every form of error, for in Him all the fulness of the Godhead dwells, and our fulness is found alone in Him. We have been identified with Him in His death, burial, and resurrection. All that was against us He has taken out of the way, paying our bond and nailing it to His cross. He Himself is now to be the portion of our souls, and as we are occupied with Him, the risen One, with mind and heart set on heavenly things, we shall manifest His life here on earth while we wait for His return, when we shall be manifested with Him in glory. What a gospel! Surely it was never conceived in the mind of man. It could not be, for it makes nothing of man but everything of Christ. May our hearts enter into it more and more as the days grow darker and the end draws near, "While we look not at the things that are seen, but at the things which are not seen," and live in daily expectation of His return to take us to be with Himself and make us fully like Himself forevermore.

> For God has fixed the happy day,
>   When the last tear shall dim our eyes,
> When He will wipe these tears away,
>   And fill our hearts with glad surprise.
> To hear His voice, and see His face,
>   And know the fulness of His grace.

This blessed consummation of all our hopes is set clearly before us in the Word of God as our goal—in order that, cheered by the glory shining from the gates of the city, we may be heartened and lifted above discouragement, and the depressing power of present sorrows, whether in the world or the Church, so that we may run the race with patience, ever "looking unto Jesus."

Part Two

PRACTICAL

Colossians 3:5–4:18

PRACTICAL HOLINESS BY CONFORMITY
TO CHRIST

Part 1: In Relation To Ourselves.

Colossians 3:5-11

> Mortify therefore your members which are upon the earth; fornication, uncleanness, inordinate affection, evil concupiscence, and covetousness, which is idolatry: for which things' sake the wrath of God cometh on the children of disobedience: in the which ye also walked some time, when ye lived in them. But now ye also put off all these; anger, wrath, malice, blasphemy, filthy communication out of your mouth. Lie not one to another, seeing that ye have put off the old man with his deeds; and have put on the new man, which is renewed in knowledge after the image of Him that created him: where there is neither Greek nor Jew, circumcision nor uncircumcision, Barbarian, Scythian, bond nor free: but Christ is all, and in all.

We come now to the consideration of the practical teaching of the Epistle, where we have emphasized for us the importance of walking in the power of the truth of the new man and our relationship to Christ as Head. And in this section,

130

which includes verses 5 to 17 and is too lengthy
to be taken up in one address, we have, first, that
which relates to ourselves, our individual judgment of the old ways, in verses 5 to 11, which we
will consider at this time. Then in verses 12 to
17, we have rather our relationship to others,
particularly our brethren in Christ; or, as we
might put it, the claims of Christian fellowship.
We must be right ourselves, in our own inner
lives, if we would be right toward others. "Keep
thy heart with all diligence, for out of it are the
issues of life." What I am when alone in the
presence of God is what I really am. What I
am before my fellows should be the outcome of
this, otherwise my public life will be largely a
sham.

There is a very suggestive lesson along this line
in connection with the fine linen in the tabernacle. The tabernacle, as we know, was primarily a wonderful type of our Lord Jesus
Christ. It was God's dwelling place; and we
read, "The Word became flesh and tabernacled
among us, and we beheld His glory, the glory as
of the Only Begotten of the Father, full of grace
and truth." Surrounding the court of the tabernacle were curtains of fine twined linen suspend-
ed from pillars. The fine linen, we learn from
Revelation 19, is "the righteous acts of the saints"
(*literal rendering*). Therefore the fine linen surrounding the court would speak of the perfect

ways of our Lord Jesus Christ as displayed before men on earth. The hangings of the court
were visible to all who drew near; but inside,
covering the upright boards of the tabernacle,
which were of acacia wood overlaid with gold,
were ten curtains also of fine twined linen. These
were not visible to men on the outside; they were
seen by God Himself and, in measure, by His
ministering priests. So if the fine linen outside
speaks of Christ's righteousness as Man on earth
visible to the eyes of other men, which led them
to exclaim, "He hath done all things well," and
which caused even Pilate to declare, "I find no
fault in Him," the ten curtains inside would
speak of His perfect righteousness as seen by
God the Father, that perfection which caused
Him to open the heavens and proclaim, "This is
My beloved Son in whom I have found all My
delight."

Now how many cubits of fine twined linen were
there forming the wall of the court? We learn
that the court was 100 cubits long and 50 cubits
wide. Subtracting 20 cubits for the varicolored
gate of the tabernacle, we have 280 cubits, 100
on each side, 50 in the rear, and 30 in front. Inside there were ten curtains joined together, and
each one was 28 cubits long. Here then we have
another 280 cubits. Note this well. There were
280 cubits of fine twined linen surrounding the
court where all could behold it, and 280 cubits

of fine twined linen forming the tabernacle itself, where only the eye of God saw it in its
completeness! How suggestive is all this, and
what a lesson for us. Our blessed Lord was just
the same before God as before men. But the fact
that the width of the curtains was different to
that of the hangings is also suggestive. The curtains were four cubits wide, and four is the number of weakness, and speaks of Christ's perfect
subjection to the will of the Father. The hangings were five cubits wide, and five, we know, is
the number of responsibility, and suggests our
Lord's taking the place of responsibility here on
earth, as meeting every claim of God which man
had flouted. When His enemies came asking,
"Who art Thou?" He answered, "Altogether
what I have said unto you." With Him profession and life were in perfect agreement, and this
is the standard which God now puts before the
believer.

Recognizing, then, our union with Christ, we
are called upon to manifest His life. There must
be first of all the judgment of the old ways in
their totality. In chapter 2 we have learned of
our identification with Him in His death; in the
cross we were circumcised with the circumcision
of Christ, therefore we are to mortify, or put to
death, our members which are upon the earth.
The believer is never told to crucify himself; he
is told to mortify the members of his body. We

have been crucified with Christ. Faith lays hold
of this, and so it is written, "They that are
Christ's have crucified the flesh with its affections
and lusts." All passed under judgment in the
cross, but in order to make this practical the flesh
must be kept, by faith, in the place of death and
its evil promptings refused in self-judgment.
The apostle insists first of all upon the importance of dealing unsparingly with the sins that
were so common in the heathen world out of
which these Colossians had been saved. Sins,
alas, almost as common in the world to-day, in
spite of increased light and civilization. The believer, recognizing his link with Christ, is to
abhor all uncleanness. He is to remember that
the body is for the Lord, and the Lord for the
body, consequently every tendency to the sins
mentioned in verse 5—fornication, lasciviousness,
inordinate affection, evil concupiscence (or, unlawful lusts), and covetousness, which is idolatry
(for in reality it is the worship of self)—all these
are to be judged in the light of the cross of
Christ at no matter what cost. No excuse must
be offered for such sins nor any palliation of their
wickedness attempted on the ground of the innate
tendencies of human nature. These things are
abhorrent to God and abhorrent to the new nature in every believer, and because of them the
wrath of God is coming on the children of disobedience; as of old, when God destroyed the

antediluvian world because of corruption and violence, and rained fire from heaven upon the cities of the plain because of unbridled lusts and passions.

In these sins, so characteristic of men away from God, the Colossians had once walked, living in them unblushingly; but that was before they knew Christ. Now, as risen with Him, these things, seen at last in their true light, must be refused as dishonoring to God and contrary to Christ. Other sins there are which in the eyes of many are far less vile and abominable than those mentioned above, but these, too, are to be put off. They were the habits of the old man, his old clothes, which are not fit to adorn the new man. And so we read, "But now ye also put off all these: anger, wrath, malice, blasphemy, filthy communication out of your mouth. Lie not one to another, seeing that ye have put off the old man with his deeds." The old man is more than the old nature. It is the man of old, the man you used to be before you knew Christ as Saviour and Lord. In other words, the old man is all that I once was as an unsaved person. I am through with that man; he has disappeared, for faith, in the cross of Christ. But if I make this profession, let me be sure that I do not manifest his ways. Sometimes those who make the loudest professions in regard to the truth of the new creation are the poorest performers of the truth, and thus they give the lie to what they say by what they do. It was Emerson, I think, who said, "What you are speaks so loudly I cannot hear what you say." It is to be feared that many a Christian has lost his testimony because of carelessness here.

Anger, which, as we know from Ephesians 4:26, may be righteous, is generally but the raging of the flesh, and even where it is warranted (and we read of our blessed Lord looking round about upon His opponents with anger because of the hardness of their hearts), still this must not be nursed or it will degenerate into wrath, which is a settled condition of ill feeling toward an offender and generally has coupled with it a desire for revenge, and so malice springs from it. We have three generations of sin here: anger cherished begets wrath, and wrath if not judged begets malice. No matter how grievously I have been wronged I am not to give place to the devil and malign, or seek to harm, the one against whom I may have been righteously indignant in the beginning. "Let not the sun go down upon your wrath, neither give place to the devil."

Blasphemy—This dreadful sin may be either Godward or manward. To impute evil to God or to seek to misrepresent Him, or to pervert the truth as to the Father, the Son, or the Spirit, these are various ways in which men blaspheme against God. But to speak injuriously of one another, to circulate wicked and untruthful reports against one's brethren, to revile rulers or governors, or to seek to harm, by evil report, servants of God, all these are included under the general term blasphemy, and here how often have sharp-tongued religious controversialists failed even at the very moment that they were endeavoring to meet the blasphemy of their opponents in regard to divine things. When the hyper-Calvinist, the father of William Hone, the one-time infidel, described John Wesley as a child of the devil because of his Arminianism, he had himself fallen into the sin of blasphemy. No wonder his son turned from such Christianity in horror, and was for years in darkness, till reached by divine grace. Railing accusations ill become those who have been saved through mercy alone and have occasion daily to confess their own sins and sue for divine forgiveness. The wrath of man worketh not the righteousness of God, and He, the Holy One, is not served by our hard speeches against His saints, nor even against men of the world.

Did we not know the corruption of our own hearts it might not seem necessary to warn redeemed saints against the vice of using unclean language or relating salacious stories, but this is what is involved in the next expression, "filthy communication out of your mouth." Questionable stories and the relating of things true or

false, the details of which only tend to feed a
corrupt nature, these are to be shunned by a
Christian. It was a wise answer and a deserved
rebuke that a brother once gave to one in my
own presence who began a story with the remark, "As there are no ladies here I want to
tell you something I heard the other day."
But the other checked him by saying, "Brother,
though there are no ladies present the Holy
Ghost is here. Is your story fit for Him?" The
first blushed in confusion and accepted the rebuke. We did not hear the story.

Were there any truth in the unscriptural theory held by some that the nature of the old man
is eradicated in the case of a sanctified believer
there would be no room whatever for the next
injunction, "Lie not one to another, seeing that
ye have put off the old man with his deeds."
Lying is one of the very first evidences of the
carnal nature. Of the wicked we read, "They go
astray as soon as they are born, speaking lies."
And untruthfulness is one of the hardest habits
for anyone to overcome. It is so natural to these
vain hearts of ours to try to make things appear
better than they really are, to cover up our own
failures and to accentuate the sins of others. Yet
these are just different forms of lying, and we
are called upon to judge all guile—untruthfulness of every character—in the light of the cross
of Christ. The old man was judged there in the

person of our Substitute, his deeds are to be refused, his habits put off as discarded garments which, as we have seen above, are in no sense fit for the new man.

In the next two verses we are told that we "have put on the new man, which is renewed in knowledge after the image of Him that created him, where there is neither Greek nor Jew, circumcision nor uncircumcision, Barbarian, Scythian, bond nor free: but Christ is all, and in all." The new man, then, is the man in Christ, even as the old man was the man in Adam. This new man has a new, divinely-imparted nature, and it is to this new nature God by the Spirit appeals. The new nature alone is capable of receiving divine instruction, and as the truth thus imparted controls the life, the believer manifests increasingly the image of Him who is the Head of the new creation. He Himself, as we have seen, is the image of the invisible God. Man was created in the image and likeness of God in the beginning, but that image became terribly marred through sin. In the new man this image again becomes manifest, and the very lineaments of Christ are seen in His people, and this is true, no matter who or what they were before receiving the new life, whether cultured Greek or religious Jew; whether within the circle of the Abrahamic covenant marked off from the rest of humanity by the ordinance of circumcision, or whether in the world outside, strangers to the covenants of promise; whether barbarian or Scythian (that is, of the wild tribes outside the pale of civilization); whether slaves or free citizens; all alike were sinners; all alike are included in the term "the old man." Now those who through grace have believed the gospel, from whichever of these classes they may have come, are members of the new creation and are seen by God as justified from all things and are possessors of a new and divine life. They belong to that new company where Christ is everything and in everyone. This is not to deny racial or class distinctions in the world—these the Christian must still recognize, and he has his responsibilities as to these distinctions—but above and beyond all these responsibilities is his new place in Christ, linked up with the new Head. It is from this that his new responsibilities flow; because he is a new creation man, he is called upon to manifest new ways and to put on new habits, new clothes suited to his new relationship. These new clothes will come before us next.

In closing let me remark that new creation is not simply individual. It is not merely that I, as a believer, am a new creature in Christ Jesus. A better rendering of 2 Corinthians 5:17 would be, "Therefore if any man be in Christ, it is new creation: old things are passed away; behold, all things are become new."

Joyful now the new creation
   Rests in undisturbed repose;
Blest in Jesus' full salvation
   Sorrow now nor thraldom knows.

Not yet do we see the manifestation of all this, but "we see Jesus crowned with glory and honor," seated above all the changing scenes of time. Till He returns, it is as members of the new creation that we are called upon by our new ways to manifest the holiness, the grace, the righteousness, the love, and the compassion of Him who is "the beginning of the creation of God."

It is not that He is the first being created. This error was exposed in an earlier lecture. But He is the first, the Prince, the Head, the Origin of the New Creation where all things are of God. "For in Christ Jesus neither circumcision availeth anything, nor uncircumcision, but a new creature [or a new creation], and as many as walk according to this rule"—the rule; the controlling principle of this new creation—"peace be upon them and mercy, and upon the Israel of God" (Gal. 6:15-16). This is the very opposite of legality. It is the spontaneous expression of the life of the Head in the members here on earth!

PRACTICAL HOLINESS BY CONFORMITY TO CHRIST

Part 2: In Relation To Others.

Colossians 3:12-17

Put on therefore, as the elect of God, holy and beloved, bowels of mercies, kindness, humbleness of mind, meekness, longsuffering; forbearing one another, and forgiving one another, if any man have a quarrel against any: even as Christ forgave you, so also do ye. And above all these things put on charity, which is the bond of perfectness. And let the peace of God rule in your hearts, to the which also ye are called in one Body: and be ye thankful. Let the word of Christ dwell in you richly in all wisdom; teaching and admonishing one another in psalms and hymns and spiritual songs, singing with grace in your hearts to the Lord. And whatsoever ye do in word or deed, do all in the name of the Lord Jesus, giving thanks to God and the Father by Him.

We now come to consider our new clothes, the garments of the new man—these things which we are to put on in place of the old habits which have been discarded. It is a striking thing that both in the Scriptures and in our ordinary Anglo-Saxon speech, we use at times the same words for clothing and behavior. We speak of a riding habit, a walking habit, habits of various descriptions, meaning of course, the clothing worn on

142

particular occasions, and we may speak of our
behavior as our habit. When in the Old Testament Solomon says, "Let thy garments be always
white," we understand him, of course, to mean,
let your habits or behavior be pure and righteous.
The wicked are depicted as clothed with filthy
garments, and self-righteousness is described as
but filthy rags. The characteristics of the new-
born man are garments of glory and beauty. It
is a common saying that you judge a man by his
clothes. It is true that this is not always just.
Many a princely character has, through poverty,
been obliged to dress in worn and unbecoming
garments, while rascals of the deepest dye have
been arrayed like princes of the blood. But the
same is true at times in regard to children of
God and the unsaved. There are wolves who
come in sheeps' clothing, there are ministers of
Satan who appear as ministers of righteousness,
and, alas, there are real believers whose garments
are often badly stained and rent by failure and
sin. But in the ordinary course of things it is
true that men are largely estimated according to
their appearance, and Christians are expected to
be adorned with good works and thus justify before men the profession they make of justification before God by faith in Jesus Christ. These
are the two sides of truth emphasized by the
Apostle Paul in Romans, and by James "the Lord's
brother" in his intensely practical letter.

Let us see just what kind of habits, or behavior should characterize the man in Christ; with what beautiful garments he should be arrayed. First of all we read, "Put on therefore, as the elect of God, holy and beloved, bowels of mercies." The elect of God are those whom He has foreknown from all eternity and who are manifest in time as believers in His Son. "Holy and beloved" is what they are as before God. They have been set apart in Christ; sanctified by the blood of the everlasting covenant, they are dear to God because they are His own children, partakers of the divine nature. How unseemly if such are ever found stern and unfeeling toward others, recipients as they are of such grace themselves. The ancients used the term "bowels" very much as we do the word "heart," to express the deepest feelings of humanity. We might read, "emotions of pity." While this may not be exactly a translation, it at least expresses in English the thought of the original. We are called upon to have hearts readily stirred to compassion and, like God Himself, delighting in mercy. Where it is otherwise we may well question whether one has been born of God. Harshness in dealing with failing brethren, on the basis of the necessity of maintaining righteousness, is anything but the spirit of Christ. Yearning love that would lead us to go to any possible length without contravening God's righteous claims, should ever characterize us in our dealings one with another. "Be pitiful," writes another apostle, and how much we need to take such an exhortation to heart. The cruelest things have been done in the name of Him who is the incarnation of infinite mercy. How He has been misrepresented in His attitude toward sin and sinners by many who profess to be His followers.

The next word is in keeping with this: "kindness." It is quite impossible to maintain fellowship with God and not show the kindness of God toward others. There may indeed be a rigid, legal type of piety which leads one to imagine that he has been appointed of God to demonstrate His justice, but this is far from the godliness which is inculcated in the New Testament. Macaulay said of some of the sterner Puritans, "As one reads their writings he wonders if they had ever read a little volume called the New Testament." The loving-kindness of the Lord will be manifest in our kindness one to another. These two garments, emotions of pity and kindness are, we might say, inner vestments. The next one is a cap for the head, "humbleness of mind." Pride is of all things to God most hateful: "The proud He knoweth afar off." "Pride goeth before destruction and a haughty spirit before a fall." The realization of one's own weakness and natural tendency to err will lead to low thoughts of self, and will make it easy to don the vesture of meekness. This is composed of rarer material than is often supposed. Our Lord was adorned with it; He could say, "I am meek and lowly in heart." How beautiful He appeared as thus arrayed. And Moses had a garment of this excellent texture, lawgiver though he was, for we read, "The man Moses was very meek above all the men that were upon the face of the earth." But so rare is this grace that in the prophet Zephaniah, chapter 2, verse 3, we are told to "seek meekness," and this is after he has said, "Seek ye the Lord, ye meek of the earth, which have wrought His judgment." So delicate is this fabric that it might readily wear away in the stress and strain of the trials of this life. One needs therefore to be constantly in the presence of God seeking for this grace, which can be found nowhere else than in communion with Him. "Take My yoke upon you and learn of Me, for I am meek and lowly in heart," suggests the necessity of coming under His control if we would be adorned with meekness. The world will never understand the value of this lowly spirit. Our own lion-hearted Theodore Roosevelt said once, "I hate a meek man." He probably did not realize that the boldest man, the most utterly unafraid man ever seen on earth, our Lord Jesus Christ, was in the fullest sense a meek man. Meekness is not inconsistent with bravery, and enables one to suffer and be strong when the world would "turn aside the way of the meek" (Amos 2:7).

Closely associated with meekness is the grace of "longsuffering," the readiness to endure grief suffering wrongfully. It is so natural for us when falsely accused to feel we must defend ourselves, or to resent such treatment; but of our blessed Lord we read that when false witnesses had risen up against Him He answered not a word, and when the adversary taunted King Hezekiah and his officers, charging them falsely and threatening severe treatment, the king's command to his people was, "Answer him not a word." God can be depended on to vindicate His own if they do not attempt to vindicate themselves, and so as they learn to commit their reputation, as well as all else that they once counted of value, to Christ Himself, they can patiently endure without resentment, praying for those who despitefully use them and who persecute them. In this they become consistent followers of the Man of Sorrows who could say, "They laid to My charge things I knew not."

We next read, "Forbearing one another, and forgiving one another, if any man have a quarrel against any: even as Christ forgave you, so also do ye." This is in exact accord with Ephesians 4:32: "And be ye kind one to another, tenderhearted, forgiving one another, even as God for Christ's sake [or, in Christ] hath forgiven you."

When teaching His disciples to pray our Lord told them to say, "Forgive us our trespasses as we forgive those who trespass against us," and He added, "When you stand praying, forgive: for if ye forgive not men their trespasses, neither will your heavenly Father forgive you." Some have thought the earlier passage is on lower ground than the later ones, but it does not seem necessary to put the one in any sense in opposition to the others. The forgiveness of which our Lord was speaking to His disciples was not the forgiveness of a sinner, but the forgiveness of a failing saint, one who could address God as "our Father," whereas the forgiveness spoken of here in Colossians and also in Ephesians is that of the sinner. Addressing His disciples our Lord says, as it were, "You are failing from day to day, you constantly need your Father's restorative and governmental forgiveness, and yet you cherish feelings of malice and enmity and an unforgiving spirit toward your brethren who offend you. If you do not forgive them you cannot expect your Father's forgiveness when you come to Him confessing your failures, and as long as this spirit of malice is cherished by you, you cannot really pray in faith." Here Paul takes it up in another way. He says, as it were, "Think how freely you have been forgiven; think how much God has cast behind His back. In the light of this how can you hold hard feelings or maintain an un forgiving spirit toward those who have sinned against you? If God had dealt with you according to your offences, how fearful would your judgment be, yet He in Christ has graciously forgiven all. He has put away every sin; thus making you fit for His holy presence. Your responsibility now is to forgive as you have been forgiven."

Some of you will remember the striking incident of the conversion of Macdonald Dubh, as narrated by Ralph Connor in "The Man from Glengarry." I understand the incident is not merely fiction, but is founded upon actual fact. The black Macdonald, a powerful, burly Highlander, living in Glengarry county, Ontario, had suffered untold anguish for years because of an injury inflicted upon him by a French Canadian some years before. He had nursed the desire to take a fearful vengeance upon his foe until it became a perfect obsession with him. Neither God nor eternity had any place in his life. It was in vain that the minister's wife tried to get him to forgive his enemy. She sought to have him repeat the Lord's Prayer, but he always balked at the words, "Forgive us our trespasses as we forgive those that trespass against us." But God wrought in power in the Glengarry country, and there was a great revival, in which real Christians were aroused, and Christless men and women reached and saved. The black Macdonald heard the story of the Cross told forth in living power in the Gaelic tongue, from the lips of the venerable Highland minister. It broke his heart and bowed him in penitence at the Saviour's feet. When next the minister's wife went to visit him and tried to stress the necessity of forgiveness, he sobbed out, as he joined with her in what is generally called the Lord's Prayer, *"Oh, it's a little thing, it's a little thing, for I have been forgiven so much!"* It is this that grips the heart and enables one to bear in patience the ill-doing and evil-speaking of others and preserves from bitterness of spirit or any desire for vengeance. How can one, forgiven so much, ever hold an unforgiving spirit against any?

And now turn to verse 14 where we have the girdle that holds all our new garments in place. It might be rendered, "And over all these things put on love, which is the girdle of perfection." Just as the Oriental binds his flowing robes about him with a girdle, or sash, so the new man binds his new habits with the controlling power of love. Whatever is contrary to love is contrary to Christ. No amount of sophistical reasoning can make anything pleasing to God which is opposed to that divine love which He Himself sheds abroad in our hearts by the Holy Spirit who is given unto us.

It would be well for some of us who are possessed with the idea that our great business on

earth is to carry out what has sometimes been
called Pauline truth, to remember that Pauline
truth does not center in 1 Corinthians 5, but rises
to its highest, experimentally, in 1 Corinthians 13.
We are not to neglect the one in order to fulfil the
other; both are right and proper in their own places.
In the portion we have been looking at we have
had what should express our attitude toward our
brethren in Christ and toward men of the world.
Now in verse 15 we get that which is distinctly
personal: "Let the peace of God," or, as some
manuscripts read, "the peace of Christ"—the same
peace that ever filled His breast when here on
earth, the peace that is His on the throne of God
in Heaven, where He sits far above all the storms
of this lower scene—let that peace bear rule, or
umpire, in your hearts. It is to this you are
called in one Body. We are to seek the things
that make for peace as members of that Body,
and things whereby we may edify one another.
But what is distinctly emphasized here is daily
abiding in the blessedness of communion with our
risen Lord, so that our hearts, like His own, may
be kept in peace despite all we may be called upon
to pass through, and thus we can fulfil the brief
injunction, "Be ye thankful." Of the many sins
of the unsaved not the least is unthankfulness.
We are called upon to give thanks in every circumstance, "Giving thanks always for all things,"
knowing that nothing can ever enter into the life
of the believer but what infinite love allows.

In the next two verses, which are very intimately linked with Ephesians 5:18-20, we read,

> Let the word of Christ dwell in you richly: in all wisdom teaching and admonishing one another: in psalms and hymns and spiritual songs singing with grace in your hea ts to the Lord. And whatever ye do in word or deed, do all in the name of the Lord Jesus, giving thanks to God and the Father by Him.

As punctuated in the Authorized Version the 16th verse does not bring out the three admonitions clearly and distinctly, but as given above each one stands out separately and in its place. First we are told to let the word of Christ dwell in us richly. This is the only place in the New Testament where this particular expression, "the word of Christ," is found. It is most suggestive. The actual teaching of Christ, whether personally here on earth or by the Spirit since He has ascended to Heaven, is to dwell in full measure in each believer. Thus equipped and controlled by the truth we will be able to bless and help others—in all wisdom teaching and admonishing one another. What we have is not given for ourselves alone. We are to be ready to communicate. Then, in the third place, as thus controlled by the Word of God, our lives will be lyrical and our hearts filled with melody, in psalms and hymns and spiritual songs, singing with grace in our hearts to the Lord. We read in Nehemiah, "The joy of the Lord is your strength." Holiness and happiness go together. Judah won a great victory when Jehoshaphat put the singers in the forefront of the army. Depend upon it, something is radically wrong with the Christian when he can no longer praise and rejoice.

Then, lastly, the entire life of the believer is summed up as subjection to the Lord. Whatever he does, whether in act or speech, all is to be in the name of the Lord Jesus, through whom he gives thanks to God, even the Father. There is no room whatever for self-will, for self-assertiveness here. As Christ in His humiliation could say, "I came not to do Mine own will but the will of Him that sent Me," so the Christian, the new man, is left on earth to represent Christ, to do the will of the Lord and not to please himself.

By comparing the Ephesian passage with this it will become evident that we have the same results from being filled with the Spirit there, and filled with the Word here. A Word-filled Christian is a Spirit-filled Christian; that is, a Christian who is so controlled by the Word of God that it dominates his entire life, and manifests that he is filled with the Holy Spirit. A careful consideration of these two passages might save from a great deal of fanaticism and misunderstanding in regard to the fullness of blessing which every truly converted soul cannot but crave.

THE EARTHLY RELATIONSHIPS
OF THE NEW MAN

Colossians 3:18—4:1

Wives, submit yourselves unto your own husbands, as it is fit in the Lord.

Husbands, love your wives, and be not bitter against them.

Children, obey your parents in all things: for this is well pleasing unto the Lord.

Fathers, provoke not your children to anger, lest they be discouraged.

Servants, obey in all things your masters according to the flesh; not with eye-service, as menpleasers; but in singleness of heart, fearing God; and whatsoever ye do, do it heartily, as to the Lord, and not unto men; knowing that of the Lord ye shall receive the reward of the inheritance: for ye serve the Lord Christ. But he that doeth wrong shall receive for the wrong which he hath done; and there is no respect of persons.

Masters, give unto your servants that which is just and equal; knowing that ye also have a Master in heaven.

In these verses the Holy Spirit, who, as we have seen, is Himself not mentioned in this Epistle, save incidentally in verse 8 of chapter 1, gives us instruction in regard to the sanctification of the natural, or earthly, relationships of the new man. It would be a great mistake to suppose, as some have done, that because we are members of the new creation we need no longer consider ordinary human ties or responsibilities. While it is quite true that in the new creation there is neither male nor female, bond or free, but all are one in Christ Jesus, it is important to remember that our bodies belong to the old creation still, and it will not be until the redemption of the body at the coming of our Lord Jesus Christ and our gathering together unto Him, that we shall be above the natural relationships in which we stand to one another as men and women here in the world. Even in the Church of God these human distinctions hold good, as we are reminded in the Epistles to the Corinthians and to Timothy and Titus. To say as some do that because there is neither male nor female in the new creation, we are to pay no attention to the divinely-given order pertaining to the respective places of man and woman in the Church of God on earth is not only to go beyond Scripture, but is positive disobedience to the Word of God. As long as we are subject to human limitations so long must we recognize our human responsibilities, and seek to maintain these in a scriptural way in order that we may commend the gospel of Christ. There is no condition in which the new life is more blessedly manifested than in circumstances sometimes hard for flesh and blood to endure, but where grace enables, brings triumph. A comparison of the instruction given in Colossians, in the verses quoted above, with similar instruction in the Epistle to the Ephesians, will show us that the apostle deals very briefly here with what he has taken up at much greater length there, and the one Epistle should be compared with the other, and both with similar teaching given in 1 Peter, in order that we may get the mind of God as fully revealed in regard to the great and important principles which govern our behavior.

It will be noticed that in each of the Scriptures referred to the weaker is dealt with first, and then the stronger; or the one subject first, and then the one in authority: so here we have wives and husbands; then children and fathers; and lastly, servants and masters. Let us examine with some degree of care what the Holy Spirit says to each one.

"Wives, submit yourselves unto your own husbands, as it is fit in the Lord." Where husband and wife are both Christians seeking to do the will of God, in whose hearts there is real mutual affection and esteem there will be no difficulty whatever in regard to such an admonition as this; but it will require true grace to yield loving obedience when perhaps the husband is a carnal, worldly, and unreasonable man, and yet we need to remember the marriage relationship is divinely ordained and as the old wedding ceremony puts it, "not to be lightly entered into," and according to the Word of God not easily to be terminated. "For better, for worse, until death do us part," are words often flippantly uttered with no real conception of their seriousness. For the Christian woman this relationship once entered into, there is no other position in conformity with the will of God than that of godly submission to the husband whom she herself has chosen. The present loose ideas in regard to easy divorce are bearing fearful fruit which will increase unto more ungodliness as the end draws near, until there will be duplicated in Christendom the corruption and vileness of the days before the flood and the unspeakable immoralities of the cities of the plain. Of all this our blessed Lord has warned us most solemnly.

For one to seek to dissolve the marriage relationship because of incompatibility of temperament is to fly in the face of the Word of the living God. Death, or what is equivalent to it, the infidelity of husband or wife, is the only scriptural ground for termination of the marriage contract, leaving the other party free to remarry. It is true that 1 Corinthians 7:11 would imply that there may be circumstances in which no self-respecting woman could continue to live in this relationship, because of unspeakable cruelty, or abominable conditions which would be ruinous to soul and body alike, but if she departs she is to remain unmarried, and if conditions change she may be reconciled to her husband. But so long as she remains with him she is responsible to recognize his headship as the one appointed by God to provide for the family, and even though conditions may sometimes be very distressing she is to seek to win her wayward spouse by manifesting the grace of Christ. "As it is fit in the Lord," suggests that gracious demeanor which ever characterized Him while He was in this scene, and also that her submission and obedience will never be such as to injure conscience or dishonor the Lord. In this she must act as before God, for after all, hers is the submission of a wife and not of a slave. It is loyalty to him who is her head that is enjoined.

In the 19th verse we read, "Husbands, love your wives, and be not bitter against them." And, right here, how many husbands fail! Imperiously demanding submission from the wife, how little do they show the love of Christ in their dealings with those thus dependent upon them! The Christian husband is to accept his place of headship as a sacred responsibility put upon him by God Himself, and is to exercise his authority for the blessing of his home in the love of Christ. And just as some wives may be united to tyrannical and unreasonable men, so there are husbands who, after marriage, find that one who in days of courtship seemed so docile and affectionate is a veritable termagant, and as unreasonable as it is possible to be. But still

the husband is to love and care for her, showing all consideration, "giving honor unto the wife
as unto the weaker vessel," as Peter puts it, without indulging in wrath or anger. How much is
involved in the exhortation, "Be not bitter against
them." God knew how petty and trying some
women's ways would be when He said to good
men, "Be not bitter against them." In the power
of the new life one may manifest patience and
grace under the most trying circumstances.

Now we come to the injunction to children:
"Children, obey your parents in all things, for
this is well pleasing unto the Lord." In childhood
days parents stand in relation to their children
as God Himself in relation to the parent. Children who do not obey their parents when young
will not obey God when older. The natural heart
is ever rebellious against authority, and perhaps
never more strikingly has this been manifested
than in these democratic days in which we live.
But Christian children should be examples of
godly submission to father and mother or whoever may be in authority over them, and parents
are responsible to instill into their hearts the
divine requirement of obedience. For young people professing piety, to ignore this principle of
obedience is to manifest utter insubjection to the
One they own as Lord.

But again we notice how carefully the Spirit
of God guards all this when He says, "Fathers,

provoke not your children to anger, lest they be discouraged." Parental rule may be of such a character as to fill the growing boy or girl with indignation and contempt instead of drawing out the young heart in love and obedience. How easy it is, when come to manhood, to forget the feelings of a child, and so to implant in the hearts of the little ones resentment instead of tender affection. Surely this is contrary to every instinct of the new man. The Christian father is to imitate Him who is our Father-God.

It is when He addresses the servants that he goes into the greatest details. These, in the days when this Epistle was written, were slaves and not free men who served for wages, but if such instruction as we have here was applicable to bondmen, how much more does it apply to those who have the privilege of selling their services and of terminating engagements at will. There is no excuse whatever for surly, dishonest service, because perhaps the master or mistress may be exasperating and unappreciative. Notice the exhortation, "Servants, obey in all things your masters according to the flesh; not with eye-service, as men-pleasers; but in singleness of heart, fearing God." How this glorifies the servant's lowly path in whatever capacity he is called upon to labor for others. He is privileged to look at all his service as done unto the Lord Himself. Thus he labors faithfully, not only under the master's eye, but when unseen by man; he carries on his appointed task conscientiously in singleness of heart, having the fear of God before his soul, according as it is written, "And whatsoever ye do, do it heartily as unto the Lord and not unto men: knowing that of the Lord ye shall receive the reward of the inheritance, because ye serve the Lord Christ." What a cheer was this to the Roman or Grecian slave, toiling on day after day with the most faithful ministrations taken perhaps but as a matter of course; yet if all were done as to the Lord one could be sure that in the coming day, the day of manifestation, He Himself would reward accordingly, accepting all the service as done unto Him.

On the other hand, if treated cruelly, and perhaps over-reached and cheated out of the due reward of his labor, the Christian servant does well to remember that God is taking note of all, and a day is coming when every wrong will be put right, and things that can never be settled here in righteousness will have a full settlement then, for, "He that doeth wrong shall receive for the wrong which he hath done: and there is no respect of persons." Whether it be the servant who is unfaithful or the master who is unappreciative, the Lord Himself will bring everything to light at His judgment-seat, or in the case of the unsaved, at the Great White Throne, when every man shall be judged according to his works.

It is unfortunate that the chapter break comes just where it does. It would seem far more suitable to close chapter 3 with the next verse, and let chapter 4 begin with verse 2, for it is evident that verse 1 concludes this particular section. It is a message to those in authority: "Masters, give unto your servants that which is just and equal; knowing that ye also have a Master in heaven." In every instance it is to the new man He speaks. Ungodly masters could not be expected to take heed to such an admonition as this, but it is addressed to one who, while master in his relationship to his servants, is himself but a servant to his own Master in Heaven. He may well give heed to what is here so impressively urged upon him. He is to treat his servants as he would have the Lord treat him. He is to be characterized by fairness, giving to those beneath him that which is just and equal, knowing that all the time his heavenly Master is looking on, and that when he comes to give account of his service, his relations to those who on earth served under him will all be carefully gone into, when everything will be brought to light.

What marvelous principles are these which we have seen so simply stated. Only one who knows something of the conditions prevailing in the Roman Empire at the time this letter was written can realize how revolutionary they were. In those days wives, children, and slaves had prac-

tically no standing before the law, except as
husbands, fathers, or masters might desire to recognize them, but this glorious truth of the new
man, this blessed unfolding of the new creation,
tinged with glory every earthly relationship in
which the Christian was found. It is like the
blue border upon the hem of the pious Israelite's
garment. Even on the lower edge where that
long flowing robe came most nearly in contact
with the earth, this ribbon of blue was seen; and
blue, as we well know, is the heavenly color. The
Israelite was to look upon it and remember that
he had owned the Lord to be His God, He who
had said, "Be ye holy, for I am holy." As he
looked upon the ribbon of blue he was to remember his responsibility to honor and to glorify the
God of Heaven in his life on the earth, and we as
Christians are to manifest the heavenly character
in every lawful relationship which God has established during the present order of things for the
blessing of mankind.

There is a story told of one of the Dauphins of
France who had an English tutor. This teacher
found his princely pupil very difficult to handle.
Proud and haughty, and impatient of restraint,
the young man submitted unwillingly to school-
room restrictions and his foreign instructor was
often at his wits' end how to deal with him. One
morning as his pupil came to him the tutor placed
upon the lapel of his jacket a purple rosette, say-

ing to him, "This is the royal color, and as you wear it I want you to remember that you are the Crown Prince of France, and that it is incumbent upon you ever to behave in a princely way. If you are wilful or disobedient I shall, of course, not attempt to punish you, as that is not in my province, but I shall simply point to the purple, and you will understand what I mean, that I do not feel your behavior is worthy of a princely lad." The appeal to the purple! How striking the suggestion, and may we not say that to us there is a similar appeal but, to use the Old Testament picture, it is the appeal to the blue! Wives, husbands, children, fathers, masters, and servants, are all alike called upon to manifest the holiness of Heaven, to display the heavenly character, even in earthly relationships.

It is in just such things as these that the power of the new life is wonderfully manifested. "Holding the Head" is not merely maintaining ecclesiastical truth, but it is shown forth in a holy godly life—in subjection of heart and mind to Christ, and never more fully than in the way we live in the family, and in connection with business and social responsibilities.

LECTURE 15

CONCLUDING EXHORTATIONS

Colossians 4:2-6

Continue in prayer, and watch in the same with thanksgiving; withal praying also for us, that God would open unto us a door of utterance, to speak the mystery of Christ, for which I am also in bonds: that I may make it manifest, as I ought to speak. Walk in wisdom toward them that are without, redeeming the time. Let your speech be alway with grace, seasoned with salt, that ye may know how ye ought to answer every man.

One of the most common sins among Christians to-day is that of prayerlessness. No doubt this has been true throughout the centuries. And yet we are again and again not only exhorted, but distinctly commanded to pray.

"Men ought always to pray and not to faint."
"Pray without ceasing."
"Praying always with all prayer and supplication in the Spirit."
"Praying in the Holy Ghost."

To these might be added many similar expressions, reminding us that prayer is in very truth "the Christian's vital breath." It is the life of the new man. One can no more have a happy, triumphant Christian experience who neglects this

165

spiritual exercise than one can be well and strong physically who shuts himself up in a close room to which the sun never penetrates and where pure air is unknown. The soul flourishes in an atmosphere of prayer.

And yet the Christian has sometimes been asked, Why do we need to pray? If God is infinitely wise and infinitely good, as the Holy Scriptures declare Him to be, why need any of His creatures petition Him regarding anything which they conceive to be either for their own good or for the blessing of others? Is it not a higher and purer faith that leads one to ignore these exercises altogether and simply to trust Him to do what He sees to be best in every circumstance? Those who reason thus manifest but little acquaintance with the Word of God, and little realize the needs of the soul.

Prayer is, first of all, communion with God. Our blessed Lord Himself, in the days of His flesh, is seen again and again leaving the company of His disciples and going out into some desert place on a mountain side, or into a garden, that His spirit might be refreshed as He bowed in prayer alone with the Father. From such reasons of fellowship He returned to do His mightiest works and to bear witness to the truth. And in this He is our great Exemplar. We need to pray as much as we need to breathe. Our souls will languish without it, and our testimony will be utterly fruitless if we neglect it. We are told to continue in prayer. This does not mean that we are to be constantly teasing God in order that we may obtain what we might think would add most to our happiness or be best for us, but we are to abide in a sense of His presence and of our dependence upon His bounty. We are to learn to talk to Him and to quietly wait before Him, too, in order that we may hear His voice as He speaks to us. We are bidden to bring everything to Him in prayer, assured that if we ask anything according to His will He heareth us. But because we are so ignorant and so shortsighted we need ever to remember that we are to leave the final disposal of things with Him who makes no mistakes. Without anxiety as to anything, we may bring everything to Him in prayer and supplication with thanksgiving, making known our requests in childlike simplicity; then, leaving all in His hands, we go forth in fullest confidence as our hearts say, "Thy will be done," knowing that He will do for us exceeding abundantly above all that we ask or think.

We need to be often reminded that we cannot pray as we should unless we are careful as to our walk before God, and so we are told not only to continue in prayer but to watch in the same, and that with thanksgiving. "Watch and pray." Here are two things which must never be separated. It is so easy to slip into a careless condition of

soul, to become entangled amid worldly and
unholy snares, so that we lose all spiritual discernment and our prayers become selfish; and
when this is the case it is vain to think that we
shall obtain anything from the Lord. But where
there is watchfulness and sobriety, with honest
confession and self-judgment when we realize
failure has come in, we can pray in fullest confidence, knowing that all hindrance is removed.
Here, as in Philippians 4, we are reminded that
thanksgiving for past mercies should accompany
prayer for present and future blessing. To receive God's good gifts as a mere matter of course
soon dries up spiritual affection, and we become
self-centered instead of Christ-centered, and fool-
ishly imagine that God is in some way bound to
lavish His mercies upon us whether we are grateful or not. In our dealings with one another we
feel it keenly if ingratitude is manifested and
kindness goes unacknowledged. Even though
we may give unselfishly we like appreciation, and
a hearty "thank you" makes one all the more
ready to minister again where there is need. And
we may be assured that our God finds joy in His
people's praises. He loves to give, but He delights in our appreciation of His benefits.

Paul, unquestionably the greatest preacher and
teacher that the Christian dispensation has
known, was not above requesting the prayers of
the people of God. He felt his need of their

prayer-help, and so he says, "Withal praying also for us that God would open unto us a door of utterance to speak the mystery of Christ, for which I am also in bonds; that I may make it manifest as I ought to speak." He did not feel that because he was in prison his work was over. Although unable to face the multitudes in public places as in past years, he was ever on the lookout for opportunities of service, and he would have the saints join with him in prayer that even in his prison cell a door of utterance might be open to him. How natural it would have been for him to give up in despair and settle down in utter discouragement, or simply to endure passively the long, weary months of imprisonment, taking it for granted that nothing could really be accomplished for God so far as gospel fruit was concerned until he should be free. But he was of another mind entirely. His circumstances did not indicate that God had forsaken him nor that He had set him to one side. He was eagerly looking for fresh opportunities to advance upon the enemy.

We are told that just before the first battle of the Marne in the World War of 1914–18, Marshal Foch, the great French General, reported: "My center is giving; my left wing is retreating; the situation is excellent; I am attacking." This was not mere military bombast, for the Marshal realized that apparent defeat could be

turned into victory by acting with resolution and
alacrity at the very moment when the enemy
seemed to be triumphant. Doubtless the devil
thought he had gained a great advantage when
he shut Paul up in prison, but from that prison cell
came at least four of the great Church Epistles, and
some of the pastoral letters, which have been the
means of untold blessing to millions throughout
the centuries. And from that cell, too, the gospel
went out; first to the prison-guards, and through
them to many more in Caesar's palace who might
not otherwise have been reached. How important it
is not to give ground to Satan, but in prayer and
faith to turn every defeat into a victory by seizing
the opportunity and advancing against the foe,
assured that our great Captain knows no retreat.

Alas, we spend so much time halting between
two opinions, debating what we should do,
and doing nothing. We need the grace of
decision that will enable us to seize the
opportune moment and act upon it in the fear
of God. And this is emphasized in the verse
that follows: "Walk in wisdom toward them that.
are without, redeeming the time." In our inter-
course with men of the world how we need to remember that opportunities, to warn of judgment
to come and to point them to Christ, once given
may never come again. Therefore the tremendous importance of buying up such privileges of
service in the light of the judgment-seat of Christ.

The day of grace is fast passing away. We meet
men once, perhaps, never to see them again, and
while it is perfectly true that we cannot be forever pestering people about what they would call
our religious notions, yet it is the part of wisdom to be on the lookout for every opening that
will give us the privilege to minister Christ to
their souls.

> To each man's life there comes a time supreme,
> One day, one night, one morning, or one noon,
> One freighted hour, one moment opportune,
> One rift through which sublime fulfilments gleam,
> One space when faith goes tiding with the stream,
> One *Once* in balance 'twixt Too Late, Too Soon,
> And ready for the passing instant's boon
> To tip in favor of uncertain beam.
>
> Ah, happy he who, knowing how to wait,
> Knows, also how to watch, and work, and stand,
> On Life's broad deck alert, and at the prow
> To seize the passing moment, big with fate,
> From Opportunity's extended hand,
> When the great clock of Destiny strikes *now!*

But if we would witness to the Lord in such a
way that our testimony will really count we must
be careful that our walk agrees with our speech.
Careless behavior when in the company of
worldlings will only make them feel that we do
not ourselves believe the tremendous truths which
we would press upon them. How careful preachers need to be in regard to this! The world is
so quick to judge, and will only turn away with

disgust from a man who is serious on the platform but frivolous among men. He who is solemn
as he preaches of divine realities but is a giggling
buffoon when out in company, need not think that
he will make any permanent impression for good
upon the hearts and consciences of those among
whom he mingles. Many a servant of Christ in
his anxiety to be accepted of men and to become
what is called to-day "a good mixer," sincerely
hoping thereby to commend his message, has found
to his sorrow that he has paid too high a price for
his popularity; he has but cheapened himself and
his ministry by coming down to the level of natural
men who know not the power of the new life.

I remember well a friend speaking once
of two preachers. One was perhaps a bit unduly
serious, not that anyone can be soo sober as he
faces the realities of eternity, but the man in
question was perhaps a bit too stern to readily
make friends among those whom he wished to
help. The other was the very soul of cordiality.
He would tell a good story, smoke a good cigar,
and make himself hail-fellow-well-met with all
and sundry with whom he came in contact.
Speaking of him my friend said, "Dr. Blank is a
fine fellow. I do enjoy an hour in his company;
he makes me forget all my troubles, but," he
added thoughtfully, "if I were dying I'd rather
have Mr. So-and-So come and pray with me." Ah,
my brethren, let us not forfeit our high and holy

calling as Christ's representatives in order that we may obtain popularity among men who have little relish for divine things. This does not mean that we are called upon to be disagreeable in our behavior or conversation, for we are told, "Let your speech be alway with grace, seasoned with salt, that ye may know how ye ought to answer every man." Gracious speech flows from a heart established in the grace of God. Of Jesus the psalmist wrote, "Grace is poured into Thy lips." He could say, "Thy gentleness hath made me great." But this did not make Him indifferent to evil, nor unfaithful in dealing with those who needed rebuke. "Seasoned with salt" suggests the preservative power of faithfulness. There is always a danger that a gracious man will become a weak man, and will lack courage to speak out faithfully when occasion demands it. In the law it is written, "Thou shalt in any wise rebuke thy neighbor; thou shalt not suffer sin upon him." We are all our brothers' keepers to a certain extent, and while nothing is more contrary to the spirit of Christ than an overweening, captious, fault-finding spirit, yet where Christ's honor is at stake, or where we realize a brother is standing in dangerous places, we need the salt of righteousness to season gracious speech in order that we may know how to speak to every man. And if we would perfect ourselves in this grace we need to live more in company with the Lord Jesus

Christ Himself. Follow Him through the Gospels in His wondrous ministry of grace and truth here on earth. See how marvelously He met each individual case. F. W. Grant has well said, "Our Lord had no stereotyped method of dealing with souls." He took up each case on its merits. He did not talk to the woman at the well in the same way as He addressed Nicodemus, the ruler of the Jews. He probed the depths of each heart and ministered according to the need.

And His devoted follower, the Apostle Paul, the author of this divinely inspired letter to the Colossians, was ever exercised in regard to the same thing. He was made all things to all men if by any means he might save some. In the Jewish synagogue he reasoned out the Scriptures like the most able rabbi or doctor of the law. When he stood on Mars Hill among the Athenian philosophers he was a master of rhetoric and showed full acquaintance with Greek thought and literature, but spake not as pleasing men, but God who trieth the hearts, until his great address was interrupted by the excited throng about him, who spurned the idea of the resurrection of the body. Addressing the idolaters of Lycaonia he met them on their own ground, and appealed from nature to nature's God, seeking to turn them from their vanities and draw their hearts to the Creator of all things. How different in all this was both the Master and the servant to many who to-day seem to pride themselves on their outspokenness and indifference to the views and opinions of others. Is it any wonder that men turn from them in disgust and refuse to listen to what seems to them but the dogmatic utterances of self-centered egotists. On the other hand, as intimated above, there are those who seek to be gracious but who utterly lack faithfulness, and who would gloss over any doctrine or evil in the lives of their hearers rather than run the risk of giving offence. How much divine wisdom is needed, and how close must the servant keep to the Master Himself, in order that he may know how to answer every man.

LECTURE 16

CLOSING SALUTATIONS

Colossians 4:7-18

All my state shall Tychicus declare unto you, who is a beloved brother, and a faithful minister and fellow-servant in the Lord: whom I have sent unto you for the same purpose, that he might know your estate, and comfort your hearts; with Onesimus, a faithful and beloved brother, who is one of you. They shall make known unto you all things which are done here. Aristarchus my fellow-prisoner saluteth you, and Marcus, sister's son to Barnabas (touching whom ye received commandments: if he come unto you, receive him); and Jesus, which is called Justus, who are of the circumcision. These only are my fellow-workers unto the kingdom of God which have been a comfort unto me. Epaphras, who is one of you, a servant of Christ, saluteth you, always laboring fervently for you in prayers, that ye may stand perfect and complete in all the will of God. For I bear him record, that he hath a great zeal for you, and them that are in Laodicea, and them in Hierapolis. Luke, the beloved physician, and Demas greet you. Salute the brethren which are in Laodicea, and Nymphas, and the church which is in his house. And when this epistle is read among you, cause that it be read also in the church of the Laodiceans; and that ye likewise read the epistle from Laodicea. And say to Archippus, Take heed to the ministry which thou hast received in the Lord, that thou fulfil it. The salutation by the hand of me Paul. Remember my bonds. Grace be with you. Amen.

This last section, though somewhat lengthy, does not require very much in the way of either exposition or explanation. It is interesting, however, to compare the references to the same persons mentioned here with those in other Epistles.

We do not know much about Tychicus, mentioned in verse 7, exceptin that in Ephesians 6: 21-22 he is again spoken of in almost the same terms. It is evident that he was one in whom the apostle had implicit confidence. He speaks of him in each passage as a beloved brother and faithful minister, adding here a third expression —"fellow-servant in the Lord." Beloved and yet faithful! What a rare but blessed combination is this! So often men who seek to be faithful become almost unconsciously stern and ungracious, thereby forfeiting the tender affection of the people of God, even though they may be looked upon with respect as men of principle who can be depended upon to do and say the righteous thing at all cost to themselves or others; and unhappily, in the last instance, they may manifest very little real concern for the peace of mind or comfort of heart of those who disagree with them. On the other hand, many a beloved brother purchases the affectionate regard of the saints at the cost of faithfulness to truth. It is far better to be true to Christ and His Word, and thus have His approval, than to be approved of men and loved because of weakness in enforcing what is according to truth.

Tychicus evidently went to neither extreme. He was undoubtedly a lovable man because of his gracious demeanor and his tender solicitude for the welfare of the saints, but at the same time he was faithful in ministering the Word of God, rebuking iniquity and also comforting the penitent. Such men are rarer than we realize. In them we see the delightful combination of the shepherd's heart and the prophet's spirit. One cannot but think how alike in character were Timothy and Tychicus. Both were loyal to the Word of God, and both sought the comfort and blessing of the people of God.

In verse 9 Onesimus is spoken of in similar terms. He is called a "faithful and beloved brother." It is evident that he did not have the gift that marked Tychicus, but the two characteristics we have noticed were manifest in him. We know much more of his history than of several others mentioned in this chapter. The brief letter to Philemon tells us a great deal regarding him. He had been a dishonest runaway slave: he had robbed his master and apparently wasted his ill-gotten gains, ere he was brought to Christ through coming in contact with Paul in Rome. Philemon himself had been converted through the same devoted servant, so we may see, in mercy being extended to the thieving slave, a wondrous picture of sovereign grace.

> Sov'reign grace o'er sin abounding;
>   Ransomed souls the tidings swell!
> 'Tis a deep that knows no sounding;
>   Who its length and breadth can tell?
>   On its glories
>   Let my soul forever dwell.

After Onesimus was brought to Christ, Paul sent him back to his master, offering himself to become his surety in the tender words, "If thou count me therefore a partner, receive him as myself. If he hath wronged thee or oweth thee aught, put that to my account; I, Paul, have written it with mine own hand. I will repay it." What a gospel picture is this! It is Christ Himself who has assumed the responsibilities of the penitent sinner. "We are all God's Onesimuses," said Luther. Christ paid our debt that we might be accepted in Him before God.

> He bore on the tree, the sentence for me,
> And now both the Surety and sinner are free.

And when thus redeemed, it is our happy privilege to serve Him in glorious liberty and say with the psalmist, "Truly I am Thy servant; Thou hast loosed my bonds."

Of Aristarchus, whom Paul here calls his fellow-prisoner, we read in Acts 19 that he was a Macedonian traveling with Paul, and endangered his very life on behalf of the gospel at the time of the uproar in Ephesus. He is also mentioned

again in Philemon 24 as a fellow-laborer with
the apostle. His name would imply that he was
of the so-called upper classes, an aristocrat of
Macedonia, who for the sake of the kingdom of
God had renounced his place of prominence in
the world to become a bondman of Jesus
Christ.

We are glad to see the affectionate way in
which Paul here writes of Marcus, the nephew
of Barnabas. Years before, this young man had
been the cause of serious contention between
these two devoted men of God. Paul had lost
confidence in John Mark because of his leaving
the work and returning to his mother in Jerusalem, upon the completion of the evangelistic
tour in Cyprus. Barnabas, kindly in spirit and
evidently moved by natural affection, wanted to
give the unfaithful helper a second chance, but
Paul was obdurate. He felt he could not afford
to jeopardize the success of their work by again
taking with them one who had proved himself
a weakling. Which one really had the mind of
God, we are not told; but we are thankful indeed
to find that Mark "made good" as we say, and
became a trusted and honored man of God; companion to Peter (see 1 Peter 5:13), and dear to
Paul as well as to his uncle, Barnabas. He is
again mentioned in Philemon 24 as a fellow-
laborer, and Paul requests Timothy to bring Mark
with him, in 2 Timothy 4:11. The fact that he

needed the spiritual commendation of this 10th verse would seem to imply that at the time of writing there were some who still stood in doubt of him, but the apostle's recommendation would remove all that.

The next name, "Jesus, which is called Justus," might well remind us of the humiliation to which our blessed Lord stooped in grace when He became a man in order to give His life for sinners. To us there is only one "Jesus." That name is now above every name, and shines resplendent in highest glory; unique and precious; a name with which none other can ever be compared. But we need to be reminded that "Jesus" represents the Hebrew name "Joshua" and was in common use when our Lord was here on earth. And so we have here a brother otherwise unknown bearing the same name as his Saviour, and not only that but surnamed The Just. This latter title was given to men because of their recognized integrity, as in the case of Joseph Barsabas of Acts 1:23, and an otherwise unknown Justus in Acts 18:7.

There is something peculiarly suggestive in the way the apostle eulogizes these brethren whose salutations he thus conveys to the Colossians. "These only are my fellow-workers unto the kingdom of God which have been a comfort unto me." It is evident that then, as now, gift and grace did not necessarily go together. There were others who were perhaps energetic enough in service but who were anything but brotherly in their attitude toward Paul.

Of Epaphras we have already had the apostle's estimate in Colossians 1:7. Here he draws special attention to this man's fervency in prayer. It was he who had come from Colosse to visit Paul and to acquaint him with the conditions that called forth this letter. That he had some ability as a preacher and teacher we know, for it was through his ministry these Colossians had been won to Christ and the assembly formed there; but his greatest ministry was evidently one of prayer. In that he labored fervently, striving earnestly in supplication before God, so deeply concerned was he for the saints that they might enter into the truth in all its fulness and thus in practical experience stand as full-grown and filled full, or complete, in all the will of God. In this prayer Paul joined, as we have seen in Colossians 1:9. This earnest apostle of prayer, Epaphras, had not confined his ministry or interest to Colosse, but he bore in his heart, in the same intense zeal, the neighboring assemblies of Laodicea and Hierapolis.

It is most pathetic to compare verse 14 with 2 Timothy 4:10-11. Here we read, "Luke, the beloved physician, and Demas greet you." But in writing to Timothy the apostle says, "Demas hath forsaken me, having loved this present world, and hath departed unto Thessalonica..Only Luke is with me." From the day he joined Paul's company (as intimated in Acts 16 where the change of the pronoun from "they" to "us" showed that Luke formed one of the party at Troas, Acts 16: 8-9), "Luke, the beloved physician," was one of Paul's most devoted helpers. He remained with him to the end, and possibly saw him martyred.

Demas and Luke seem to have been intimately associated, for both here and in Philemon 24 the two names are found together, but upon the occasion of Paul's second imprisonment we learn that the love of the world had been too much for Demas. He found the itinerant preacher's lot too hard, and he left the apostle in his hour of need and went off to Thessalonica. There is no hint that he plunged into a life of sin. He may have gone into some respectable business; but the Holy Ghost relentlessly exposes the hidden springs of his changed behavior. He loved this present world. No longer are he and Luke joined in devoted service. Demas had chosen an easier path.

Salutations are sent to the Laodicean brethren; and Nymphas, who was evidently prominent among them and in whose house they met for worship, is especially mentioned. We may gather from verse 16 how the apostolic letters were early circulated among the churches. This Colossian Epistle was not only to be read locally but

was to be read also in the assembly of the Laodiceans. And a letter sent to the latter church
was to be sent on to Colosse. This Epistle from
Laodicea (observe not *to* Laodicea) is probably
our Epistle to the Ephesians, and is generally
regarded as a circular letter that went first to
Ephesus and then to other churches in the Roman
proconsular province of Asia, thus reaching
Colosse from Laodicea. We have already seen
how important it is to study the two together
as they are divinely linked in such a wonderful
way.

In verse 17 Paul gives a special admonition
to Archippus, also mentioned in the letter to
Philemon, who was apparently a servant of Christ
ministering the Word at Colosse, but had a tendency not uncommon in some young preachers to
settle down comfortably and take things easily.
To him the apostle sends the message, "Take heed
to the ministry which thou hast received in the
Lord that thou fulfil it.'. Promptness and energy
are as important in spiritual service as in anything else. There is an incident related in connection with two leading generals of the Southern
Confederacy of America that might well speak
to every servant of Christ. General Robt. E. Lee
once sent word to General Stonewall Jackson that
he would be glad to talk with him at his con-
venience on some matter of no great urgency.
General Jackson instantly rode to headquarters,

through most inclement weather. When General Lee expressed surprise at seeing him, Jackson exclaimed, "General Lee's slightest wish is a supreme command to me, and I always take pleasure in prompt obedience." It is to be hoped that this same spirit laid hold of Archippus, and that he profited by the prodding of the aged apostle.

The Epistle was signed in accordance with Paul's usual custom with his own hand. According to the note at the end Tychicus and Onesimus acted as his amanuenses in producing this letter but he appended his signature. How much would one give to have an autographed copy of this or any other of his letters! He would have them remember his bonds both as stirring them up to prayer and to remind them that the servant's path is one of suffering and rejection.

He closes with the customary benediction, "Grace be with you. Amen." This is not so full as that in the last verse of 2 Thessalonians, which he tells us is the token of genuineness in every Epistle of his, but as we go over all the thirteen letters that bear his name and the anonymous letter to the Hebrews we see that in every one there is some message about grace at the end. He was preeminently the apostle of grace, and it is no matter of surprise that this precious word should be his secret mark, as it were, thus authenticating every letter. May that grace abound in us as it already has abounded toward us through the abundant mercy of our God.

> Grace is the sweetest sound
>   That ever reached our ears,
> When conscience charged and Justice frowned,
>   'Twas grace removed our fears!

We began with grace, we are kept by grace, and it is grace that will bring us home at last.

Thessalonians

PREFATORY NOTE

These addresses on the Thessalonian Epistles consist of expository messages on these two letters, given over a period of ten weeks on the Lord's Days at the Moody Memorial Church in Chicago. They were stenographically reported, but have been abbreviated somewhat by the elimination of considerable matter that was not deemed suitable for the general reader, and also because of repetition which can hardly be avoided in addressing changing audiences but would be needlessly redundant in a book. Even as it is, some things are repeated because of certain truths treated or alluded to in both Epistles. It is hoped that these will not mar the effectiveness of the attempt to elucidate the great lessons that St. Paul was used of God to present to this particular church.

—H. A. IRONSIDE.

Chicago
February, 1946

FIRST EPISTLE TO THE THESSALONIANS

ADDRESS ONE

SERVING AND WAITING

✓ ✓ ✓

"Paul, and Silvanus, and Timotheus, unto the church of the Thessalonians which is in God the Father and in the Lord Jesus Christ: Grace be unto you, and peace, from God our Father, and the Lord Jesus Christ. We give thanks to God always for you all, making mention of you in our prayers; remembering without ceasing your work of faith, and labour of love, and patience of hope in our Lord Jesus Christ, in the sight of God and our Father; knowing, brethren beloved, your election of God. For our gospel came not unto you in word only, but also in power, and in the Holy Ghost, and in much assurance; as ye know what manner of men we were among you for your sake. And ye became followers of us, and of the Lord, having received the Word in much affliction, with joy of the Holy Ghost: so that ye were ensamples to all that believe in Macedonia and Achaia. For from you sounded out the Word of the Lord not only in Macedonia and Achaia, but also in every place your faith to God-ward is spread abroad; so that we need not to speak any thing. For they themselves show of us what manner of entering in we had unto you, and how ye turned to God from idols to serve the living and true God; and to wait for His Son from heaven, whom He raised from the dead, even Jesus, which delivered us from the wrath to come"—1 Thess. 1: 1-10.

✓ ✓ ✓

THE Thessalonian Epistles are the earliest of Paul's writings, under the guidance of the Holy Spirit, which the Lord in His grace has preserved for the edification of the Church. It is evident that they were written from Corinth after Paul had left Berea because of persecution. Timothy and Silas, at his request, had remained behind

9

and gone on to Thessalonica. They then came to Paul to report on the condition of the young church. According to Luke's account in the book of Acts, Paul had preached the gospel on three successive Sabbath days in the Jewish synagogue at Thessalonica. How much longer he remained in the city we are not told, but it could not have been very long. The results of his short visit were remarkable. Quite a group were brought to a saving knowledge of the Lord Jesus Christ. Some of these were Jews, but the majority were evidently Gentiles who had been brought to see the folly of idolatry and led to put their trust in the living God as manifested in His Son.

Paul was deeply concerned about these young converts. They seemed to be as sheep without a shepherd, though of course he realized the great Shepherd was ever watching over them. Paul tells us he had no rest in his spirit while he waited for the coming of Timothy and Silas, because he feared lest Satan might take advantage of those so recently brought to Christ. The word, however, that came to him was most encouraging and led to the writing of this letter.

It is an interesting fact that the second coming of our Lord Jesus Christ is referred to in some way in every chapter of this Epistle. Although the letter was addressed to babes in Christ, the apostle realized the importance of giving them clear instruction regarding this great theme. Often today we are told that the second advent is a doctrine with which generally Christians are not to be occupied. Many ministers never preach on it at all; many have no clear convictions regarding it. In the classroom of theological seminaries this doctrine often becomes just a theme for an academic discussion. But to Paul it was a tremendously important and exceedingly practical truth which needed emphasis because of its bearing on the hearts and lives of God's beloved people.

The first chapter tells how the gospel was received in Thessalonica. It closes by picturing for us a group of happy believers earnestly serving God while waiting expectantly for the return of Jesus Christ.

We have the apostolic salutation in the first verse: "Paul, and Silvanus, and Timotheus, unto the church of the Thessalonians which is in God the Father and in the Lord Jesus Christ: Grace be unto you, and peace, from God our Father, and the Lord Jesus Christ." Note that Paul's fellow-laborers are linked with him in this greeting which he extends to these young converts. The expression, "The Church . . . which is in God the Father and in the Lord Jesus Christ," is peculiar to the Thessalonian letters. Of course, it refers to the same Church which elsewhere is spoken of as *the Body of Christ*. But here the emphasis is upon the new relationship into which these young Christians had come. They were now linked up in infinite grace with God the Father; they were His children. They owed it all to the Lord Jesus Christ, who had given Himself for them.

It is not the grace that saves from judgment of which Paul speaks but grace that sustains from day to day. Neither is it peace with God that he has in view. That was settled already. He refers to the peace *of* God which is the abiding portion of all who trust in the loving Father and seek to walk in obedience to the Lord Jesus Christ.

Vers. 2 to 4 are introductory. "We give thanks to God always for you all, making mention of you in our prayers; remembering without ceasing your work of faith, and labor of love, and patience of hope in our Lord Jesus Christ, in the sight of God and our Father; knowing, brethren beloved, your election of God."

It is remarkable how often the apostle speaks of bearing up God's people in prayer. He was a man of intense activity: preaching, visiting from house to house, often working at tent-making for his daily bread; and yet he found time to intercede with God in behalf of all the churches which he was used of the Lord to found, as well as remembering in prayer those of whom he learned, though they had not seen his face, as in the case of the Colossians. He links together in the third verse the three graces of which he was to write later in the Corinthian Epistle: faith, hope, and love. Here the order is different, and he speaks not simply of these graces as such, but of the spiritual realities connected with them: the work of faith, the labor of love, the patience of hope. Faith, we are told elsewhere, worketh by love. James insists that faith without works is dead. These young converts manifested their faith by their work.

Love to be real must be self-sacrificing. Therefore we read here of the labor of love. It is one thing to talk about loving our brethren, loving Israel, loving lost souls in general, but our love is not genuine unless we are willing to labor earnestly for the blessing of those for whom we profess to have this deep concern.

The hope of the believer is the coming of our Lord Jesus Christ, but here the apostle speaks of the patience of hope. Often we may well long for the day when trial and tribulation will be ended, and Christ will take us to be with Himself; but we are not to be impatient as we await that glad consummation. He Himself is the Man of Patience, seated upon the throne of God. "The husbandman waiteth for the precious fruit of the earth, and hath long patience for it, until he receive the early and latter rain." During all the centuries since He ascended to heaven, as we count time on earth, He has waited patiently for the end of the Church's testimony. Then the Lord will descend in the air to call His own to be with Him. Thereupon that change which the poet has expressed will be true of all believers:

> "He and I in that bright glory
> One deep joy shall share:
> Mine to be forever with Him,
> His, that I am there."

The fourth verse is particularly interesting: "Knowing, brethren beloved, your election of God." How did he know this? Had he been permitted to look into the books of eternity and there behold their names written before the foundation of the world? Had God revealed to him His divine sovereign decrees? Not at all! He saw in their lives such evidence of the new birth that he had no question concerning their election. Paul knew that the fruit of the Spirit which was manifested in their lives was not of nature, but was the outflowing of the new life in the power of the Holy Ghost. It is in this way that our election may be made manifest.

In verses 5 to 10 the apostle epitomizes the effects of his ministry among these Thessalonians. "Our gospel," he says, "came not unto you in word only, but also in power, and in the Holy Ghost, and in much assurance; as ye know what manner of men we were among you for your sake." The gospel of course must come in word. It is the business of the servants of Christ to proclaim the Word of the truth of the gospel to a lost world. "It has pleased God by the foolishness (the simplicity) of preaching to save them that believe." But the mere statement of gospel truth, apart from the power of the Holy Spirit, is not likely to produce such results as were seen in Thessalonica. It is true that God in His sovereignty may use His own Word, no matter who proclaims it, or even if it is found on the printed page; He has often done so. His general method however is to empower devoted men to set forth the Word with clearness and in the energy of the Holy Spirit. Then the results are assured. The Lord Jesus told His disciples, as recorded in Acts 1:18, "Ye shall receive the power of the Holy Ghost coming upon you, and ye shall be witnesses unto Me" (*marginal reading*). Speaking in the power of the Holy Spirit is something that should never be ignored. To mistake human eloquence or oratory for preaching in the power of the Spirit of God is a great mistake. Someone has well said that, "Preaching is eloquence touched with fire." It was in this way that Paul and his companions proclaimed the gospel as they went from place to place, and the result of such a proclamation was not only that people were led to trust in Christ, but they also received "much assurance." It is a lamentable fact that a great deal that passes for gospel preaching today would never give assurance of salvation to anyone. Sermons may be theologically correct, but they make no true application to the needs of the hearers, and are, as someone has said, "clear as crystal, but cold as ice." When the Word is preached in simplicity and in the energy of the Holy Spirit, those who believe it receive the full assurance of faith.

The last part of the verse is exceedingly significant. "Ye know what manner of men we were among you for your sake." They were careful to walk before God in holiness of life and in righteousness toward their fellow-men. A holy minister is a tremendous weapon in the hands of God for the pulling down of strongholds of sin. Emerson said of another, "What you are speaks so loudly that I cannot hear what you say." What a pitiable thing if this should ever be true, as, alas, it has often been true of ministers of Christ. Integrity of life, devotedness of heart, holiness of spirit should characterize the proclaimers of the gospel of grace.

The self-denying ways of Paul and his companions made a deep impression on these Thessalonians. He writes, "Ye became followers of us (imitators of us), and of the Lord, having received the Word in much affliction, with joy of the Holy Ghost." It may seem strange that he speaks here of himself and his companions before he speaks of the Lord, but we need to remember that these Thessalonians had never heard of the Lord, probably never would have heard of Him, if Paul and his companions had not gone to them. It was what these Thessalonians saw in Paul and his companions that led them to be interested in the things of the Lord, and so having trusted in Christ they took His servants as their examples, and in imitating them they were really following the Lord.

They received the Word in much affliction and yet in joy. This sounds paradoxical, and indeed it is; but the Christian may be sorrowful yet always rejoicing. The affliction to which the apostle refers may have been twofold. There was of course deep contrition as they recognized their sinfulness and mourned over their years of ungodliness and idolatry. Then, too, they knew that to decide for Christ would mean, in many instances, separation from loved ones, grievous misunderstandings, and even bitter persecution. But they were prepared for all this. They counted the cost and considered that Christ would mean far more to them than temporal comfort or worldly prosperity, and so they joyfully received the message which told them of sins forgiven and the hope of heaven.

So great was the change in their lives that others soon noticed it. They "were ensamples," as we are told, "to all that believe in Macedonia and Achaia." Thessalonica was one of the chief cities of Macedonia; Achaia was the neighboring province. To

one city after another the word went forth of what
had happened in Thessalonica, where Paul had
labored so earnestly. They who had been converted through his preaching became, in turn,
preachers themselves. From these preachers
sounded out the Word of the Lord. Not only in
Macedonia but in other places as well, the news
was spread of what had taken place. It was not
necessary for anyone to insist on the reality of their
conversion; their lives made it evident that they
were in touch with God.

In the last two verses we have two words which
cover the whole Christian life—"serve" and "wait."
Note the connection. "They themselves show of us
what manner of entering in we had unto you, and
how ye turned to God from idols to serve the living
and true God! and to wait for His Son from
heaven, whom He raised from the dead, even Jesus,
which delivered us from the wrath to come." This
was real conversion. They turned to God, and in
turning to God they turned from idols. We have
a different order in Acts 14:15. In speaking to the
men of Iconium, Paul says, We "preach unto you
that ye should turn from these vanities unto the
living God." The two passages are not contradictory; both suggest true repentance upon which
conversion rests. To repent is to change the mind:
that is, to reverse one's attitude; and so these who
had been idolators turned to the true and living God;

they were through with idolatry. Today when men
trust in Christ and bow before God in repentance
they turn from the things of a godless world and
yield themselves to the One who died to redeem
them. Following the conversion of these Thessalonians, as intimated above, two words set forth
their new attitude. They sought to *serve* the living
and true God while they *waited* for His Son from
heaven. We are sometimes told that occupation
with the second coming of the Lord has a tendency
to throttle Christian activities. People become
dreamers, become taken up with prophetic questions, and they are interested no longer in living
for God or seeking to win others for Christ. Frank-
ly, my own experience teaches me the contrary to
be true. The more this blessed truth grips the soul,
the more one would be concerned not only about
serving God but also winning others to Christ. It
was true of these young believers. They lived day
by day in the expectation of Christ's return; they
looked for Him—the risen and ascended One—to
come back again as their Deliverer from coming
wrath. The wrath referred to here, I take it, is
not eternal judgment. From that they have already been delivered. But he refers to the wrath
that is coming upon the world. This wrath is still
in the future. But the Lord has promised to take
away His own before the trumpets of wrath begin
to sound and the judgments of the great tribulation

fall upon the world. It is evident, to some extent at least, that Paul had intimated that such a time of trouble was in the future, but he also told them that Jesus would come to snatch His own away ere that wrath is let loose. His coming for His own is still the hope of His saints.

A CHRIST-LIKE MINISTRY

✓ ✓ ✓

"For yourselves, brethren, know our entrance in unto you, that it was not in vain: but even after that we had suffered before, and were shamefully entreated, as ye know, at Philippi, we were bold in our God to speak unto you the gospel of God with much contention. For our exhortation was not of deceit, nor of uncleanness, nor in guile: but as we were allowed of God to be put in trust with the gospel, even so we speak; not as pleasing men, but God, which trieth our hearts. For neither at any time used we flattering words, as ye know, nor a cloke of covetousness; God is witness: nor of men sought we glory, neither of you, nor yet of others, when we might have been burdensome, as the apostles of Christ. But we were gentle among you, even as a nurse cherisheth her children: so being affectionately desirous of you, we were willing to have imparted unto you, not the gospel of God only, but also our own souls, because ye were dear unto us. For remember, brethren, our labor and travail: for laboring night and day, because we would not be chargeable unto any of you, we preached unto you the gospel of God. Ye are witnesses, and God also, how holily and justly and unblameably we behaved ourselves among you that believe: as ye know how we exhorted and comforted and charged every one of you, as a father doth his children, that ye would walk worthy of God, who hath called you unto His kingdom and glory"—1 Thess. 2: 1-12.

✓ ✓ ✓

IN these twelves verses the apostle reviews the ministry of himself and his companions, in the city of Thessalonica. He reminds the believers how he had come to them from Philippi where he had been "shamefully entreated." In the sixteenth chapter of the book of Acts, we find the record of that shameful treatment, and we learn that Paul and Silas were unjustly arrested, beaten with thongs and cast into a dungeon. Their feet were put in the stocks; and there in the night they prayed and sang praises unto God. Someone has said that the gospel entered Europe in a sacred concert! There were two artists, one was Paul and the other Silas, possibly a tenor and a bass! What hymns they sang we are not told, but the concert was given, and it was so effective that it brought down the house! There was a great earthquake and down came the jail. That was the result of the first gospel concert of which we have any record in the New Testament. The day following the conversion of the jailer the city authorities sent to Paul and Silas and wanted to release them, but Paul said, "They have beaten us openly, uncondemned, being Romans, and have cast us into prison; and now do they thrust us out privily?" So Paul, for the gospel's sake, in order that no dishonor might be connected with the message, refused to go out in that way. He demanded, "Let them come themselves and fetch us out." To this the magistrates eventually agreed.

When Paul and Silas were released from prison they left Philippi after a farewell meeting with the brethren in Lydia's house. They went on down the highway to the city of Thessalonica and there preached the Word, and many were brought to a saving knowledge of the Lord Jesus Christ.

The apostle, in verse 3, mentions the holiness of
life which should characterize the one who proclaims the message of God. He says, "For our exhortation was not of deceit, nor of uncleanness, nor
in guile." He was not careless as to his own life.
It is most important that the man who preaches
the gospel should live the gospel. There should be
no hidden evil, nothing unclean in his life, nothing
that grieves the Holy Spirit of God. Paul was very
careful as to this. He declared that there was no
deceit, no uncleanness, nor any guile with him and
his companions. They were perfectly open about
everything; they had no hidden schemes. They did
not go out preaching in order to make money, but
to exalt Christ and to win souls.

We recognize the fact that the ministers of Christ
have to live, and the Bible says, "They that preach
the gospel should live of the gospel." But when
ministers preach Christ simply as a means of livelihood they have missed their path altogether. The
Lord will support those who faithfully carry on His
work, but if they make personal gain their object,
their ministry becomes obnoxious to God. So Paul
repudiated any selfish motive in his own preaching.
He says, "But as we were allowed of God to be put
in trust with the gospel." That is a striking expression! Not man's choice but God's. It was
God's permission and Paul looked upon it as a privilege—this business of preaching the gospel. He

says, "As we were allowed of God (permitted by God) to be put in trust with the gospel, even so we speak; not as pleasing men, but God, which trieth our hearts." Notice this: they were put in trust with the gospel, and that is the one great message which the servant of Christ has to give to a lost world. We find people suggesting all kinds of themes to ministers on which to preach; and it is true that a minister of Christ should be interested in everything that is for the betterment of mankind; but on the other hand, his business is to preach just the gospel and the Word of the Lord. If we can only get men saved, then all else will soon be straightened out. If we can get men right with the Lord, there will be no trouble with other things. And so Paul's object was not to give a political address, nor some scientific lecture. He had but one object, and that was that men might know the gospel of the grace of God. "For I am determined," he says to the Corinthians, "not to know any thing among you, save Jesus Christ, and Him crucified."

Notice how strongly he speaks in verses 5 and 6, as to his single-hearted devotion to God: "For neither at any time used we flattering words, as ye know, nor a cloke of covetousness; God is witness: nor of men sought we glory, neither of you, nor yet of others, when we might have been burdensome, as the apostles of Christ." Paul and his com-

panions were absolutely disinterested, so far as
their own welfare was concerned. They did not
think primarily of that but of the welfare of others
and of the glory of God. This is the right attitude
for every missionary and every minister of Christ.

In verse 7 he says, "But we were gentle among
you, even as a nurse cherisheth her own children."
This is the better reading: There might be a difference in the way a nurse would treat the children of
someone else, and in the way she would treat her
own children. Paul looked upon these Thessalonian believers, these young Christians who had
so recently come to know Christ, as his own children in the faith. He exerted himself in every possible way to build them up in Christ. He might
have said, "Now that you are converted, the least
you can do is to be concerned about my support,"
but he did not do that. He would not bring the
gospel down to that low level. And so we know
that on many occasions when the end of his finan-
cial resources came, he turned to tent-making in
order to provide for himself and his companions.
When the saints realized their responsibility and
counted it a privilege to care for Paul, he was willing to accept it, but he never put them to this test.

"So being affectionately desirous of you, we were
willing to have imparted unto you, not the gospel
of God only, but also our own souls, because ye
were dear unto us." He literally laid himself out

for them. He asks them to recall what had actually taken place. He says, "For ye remember, brethren, our labor and travail: for laboring night and day, because we would not be chargeable unto any of you, we preached unto you the gospel of God." The word "travail" refers to birth-pangs. In writing to the Galatians, Paul says, "My little children, of whom I travail in birth again until Christ be formed in you." Oh, if we only knew more of this earnest purpose that characterized Paul, this agony of soul, in order that people might be brought to Christ, how many more we might see confess His name! The trouble is, we take things in such a matter-of-fact way. It was otherwise with Paul. He was so deadly in earnest that he went through real agony of soul if people did not come to Christ, for he felt keenly responsible for them.

He could say without fear of contradiction: "Ye are witnesses, and God also, how holily and justly and unblameably we behaved ourselves among you that believe: as ye know how we exhorted and comforted and charged every one of you, as a father doth his children, that ye would walk worthy of God, who hath called you unto His kingdom and glory." He followed Christ that they might see in him what it meant to be a true servant of the Lord.

"For this cause also thank we God without ceasing, because, when ye received the word of God which ye heard of us, ye received it not as the word of men, but, as it is in truth, the word of

God, which effectually worketh also in you that believe. For ye, brethren, became followers of the churches of God which in Judea are in Christ Jesus: for ye also have suffered like things of your own countrymen, even as they have of the Jews: Who both killed the Lord Jesus, and their own prophets, and have persecuted us; and they please not God, and are contrary to all men: Forbidding us to speak to the Gentiles that they might be saved, to fill up their sins always: for the wrath is come upon them to the uttermost" (vers. 13-16).

In verses 13-16 he reminds them of the result of his work among them: "For this cause also thank we God without ceasing, because, when ye received the Word of God which ye heard of us, ye received it not as the word of men, but as it is in truth, the Word of God, which effectually worketh also in you that believe. For ye, brethren, became followers of the churches of God which in Judea are in Christ Jesus: for ye also have suffered like things of your own countrymen, even as they have of the Jews: who both killed the Lord Jesus, and their own prophets, and have persecuted us; and they please not God, and are contrary to all men: forbidding us to speak to the Gentiles that they might be saved, to fill up their sins alway: for the wrath is come upon them to the uttermost." Notice what the gospel had done for these Thessalonians. They saw such evidence of reality in Paul's life that they felt constrained to give heed to his message, and as they listened it went home to their hearts, and it exercised their conscience and they believed the message. Note that they became Christians and received the gospel not as "the word of men," but

as the Word of the living God, and it worked
effectually in them. It is by the Word that we are
brought to repentance, and by that Word they were
regenerated; as Peter says, "Being born again . . .
by the Word of God, which liveth and abideth forever." It is the Word of the gospel that brings the
message home to the hearts and consciences of men,
and by that same truth they are sanctified. Jesus
said, "Sanctify them by Thy truth, Thy Word is
truth." It was this truth received into the hearts
of these Thessalonians that led them to take that
same stand. Those who were Jewish by birth had
to turn away from their own loved ones; they had
to turn away from their dearest friends, endure
bitter persecution and bear the reproach of Christ.
Those who turned from heathenism always suffered
from their heathen relatives and former friends,
just as the Christian Jews in Judea suffered from
their Jewish friends and relatives. There is no
limit to what religious prejudice will really do
when men's eyes become blinded. The unconverted
Jews tried to hinder the apostle Paul from going to
the Gentiles with the message of salvation through
faith in Christ; and so they gave evidence that
wrath had come upon them to the uttermost. God
is going to deal with those who reject His Son and
seek to hinder those who believe in Him.

"But we, brethren, being taken from you for a short time in
presence, not in heart, endeavored the more abundantly to see your

face with great desire. Wherefore we would have come unto you, even I Paul, once and again; but Satan hindered us. For what is our hope, or joy, or crown of rejoicing? Are not even ye in the presence of our Lord Jesus Christ at His coming? For ye are our glory and joy" (vers. 17-20).

In verses 17-20 the apostle expresses the earnest desire of his heart to see these young converts again, and he tells them how he looks forward with joy to their manifestation at the judgment-seat of Christ. He says, "But we, brethren, being taken from you for a short time in presence, not in heart, endeavored the more abundantly to see your face with great desire. Wherefore we would have come unto you, even I Paul, once and again; but Satan hindered us." He wanted to get back but Satan hindered. How may we know when Satan hinders or God hinders? Satan hindered the apostle by stirring up such persecutions against him that he could not get back to Thessalonica at that time. All the efforts of the devil, however, would avail nothing if God did not permit him to work. We do well to distinguish between God's direct will and that which God allows—His permissive will. Very often people suffer from Satan and his emissaries, but it is always by God's permission. We may therefore take all things as from God Himself.

"For what is our hope, or joy, or crown of rejoicing? Are not even ye in the presence of our Lord Jesus Christ at His coming? For ye are our glory and joy." Even if he never saw them again

on earth he would see them in that day when the
Lord returns. In that day they will be his crown
of rejoicing. This would be the abundant reward
because of the preaching, self-sacrifice, and devotedness of his life. Every soul we lead to Christ goes
to make up our crown of rejoicing. Would not it
be a sad thing, when you meet the Lord, if you have
no crown of rejoicing, because you have failed to
lead someone to Him on earth? Have you ever
talked to people about your Saviour? Have you
written letters to friends, telling how the Lord has
saved you? Have you given the gospel message to
others? Oh, the joy of winning men and women,
yes, and little children, to Christ! When in that
day we stand in His presence, how precious to be
able to say, "Behold I and the children whom Thou
hast given me"! What a host will surround the
apostle Paul in that day of manifestation! Do you
know someone to lead to Christ? If you have never
led anyone to Him, won't you go out this day determined, by the grace of God, to point someone to
the Saviour who means so much to you?

STEADFASTNESS IN THE FAITH

✓ ✓ ✓

"Wherefore when we could no longer forbear, we thought it good to be left at Athens alone; and sent Timotheus, our brother, and minister of God, and our fellow-laborer in the gospel of Christ, to establish you, and to comfort you concerning your faith: that no man should be moved by these afflictions: for yourselves know that we are appointed thereunto. For verily, when we were with you, we told you before that we should suffer tribulation; even as it came to pass, and ye know. For this cause, when I could no longer forbear, I sent to know your faith, lest by some means the tempter have tempted you, and our labor be in vain. But now when Timotheus came from you unto us, and brought us good tidings of your faith and charity, and that ye have good remembrance of us always, desiring greatly to see us, as we also to see you: therefore, brethren, we were comforted over you in all our afflictions and distress by your faith: for now we live, if ye stand fast in the Lord. For what thanks can we render to God again for you, for all the joy wherewith we joy for your sakes before our God; night and day praying exceedingly that we might see your face, and might perfect that which is lacking in your faith? Now God Himself and our Father, and our Lord Jesus Christ, direct our way unto you. And the Lord make you to increase and abound in love one toward another, and toward all men, even as we do toward you: to the end He may stablish your hearts unblameable in holiness before God, even our Father, at the coming of our Lord Jesus Christ with all His saints"— 1 Thess. 3: 1-13.

✓ ✓ ✓

AS we have noticed, this letter links very intimately with chapters 16 and 17 of the Book of Acts. In chapter 16 we have Paul's visit to Philippi, and because of persecution there he went on to Thessalonica, where he did a great work in a short time. However, persecution broke out, and the brethren sent Paul to Berea. Here he

31

found a company of open-minded Jews who were
ready to listen to and walk in the light of Holy
Scripture, for we read, "These were more noble
than those in Thessalonica, in that they received
the Word with all readiness of mind, and searched
the Scriptures daily, whether those things were so.
Therefore, many of them believed." These Bereans
may well be models for all of us. Sometimes we
hear things that are new to us, and we reject them
without investigation. In this Epistle we are told
to prove all things and hold fast that which is good.
The test, of course, is by Holy Scripture. No matter
what doctrine is taught we are to compare it with
the Word of God: if it is according to Scripture we
are to receive it; if it is contrary to Scripture then
we are just as responsible to reject it. The Jews
who had resisted Paul at Thessalonica came down
to Berea and stirred up the people against him
there, and the Berean brethren sent him to Athens.
Paul left Silas and Timothy behind. We are not
told in the Book of Acts that he asked them to return to Thessalonica to see how these young converts were progressing. But when he went on to
Athens his heart was in deep exercise, and he remained there alone and sent Timothy to Thessalonica to find out whether these young converts
were making progress in the things of the Lord;
or whether they had become despondent and discouraged.

Notice how Paul speaks of his fellow-laborers. I always revel in the delightful way in which he refers to them. He says, "Timotheus, our brother, and minister of God, and our fellow-laborer in the gospel of Christ." What more could be said of any servant of the Lord: a beloved brother in Christ, a dear fellow-laborer—Timothy was all this to Paul. So he sent Timothy to establish and comfort these young Christians concerning their faith. They needed comfort; they were in the midst of a godless, pagan world. It meant a great deal in those days to come out for Christ. Sometimes it does not seem to mean so much now, and yet we find people afraid to take this step. These people came out from idolatry; they were surrounded by bitter enemies; yet they surrendered their lives to the Lord and bore a bright testimony for Him. Paul was concerned lest they should become discouraged; so he sent Timothy to exhort them that no one should be moved by these afflictions, because, after all, this was what they were to expect, what all Christians are to expect in the world. He adds, "For yourselves know that we are appointed thereunto." How often people, who become Christians, wonder if perhaps they have made a mistake when trouble and sorrow come upon them; they wonder whether or not God has actually forgiven their sins, and if they are really born again. But hear the word of the apostle: "For verily, when we were

with you, we told you before that we should suffer
tribulation; even as it came to pass, and ye know."
Our Lord Jesus said to His disciples before He
went away, "These things I have spoken unto you,
that in Me ye might have peace. In the world ye
shall have tribulation: but be of good cheer; I have
overcome the world" (John 16:33). Elsewhere
Paul tells us we must pass through much tribulation to enter into the kingdom of God. Do not be
discouraged, dear suffering Christians; do not question your Father's love because you are passing
through sorrows, or have to face disappointing circumstances. The Apostle Peter says, "That the
trial of your faith, being much more precious than
of gold that perisheth, though it be tried with
fire, might be found unto praise and honor and
glory at the appearing of Jesus Christ" (1 Peter
1:7).

"For verily, when we were with you, we told you
before that we should suffer tribulation; even as it
came to pass, and ye know. For this cause, when
I could no longer forbear, I sent to know your faith,
lest by some means the tempter have tempted you,
and our labor be in vain." There is always the
possibility that people will make a Christian profession without genuine repentance and implicit
faith in Christ. Sometimes it is easy to go along
with a crowd when many are turning to the Lord;
it is easy under such circumstances to make a pro-

fession, but with no real work of God in the soul. Paul feared lest there might be some who had made such a profession of Christ, but who were not truly regenerated, so he sent Timothy to know their faith.

In verses 6 to 10 we learn of the good report brought. "But now when Timotheus came from you unto us, and brought us good tidings of your faith and charity": that is, your faith and love. One can well understand what it must have meant to Paul to be in Athens in utter loneliness for some time. He had walked about the streets of that great city; his heart stirred within him as he beheld idolatry on every side. An ancient Greek writer has said, "In Athens it is easier to find a god than a man." Evidences of idolatry were everywhere, and not a single light shining for Christ until Paul entered that city, and he did not find many interested until he was urged to go up to Mars Hill. This he did, and we have that address recorded in Acts 17. However, all the time, there was this anxiety, this concern for these young Christians at Thessalonica, but when Timothy came he reported that they were going on beautifully; they were living for God: in fact, many had turned preachers! "Therefore, brethren, we were comforted over you in all our affliction and distress by your faith." When this word came to Paul it gladdened his heart, because he was so definitely linked in spirit with these young converts that he could say, "For now we live, if ye stand fast in the Lord." I think every real soul-winner knows something of the meaning of those words. When we have the joy of bringing sinners to Christ, how it cheers the heart, but how much it means afterward to learn that they are going on brightly and maintaining a consistent testimony. Oh, how it refreshed Paul's soul to get this good word as to these young converts! Exuberantly he wrote, "Now we live, if ye stand fast in the Lord." Young believers sometimes imagine that those who are older and stand in the place of guides and teachers, are often too severe if they warn concerning worldly things that militate against a real Christian testimony, but if they would only understand how fervent is the love of God put into the hearts of those who are soul-winners and have pastoral or shepherd hearts, they would not wonder that sometimes leaders have to say very strong things in order to impress upon the young the importance of being wholly yielded to Christ. Let me assure you of this: in that coming day when we stand at the judgment-seat of Christ, no one will be sorry because he was so completely yielded to the Lord; but in that day there will be many, I am sure, who would give worlds, if they possessed them, if they had only been more devoted, more truly separated from the world, more out-and-out for their Saviour in this scene below. This is what Paul wanted to see in his converts; it is what all faithful ministers of Christ long to see in the souls of those who profess faith in His name.

Paul opened his heart to them. He says, "For what thanks can we render to God again for you, for all the joy wherewith we joy for your sakes before our God; night and day praying exceedingly that we might see your face, and might perfect that which is lacking in your faith." Preaching the gospel was no mere profession with Paul. He did not go from town to town, holding a series of meetings, and pass on and forget his converts. He carried them in his heart, and always hoped that he might return to them to give them additional instruction in the faith and lead them further along in the ways of Christ; and he remembered them in prayer night and day, that they might continue in the will of God and learn to walk faithfully as the truth was opened up to them.

Verses 11 to 13 express his prayerful desire for these young Christians. I am sure these words might well be looked upon as a prayer for every Christian down to the end of this dispensation: namely, "God Himself and our Father, and our Lord Jesus Christ, direct our way unto you. And the Lord make you to increase and abound in love one toward another, and toward all men, even as we do toward you: to the end He may stablish your hearts unblameable in holiness before God, even our Father." When? Will we ever reach that place here on earth? The apostle does not say that we will; he does not even suggest that. As long as we are down here there will always be higher heights to reach, deeper depths to sound; there will always be sins over which we will need to have victory. But it is the will of God that by prayer we shall continually make progress here on earth until at last we stand before our blessed Lord at the judgment-seat when we shall be "found unblameable in holiness before God, even our Father, at the coming of our Lord Jesus Christ with all His saints."

We have already noticed that the second coming of the Lord is presented in some aspect in each chapter of this Epistle. In the first chapter he tells us how they had turned to God from idols to serve the living and true God and wait for His Son from heaven. That was their daily attitude; they lived in constant expectation of the return of the Lord Jesus Christ from heaven, and that should be our attitude also. When we rise in the morning we should say, "The Lord Jesus may be back before night;" and when we commit ourselves to God ere retiring we should remind ourselves, "Before morning comes I may hear His voice and see His face." This should be the attitude of every Christian: ever waiting for the Son from heaven. In the second chapter we find that all these whom we win to Christ will be our crown of rejoicing when the

Lord returns to call His saints to be with Himself. At His return He will sit upon the Bema, and believers (no unsaved ones will be there) will stand before that judgment-seat; and all our works will be made manifest. Everything that was of God— everything which was the result of the Spirit's working in and through the believer, everything that was in accordance with the will of God—will bring its reward. The reward is pictured as a crown: the crown of life for those who have suffered for Christ's sake; the crown of righteousness for those who loved His appearing; the crown of glory for those who fed the lambs and the sheep of His flock; the incorruptible crown for those who press on steadfastly in the Christian race; and, as mentioned here, the crown of rejoicing for those who win souls. These Thessalonian believers would constitute Paul's crown of rejoicing in that day when he himself should receive his reward. He will see gathered there all those whom he had led to Christ. Then they would be stablished and unblameable in holiness before God.

Until that great day, however, we are to press on; we are to put away every known sin, and purge our lives from all filthiness. If one says, "I have already attained to perfect holiness," you may know he is simply deceiving himself, for Scripture says, "If we say that we have not sinned, we make Him a liar, and His word is not in us" (1 John 1:10.

Holiness will be attained only when we meet our Saviour, gaze on His face, and in that glorious moment become like Him; for we shall see Him as He is.

ADDRESS FOUR

THE RAPTURE OF THE CHURCH

✓ ✓ ✓

THIS fourth chapter consists of two parts: the first consisting of a series of exhortations, and the second having to do with the second coming of our Lord for His Church. Let us consider the first section:

"Furthermore then we beseech you, brethren, and exhort you by the Lord Jesus, that as ye have received of us how ye ought to walk and to please God, so ye would abound more and more. For ye know what commandments we gave you by the Lord Jesus. For this is the will of God, even your sanctification, that ye should abstain from fornication: that every one of you should know how to possess his vessel in sanctification and honour; not in the lust of concupiscence, even as the Gentiles which know not God: that no man go beyond and defraud his brother in any matter: because that the Lord is the avenger of all such, as we also have forewarned you and testified. For God hath not called us unto uncleanness, but unto holiness. He therefore that despiseth, despiseth not man, but God, who hath also given unto us His holy Spirit. But as touching brotherly love ye need not that I write unto you: for ye yourselves are taught of God to love one another. And indeed ye do it toward all the brethren which are in all Macedonia: but we beseech you, brethren, that ye increase more and more; and that ye study to be quiet, and to do your own business, and to work with your own hands, as we commanded you; that ye may walk honestly toward them that are without, and that ye may have lack of nothing"—1 Thess. 4: 1-12.

In this section the apostle sets forth the walk that pleases God. Notice the opening verse: "Furthermore then we beseech you, brethren, and exhort you by the Lord Jesus, that as ye have received of us how ye ought to walk and to please God, so ye would abound more and more." During his ministry among them Paul had been careful to dwell on the practical side of Christianity. Sometimes we are apt to neglect this. We become so taken up with the doctrinal side that we do not sufficiently stress that which has to do with our responsibility as believers. Both lines of truth are important. Here there is special warning against sins of impurity. Immorality was so common among the heathen that even Christians were apt to look upon it with a measure of indifference, or even complacency. You remember what one of our poets has written:

> "Vice is a monster of such frightful mien,
> That to be hated needs but to be seen;
> Yet seen too oft, familiar with her face,
> We first endure, then pity, then embrace."

Among pagan nations the vilest kind of lasciviousness was connected even with the worship of their false gods. Ours is a God infinitely holy, and we who know Him are called to be careful to avoid every tendency to uncleanness. "For," says the apostle, "this is the will of God, even your sanctification, that ye should abstain from fornication." We often find this verse quoted in part only, particularly by those who misunderstand the meaning of sanctification; they think of it as though it were a second definite work of grace in the soul that follows justification. Building on a false premise they attempt to find scriptural endorsement by reading, "This is the will of God, even your sanctification."

But the apostle is speaking here of God's will that believers should walk in separation from all that is vile and immoral, from the lasciviousness and licentiousness which had characterized many of them while still unsaved. It is the will of God that believers should walk in purity; that they should look upon the body as devoted to Him. "That everyone of you should know how to possess his vessel in sanctification and honor; not in the lust of concupiscence, even as the Gentiles which know not God." We might say, "Well, we live in a civilized land where men have learned the difference between clean and unclean living; we do not need such an exhortation as this." But a little acquaintance with conditions in and out of the professing church will emphasize the importance of the admonition given here. There is always the temptation to lower the Christian standard in regard to things that are immoral and unclean. We need to be constantly reminded of the importance of living pure lives.

It is impossible to sin in the manner of which Paul writes without wronging others; you cannot do it. These are sins that cannot be committed alone; others are injured by such unholy deeds. The apostle, therefore, warns these Thessalonians, "That no man go beyond and defraud his brother in any matter: because that the Lord is the avenger of all such, as we also have forewarned you and testified. For God hath not called us unto unclean-

ness, but unto holiness." The believer's body is the
temple of the Holy Spirit, and it is to be devoted
to the glory of our blessed Lord. If men despise
such admonitions, they despise not man but God,
who has given us His Spirit.

"But as touching brotherly love ye need not that
I write unto you: for ye yourselves are taught of
God to love one another." Love is the manifestation of that new nature given to all who are born
of God. It was seen in these young converts in a
marked degree. "And indeed ye do it toward all
the brethren which are in all Macedonia: but we
beseech you, brethren, that ye increase more and
more." In this as in every other grace there should
be continuous progress.

Next we have a very practical word: "And that
ye *study* to be quiet, and to do your own business."
The word translated "study" means to be "ambitious." We are to be ambitious to do our own business: that is, to mind our own business! There are
many who seem to have an ambition to mind any
other business but their own. This always makes
for strife and dissension. "And to work with your
own hands, as we commanded you; that ye may
walk honestly toward them that are without, and
that ye may have lack of nothing." In other words,
the Christian is not to be dependent upon others,
but he is to secure his own livelihood by every possible honest means; he is to be self-supporting,

rather than looking to his brethren to sustain and maintain him in idleness.

Following these exhortations, the apostle turns to consider a matter that was troubling these young Christians. Some of their number had died since he had left them: what about these departed ones when Christ comes again? Timothy had informed Paul that the Thessalonians were concerned over this question. When Paul was with them he had told them that Jesus was coming again to set up His kingdom on this earth, and they had leaped to the conclusion that those who had died before the Lord's return might not share in His kingdom, but that only those who were living at His return would welcome Him and have a part in it. Paul writes these words to correct and instruct them:

"But I would not have you to be ignorant, brethren, concerning them which are asleep, that ye sorrow not, even as others which have no hope. For if we believe that Jesus died and rose again, even so them also which sleep in Jesus will God bring with Him. For this we say unto you by the word of the Lord, that we which are alive and remain unto the coming of the Lord shall not prevent them which are asleep. For the Lord Himself shall descend from heaven with a shout, with the voice of the archangel, and with the trump of God: and the dead in Christ shall rise first: then we which are alive and remain shall be caught up together with them in the clouds, to meet the Lord in the air: and so shall we ever be with the Lord. Wherefore comfort one another with these words" (vers. 13-18).

Observe that the apostle is here making known a new revelation that the Lord had unfolded to him. They knew that when Christ returns to reign as

King, those who are ready to receive Him will enter with Him into His kingdom, but the thing that troubled them was this: these who have died are no longer in the world, so how can they reign with Him? They looked for Christ to come back to this earth as He promised; they believed His word and expected Him to return to set up His kingdom, but what about those who have died before He comes back again? Paul says, "I would not have you to be ignorant, brethren, concerning them which are asleep." When he uses the expression "asleep," he means "dead." When he speaks of Jesus, he says "died;" but when he speaks of believers, he says they "sleep." Christ died; He went into death and all that it involved when He took our place in judgment on the cross, but now we who trust in Him shall never see death. If we enter the realm of that which we call death, our bodies will be just asleep until the Lord Jesus returns. The spirit leaves the body and goes to be with Christ: "Absent from the body, and to be present with the Lord" (2 Cor. 5:8). Several times in this passage the apostle uses the expression "sleep" as applied to believers who have died. "But I would not have you to be ignorant, brethren, concerning them which are asleep, that ye sorrow not, even as others which have no hope." He does not rebuke believers for sorrowing when they lose their loved ones in Christ, but we are not to sorrow as others who will have no reunion at the coming of our Lord Jesus Christ. "For if we believe that Jesus died and rose again" —and we do; we are not Christians if we do not! This is the foundation truth of Christianity. "For I delivered unto you first of all that which I also received, how that Christ died for our sins according to the Scriptures; and that He was buried, and that He rose again the third day according to the Scriptures." In Romans 4:25 we read, "Who was delivered for our offences, and was raised again for our justification." The body of Jesus came up from the tomb: in that body He ascended into heaven; and in that body He now sits on the throne of God. We believe He died, rose again, and has ascended into heaven. "That if thou shalt confess with thy mouth the Lord Jesus, and shalt believe in thine heart that God hath raised him from the dead, thou shalt be saved. For with the heart man believeth unto righteousness; and with the mouth confession is made unto salvation" (Romans 10:9, 10). Where this is not believed, no one has the right to the name "Christian." "For if we believe that Jesus died and rose again even so them also which sleep in Jesus will God bring with Him." Or, as it might be better translated, "Them which have been put to sleep by Jesus will God lead forth with Him." It is the blessed Lord Himself who takes His tired, weary saints and puts them to sleep until that glorious resurrection morning when they will

be awakened at the sound of His voice. Then God
will lead them forth with Him. Of what is He
speaking? When the Lord Jesus Christ returns to
establish His kingdom, He will come with all His
saints. How can He do that if some are in heaven
and some are on the earth? This is what Paul
makes clear. When He comes He will raise the
dead and change the living, and they will be caught
up together unto Him in the clouds, "to meet the
Lord in the air." Then God will lead them forth
with the Lord Jesus when He descends in power
and glory. "For this we say unto you by the word
of the Lord (it was a new revelation), that we which
are alive and remain unto the coming of the Lord
shall not prevent (or, precede) them which are
asleep."

There is not one word, so far as I can find, in the
three Synoptic Gospels—Matthew, Mark, and Luke
—of this aspect of the Lord's coming for His saints.
Whenever we have the Lord's own words concerning
His second coming in the Synoptics, it is the coming
of the Son of God with His saints to the earth to set
up His kingdom that is in view. John tells us that ere
the Lord went away He gave a brief word to the
apostles in the upper room which links with what
we have here. He said, "I go to prepare a place for
you. And if I go and prepare a place for you, I will
come again, and receive you unto Myself; that
where I am, there ye may be also" (John 14:3).

They knew He was coming again to set up His kingdom; He had told them that before, but now He gave them information as to a secret which He had kept in His heart till this time. He said, "I will come again, and receive you unto Myself; that where I am, there ye may be also." It is this aspect of His coming that was given by revelation to the Apostle Paul and through him to us. "That we which are alive (and there will be a generation of Christians living on the earth in their natural bodies when the Lord comes again) shall be caught up together with them in the clouds, to meet the Lord in the air." We have no way of knowing when this blessed event will take place. It might please Him to defer His coming until we have left this scene, but we are to live in daily expectation of His return. "We which are alive and remain unto the coming of the Lord shall not prevent them which are asleep." The English word "prevent" has quite changed its meaning in the last three hundred or more years. When this Bible was translated in 1611, "to prevent" meant "to go before." David, you remember, when he was speaking of his morning prayer in Psalm 119: 147, said, "I prevented the dawning of the morning." He did not mean he prevented the sun from rising, but that he was up and praying before the sun rose. The word "prevent" now means "to hinder." What the apostle said was, "We which are alive and remain unto the coming of the Lord shall not *precede*

them which are asleep." We who are alive shall not
enter the kingdom one moment ahead of them; we
shall all go in together. "For the Lord Himself shall
descend from heaven with a shout." I like those
words — *The Lord Himself!* He is the one for whom
I am waiting! The angels said, "This same Jesus,
which is taken up from you into heaven, shall so
come in like manner as ye have seen Him go into
heaven" (Acts 1:11). It is the Lord Himself for
whom we look. He "shall descend from heaven with
a shout, with the voice of the archangel, and the
trump of God." The archangel in the Old Testament
is connected with the Jewish people in a very special way. "And at that time shall Michael stand up,
the great prince which standeth for the children of
Thy people" (Dan. 12:1). When the Lord Jesus
comes, in fulfilment of these words, not only the
saints of this age but also the saints of all past ages
will be included. So the voice of Michael the archangel will be heard at the same time that the Lord
gives that awakening shout. When the trump of
God sounds, then "the dead in Christ shall rise
first." Literally, it might be translated, "the dead
in Christ shall *stand up* first." Millions whose bodies
are sleeping in the earth will hear His voice. Laz-
arus heard it when he was in the tomb, and he immediately sprang to life. So all the saved who have
died will stand up, come back to life, in the first
resurrection. Then we which are alive and remain

in the body shall be "caught up together with them
in the clouds, to meet the Lord in the air." The definite article before clouds obscures the sense. We
shall be caught up in clouds. I do not think it means
that we are going to ascend to the fleecy clouds
above our earth. Even our airmen go higher than
that. But we shall go up in clouds; there will be so
many millions of us! This is what we call the Rapture of the Church, when we shall be rapt away to
meet the Lord in the air. The word "meet" really
means to go out to meet one in order to return with
him, as in Acts 28:15. We shall stand before His
judgment-seat in our glorified bodies to receive rewards according to the deeds done in this life. Then
when He descends to take His kingdom—as in Revelation 19:14 (where He is seen under the symbol
of a Rider on a white horse) we read, "And the
armies which were in heaven followed Him upon
white horses"—so we are coming with Him to share
in His glory in that triumphal day. This is our
hope; this is the hope of the Church.

Notice that word "together." We have had fellowship *together* down here; we have been workers *together* under our Lord's authority, and when
He returns we will be caught up *together* to meet
the Lord in the air. People ask me sometimes,
"Shall we know one another in heaven?" Know one
another! Why we have never known as we shall
know then. "Then shall I know even as also I am

known" (1 Cor. 13:12). We shall know as God Himself has known us.

"And so shall we ever be with the Lord." You might ask, "What comes afterward?" There are wonderful events to be unfolded through the ages to come, but whatever comes afterward we shall always be with the Lord. "Wherefore," said the apostle, "comfort one another with these words."

Do they bring comfort to your heart? They should if you are living for Him. If you are not, there will be no comfort in them for you.

THE DAY OF THE LORD

✓ ✓ ✓

"But of the times and the seasons, brethren, ye have no need
that I write unto you. For yourselves know perfectly that the
day of the Lord so cometh as a thief in the night. For when they
shall say, Peace and safety; then sudden destruction cometh upon
them, as travail upon a woman with child; and they shall not
escape. But ye, brethren, are not in darkness, that that day should
overtake you as a thief. Ye are all the children of light, and the
children of the day: we are not of the night, nor of darkness.
Therefore let us not sleep, as do others; but let us watch and be
sober. For they that sleep sleep in the night; and they that be
drunken are drunken in the night. But let us, who are of the
day, be sober, putting on the breastplate of faith and love; and
for an helmet, the hope of salvation. For God hath not appointed us to wrath, but to obtain salvation by our Lord Jesus
Christ, who died for us, that, whether we wake or sleep, we should
live together with Him. Wherefore comfort yourselves together,
and edify one another, even as also ye do"—1 Thess. 5: 1-11.

✓ ✓ ✓

AFTER unfolding the truth concerning the
rapture—which will take place when our
blessed Lord rises from the Father's throne,
descends in the air and gives that awakening shout,
and the dead in Christ shall rise first; then we which
are alive and remain will be changed, and we will
be all caught up together to meet Him in the air—
the apostle turns to consider the Day of the Lord.

Following the catching away of the saints there
will come upon this world the darkest period it has
ever known—that which is designated in many
places in the Old Testament as the "day of the

Lord;" and also the "time of trouble," or "great tribulation," as it is called in both the Old and New Testaments. Concerning this we are told, "But of the times and the seasons, brethren, ye have no need that I write unto you. For yourselves know perfectly that the day of the Lord so cometh as a thief in the night." The subject of the day of the Lord, then, is included in that expression "of the times and the seasons." May I say that times and seasons—prophetic times and seasons—never have to do with the hope of the Lord's return for His Church. The times and seasons have to do always with events preceding and culminating in the Lord's coming to set up His kingdom here on the earth. It has led always, and will ever lead, to confusion to try to work out the time when the Lord will return for His own. The times and the seasons have nothing to do with that. We get this expression twice elsewhere in the Scriptures, once in the Book of Daniel, and once in the Book of Acts. In the Book of Daniel, 2: 19-22, we are told, "Then was the secret revealed unto Daniel in a night vision (this was the secret concerning Nebuchadnezzar's dream). Then Daniel blessed the God of heaven. Daniel answered and said, Blessed be the name of God for ever and ever: for wisdom and might are His: and He changeth the times and the seasons: He removeth kings, and setteth up kings: He giveth wisdom unto the wise, and knowledge to them that know understanding:

He revealeth the deep and secret things: He knoweth what is in the darkness, and the light dwelleth with Him." It is clear that the times and the seasons had to do with affairs upon the earth. God changes the times and the seasons. If He has determined to visit judgment upon a nation and that nation repents and turns to God, He will postpone the judgment, as in the case of Nineveh when Jonah was commanded to go to Nineveh and announce judgment to fall in forty days; but Nineveh repented, and God changed the times and the seasons, and the destruction was put off for something like two centuries. Then at last her doom came because of her further rejection of the Word of the Lord. God dealt in the same way with Israel and Judah on divers occasions: postponing judgment upon repentance.

In the first chapter of the Book of Acts the disciples asked the Lord, "Lord, wilt Thou at this time restore again the kingdom to Israel?" They were speaking of times and seasons which God had predicted in the Old Testament—the time when the kingdom would be restored to Israel; but Jesus said to His disciples: "It is not for you to know the times or the seasons, which the Father hath put in His own power. But ye shall receive power, after that the Holy Ghost is come upon you: and ye shall be witnesses unto Me both in Jerusalem, and in all Judea, and in Samaria, and unto the uttermost part

of the earth" (vers. 6-8). Nothing could be plainer
than the Lord's words. It is not for us to know the
times and the seasons. Our business is to preach the
gospel; going from people to people and from nation to nation until the entire world has heard. So
here in the fifth chapter of 1 Thessalonians, the
apostle says, "But of the times and the seasons,
brethren, you have no need that I write unto you.
For yourselves know perfectly that the day of the
Lord so cometh as a thief in the night." The Lord
had spoken already of these things. They had
learned from Paul's instruction when he was with
them that the day of the Lord will come as a thief
in the night. The Old Testament predicts that. But
the day of the Lord has to do with the times and
the seasons, and therefore it could never take place
so long as the Church of God is still in the world.

This expression "the day of the Lord" refers
then, not as some have supposed to the descent of
the Lord in the air to call His Church away, but
to the manifestation of the Lord in visible glory to
set up His kingdom. It has to do also with events
to take place after the rapture of the Church, prior
to the revelation of the Lord in judgment. Let us
look at some Old Testament scriptures which will
make this clear. I have selected only four or five:

Turn first to the Book of Amos, 5: 18-20. "Woe
unto you that desire the day of the Lord! To what
end is it for you? the day of the Lord is darkness,

and not light. As if a man did flee from a lion, and
a bear met him; or went into the house, and leaned
his hand on the wall, and a serpent bit him. Shall
not the day of the Lord be darkness, and not light?
even very dark, and no brightness in it?" There
were those in Israel who hoped the day of the Lord
was but a step ahead and then they would be out of
their troubles; but the prophet said, "The day of
the Lord will not be light for you; it will be darkness," as if to flee from one danger meant only to
go into a greater one; as we say, "from the frying-
pan into the fire." Or as a man fleeing "from a lion,
and a bear met him; or went into the house, and
leaned his hand on the wall, and a serpent bit him."
It will be a time of judgment. God will deal with
the world, including apostate Israel as well as the
Gentiles, because of folly and sin; and in that sense,
it is not to be desired by those who are still living
in their sins. It means judgment and sore distress
for the people who will be living on the earth in
that day.

Look at another scripture, Zephaniah 1:14-18:
"The great day of the Lord is near, it is near, and
hasteth greatly, even the voice of the day of the
Lord: the mighty man shall cry there bitterly. That
day is a day of wrath, a day of trouble and distress,
a day of wasteness and desolation, a day of darkness and gloominess, a day of clouds and thick
darkness." It is a somber picture indeed which sets

forth in detail the conditions that will prevail here upon the earth in that day of the Lord.

The Prophet Joel adds his testimony. We read in 2: 1-3: "Blow ye the trumpet in Zion, and sound an alarm in My holy mountain: let all the inhabitants of the land tremble: for the day of the Lord cometh, for it is nigh at hand; a day of darkness and of gloominess, a day of clouds and of thick darkness, as the morning spread upon the mountains: a great people and a strong; there hath not been ever the like, neither shall be any more after it, even to the years of many generations. A fire devoureth before them; and behind them a flame burneth: the land is as the garden of Eden before them, and behind them a desolate wilderness; yea, and nothing shall escape them." Our Lord Jesus refers to this time when He says: "For then shall be great tribulation, such as was not since the beginning of the world to this time, no, nor ever shall be. And except those days should be shortened, there should no flesh be saved: but for the elect's sake those days shall be shortened" (Matthew 24: 21, 22). We should not have any difficulty about this in view of the terrible events that have taken place so recently. Since the discovery and use of the atomic bomb we can readily see that another world war might entail the destruction of all flesh. The Lord says, "And except those days should be shortened, there should no flesh be saved: but for the elect's sake those days shall be shortened." Here "the elect" refers to the remnant in Israel and those of the nations who will be waiting for the Lord in that day.

We turn to the Prophet Jeremiah, 30:7, and read: "Alas! for that day is great, so that none is like it: it is even the time of Jacob's trouble, but he shall be saved out of it." It will be noticed in this passage that it is "Jacob's trouble," that is, Israel's, "but he shall be saved out of it." The prophets show us that God will have upon the earth a remnant from Israel that will turn to the Lord, and He will use them as witnesses to the Gentile world; and as a result many will be prepared to welcome the Lord when He descends to take His kingdom.   ..

Another scripture that brings this truth before us is found in Malachi 4:1: "For, behold, the day cometh, that shall burn as an oven; and all the proud, yea, and all that do wickedly, shall be stubble: and the day that cometh shall burn them up, saith the Lord of hosts, that it shall leave them neither root nor branch": that is, the ungodly Gentile world and apostate Judaism. They will all be destroyed in that day. The prophet says to those who turn to the Lord, "But unto you that fear My name shall the Sun of Righteousness arise with healing in His wings; and ye shall go forth, and grow up as calves of the stall." The day of the Lord is the time when—the day of grace having ended—

God will visit the world in judgment, and that day will come upon the earth as a thief in the night.

The first great event that will startle the world, prior to that day of wrath, will be the disappearance of millions of people who have known and loved the Lord Jesus Christ. At one instant they will be on the earth: some perhaps sleeping, some suffering in hospitals and other places, enduring pain, grief, and distress; others will be gathered together for worship. But in a moment, in the twinkling of an eye, these redeemed ones will be changed and will disappear. The world will waken to find them gone.

I remember reading years ago of a gentleman who said that one day in every month he went to a certain city, a place where there were great steel mills. These mills were going constantly, pounding, pounding, pounding, and he wondered how people could sleep; but the citizens were so used to the noise that it did not bother them. He could get no sleep during the one night a month which he spent in that town. Then one time, in the middle of the night, something happened to the electric power, and in a moment the mills stopped. Suddenly the whole town woke up. They were so used to the noise that it put them to sleep. Well, the world has heard the gospel down through the centuries and still sleeps on. But some day the Church of God will be gone, and the gospel as now preached will be silenced. Then the world will wake up to find that it is just entering upon the day of the Lord. The day of the Lord will so come as a thief in the night: "For when they shall say, Peace and safety; then sudden destruction cometh upon them, as travail upon a woman with child; and they shall not escape."

The apostle turns to comfort believers. He says, "But ye, brethren, are not in darkness, that that day should overtake you as a thief." For those who are saved, who are waiting expectantly for the coming of the Lord, His return will not be as a thief that cometh in the night. "Ye are all the children of light and the children of the day: we are not of the night, nor of darkness." We used to be children of darkness, but God has brought us out of darkness into light, and so we are no more children of darkness. The world sleeps; but we should be alert, awake, ever seeking to serve the Lord Jesus, making His truth known to others, and seeking to get people ready to welcome Him when He returns. "Therefore let us not sleep, as do others; but let us watch and be sober. For they that sleep sleep in the night; and they that be drunken are drunken in the night." Oh, that Christian people everywhere might be awakened out of their lethargy and out of their carelessness and frivolity, and brought to realize the seriousness of the times in which we live! What a solemn thing it is to be a Christian in a world like this, in view of the fact that we will soon give an account of our works to the Great Judge. "But let us, who are of the day, be sober, putting on the breastplate of faith and love; and for an helmet, the hope of salvation." Faith and love to protect our hearts, garrisoned by confidence in God, even as the world is drifting on to this time of great trouble of which we have been reading. We will not be here to share in that day of wrath. We have the helmet, the hope of salvation. It is our final salvation that is in view. "For God hath not appointed us to wrath." The world is drifting on to this; and some day the wrath of God will be poured out from heaven, and Satan will be cast down to earth having great wrath. The wrath of the devil will be manifest in opposition to the wrath of God. But "God hath not appointed us to wrath (we will not be here) but to obtain salvation (deliverance out of this world) by our Lord Jesus Christ, who died for us, that, whether we wake or sleep, we should live together with Him." That is, whether we live till He returns or die before He comes, "We should live together with Him." When this hour of judgment strikes we will not be here to go through it; we will be taken away in accordance with the promise to the church of Philadelphia: "Because thou hast kept the word of My patience, I also will keep thee from the hour of temptation, which shall come upon all the world, to try them that dwell upon the earth"

(Rev. 3: 10). As Christians we do not dwell on the earth; our citizenship is in heaven from whence we look for the Saviour who is coming to snatch us away from the wrath to come.

The apostle concludes this section by saying, "Wherefore comfort yourselves together, and edify one another, even as also ye do." For those who are not yet saved there is no comfort in this message. There can be none unless they come to Christ. Some living now may be numbered among those who will be caught up when the Lord comes to take His saints to be with Himself before the day of judgment begins for this world. "Now is the day of salvation." While the gospel is preached, God wants all to believe and live. If men persistently reject His Son then only judgment awaits them. It is their own fault if they are left behind in that great day, because God has made a way of escape, and they have failed to avail themselves of it. For those who are saved and are expecting and waiting for the Lord's return, what comfort it is to know that we shall have no part in the woes of this world in that terrible hour! We will be with Him in the Father's house. When He descends to the earth to set up His kingdom we shall come with Him, and He will appoint His redeemed ones to places of authority over this lower universe to reign with Him: "Do ye not know that the saints shall judge the world: and if the world shall be judged by you, are ye unworthy to judge the smallest matters? Know ye not that we shall judge angels?" (1 Cor. 6: 2, 3). So we should be looking expectantly, not for the day of Jehovah, but for the coming of the Lord Jesus to take us to be with Him and to be like Him forever. We are told in Hebrews 9: 27, 28. "And as it is appointed unto men once to die, but after this the judgment: so Christ was once offered to bear the sins of many; and unto them that look for Him shall He appear the second time without sin unto salvation."

"We're watching for Jesus who entered within
The Holiest of all when He put away sin:
A place in the glory He's gone to prepare,
Where we shall be with Him; but will you be there?"

ADDRESS SIX

SANCTIFICATION COMPLETE AT THE LORD'S RETURN

✓ ✓ ✓

"And we beseech you, brethren, to know them which labor among you, and are over you in the Lord, and admonish you; and to esteem them very highly in love for their work's sake. And be at peace among yourselves. Now we exhort you, brethren, warn them that are unruly, comfort the feebleminded, support the weak, be patient toward all men. See that none render evil for evil unto any man; but ever follow that which is good, both among yourselves, and to all men. Rejoice evermore. Pray without ceasing. In every thing give thanks: for this is the will of God in Christ Jesus concerning you. Quench not the Spirit. Despise not prophesyings. Prove all things; hold fast that which is good. Abstain from all appearance of evil. And the very God of peace sanctify you wholly; and I pray God your whole spirit and soul and body be preserved blameless unto the coming of our Lord Jesus Christ. Faithful is He that calleth you, who also will do it. Brethren, pray for us. Greet all the brethren with an holy kiss. I charge you by the Lord that this Epistle be read unto all the holy brethren. The grace of our Lord Jesus Christ be with you. Amen."—1 Thess. 5: 12-28.

✓ ✓ ✓

THIS section of the Epistle consists largely of exhortations based upon truth revealed already. In verses 12, 13 we have a word of admonition for those who are members of the Body of Christ, concerning their attitude toward those whom God has set in their midst as guides in spiritual things. The apostle says, "We beseech you, brethren, to know them which labor among you, and are over you in the Lord, and admonish you." It is God who calls men to be His servants, and

65

entrusts to them various gifts of teaching, preaching, or administration, and gives these servants to His people in order to build them up and lead them on in Christ. True pastors are spiritual shepherds who are responsible to care for the sheep and lambs of Christ's flock. Such are to be recognized and reverenced as they seek to fulfil their ministry. "Esteem them very highly in love for their work's sake." It is not a question of simply approving their personality, but it is a question of recognizing that God has entrusted to them the ministry of teaching, preaching, and exhorting the saints.

We have an added word which we as Christians need to remember always, "And be at peace among yourselves." It is so easy to allow little things to set one Christian against another, and thus bring in strife and a spirit of quarrelsomeness among God's people. When we realize that anything like this is in our hearts we should take it immediately to the Lord in humiliation and self-judgment, and seek grace not to say or do anything wilfully that is likely to cause contention among God's children.

In vers. 14-22 we have twelve distinct exhortations. They are so plain and clear that one does not need to use many words in an attempt to explain them; they are self-explanatory. First the apostle says, "Now we exhort you, brethren, warn them that are unruly." There is always the probability that some will be found in a local church or assembly of saints who are naturally rebellious, always wanting to run things to suit themselves. Some people have a splendid disposition as long as they can have everything their own way, but just cross them and the old nature soon manifests itself. Such are to be warned, because they are hindrances to blessing.

Next, we read "Comfort the feebleminded," or "faint-hearted," as others would render it. All are not courageous and quick to act. We must be considerate toward those who are lacking in confidence and boldness. "Support the weak." Instead of censuring these we should assist them and bear with their infirmities. There is an inclination to condemn those who are not so strong in faith, or in other ways, as we may fancy ourselves to be. But that is not the spirit of Christ. "Be patient toward all men." There are many things which try our patience, even in Christian circles; much that might arouse ill-temper, but we are called to be considerate on all occasions. "See that none render evil for evil unto any man; but ever follow that which is good, both among yourselves, and to all men." The Christian is not to retaliate. Savonarola said years ago, "A Christian's life consists in doing good and suffering evil." The Lord has taught us what our attitude should be when we come up against evil: "And unto him that smiteth thee on the one cheek offer also the other; and him that taketh away thy cloke forbid not to take thy coat also." The Apostle Paul has said, "Recompense to no man evil for evil" (Romans 12:17). We are even to return good for evil.

The sixth exhortation is, "Rejoice evermore." He who knows Christ can rejoice even in the midst of sorrow. "The joy of the Lord is your strength." If his joy disappears we may be sure that something is wrong; something needs to be put right. George Mueller, that great apostle of faith of the nineteenth century, said on one occasion, "I never allow myself to begin the day without facing before God anything that has left me unhappy or distressed, because I want to be before Him always in the spirit of joyfulness." We may blame others for our lack of this, but the truth of the matter is if our joy has gone we have no one to blame but ourselves. It shows that we are out of fellowship with God. Our blessed Lord has set the example here. In spite of the fact that He was rejected by men His spirit was always one of joyfulness and gladness as He communed with His Father.

In the seventh instance we are exhorted to "Pray without ceasing." I cannot always be uttering words of prayer, but I can be in the attitude of prayer continually: that is, I am to be ever in the spirit of dependence upon God. "Prayer is the soul's sincere desire, uttered or unexpressed." We are to go through life with our hearts looking up to God no matter how much we may be occupied with other affairs.

The next exhortation is one we all need to have in mind: "In every thing give thanks: for this is the will of God in Christ Jesus concerning you." "Thankfulness" and "holiness" go together. It was when men began to be unthankful that they turned away from God and went into idolatry. "We know that all things work together for good to them that love God, to them who are the called according to His purpose" (Romans 8: 28). Giving thanks should do away with all complaint. We have seen people go to the dinner-table and give thanks for the food God has provided, and their eyes are hardly open before they begin to complain about it all. The very lips which a few moments before gave thanks for the meal are now finding fault with it! Yet there are vast numbers of poverty-stricken people in the world to whom that very food would seem most delicious and even luxurious. Giving thanks "in every thing" is to recognize that all our circumstances come from God. One may ask, "But does not Satan bring evil things into my life?" Yes; it was Satan who was permitted to afflict Job, but Job looked beyond Satan to the One who had allowed the enemy that liberty; and he said "The Lord gave, and the Lord hath taken away; blessed be the name of the Lord" and, "Shall we receive good at the hand of the Lord and shall we not receive evil" (Job 1:21; 2:10). If I remember that it is the Lord who permits the unpleasant things for my good then I should be enabled to thank Him for them all. I should seek to learn the lessons He has for me.

"Quench not the Spirit." The unsaved may resist the Spirit, but it is only believers who quench the Spirit. We may also grieve the Spirit. He is a Divine Personality, and He dwells within our hearts. To quench the Spirit is to fail to respond to His guidance.

The tenth exhortation is, "Despise not prophesyings." That is, we are to be ready to recognize the messages of God when His servants speak. In 1 Cor. 14:3 we read, "He that prophesieth speaketh unto men to edification, and exhortation, and comfort." One who prophesies is not necessarily a foreteller but a forthteller, one who tells forth the mind of God; and of course that always will be based on the Word of God.

Next we have, "Prove all things; hold fast that which is good." That is, prove the different lines of teaching. The only test is the Word of God. We are to prove all we hear by the Scriptures, and then hold fast to that which is good, and reject all else.

The last of these exhortations is one which we are prone to forget because of the independence of our spirits: "Abstain from all appearance of evil." You may have some habit; or you may be doing something by which you mean no harm, and you may say that no one has a right to judge you in regard to it, but a weaker person may think of it as an evil. We are to remember that others are looking to us and taking note how we behave. We are to abstain from all that looks like evil—from the very appearance of evil, or literally, from every form of evil.

Now we come to a text which has troubled many people. "And the very God of peace sanctify you wholly; and I pray God your whole spirit and soul and body be preserved blameless unto the coming of our Lord Jesus Christ." To sanctify, as we have seen, means to set apart, to separate from that which is evil. A Christian is to be separated from worldly things, from all that is unholy. Some have taken for granted that sanctification means the absolute eradication of all inbred sin. But as we saw in considering chapter 4:3, there is not one scripture which treats sanctification from that standpoint. Sanctification is presented in three very different ways in Scripture. Every believer is sanctified by the Holy Spirit; that is a work which begins before we ever come to a definite knowledge of salvation. We read in the first Epistle of Peter that we are "Elect according to the foreknowledge of God the Father, through sanctification of the Spirit, unto obedience and sprinkling of the blood of Jesus Christ." In 2 Thessalonians 2:13 we read, "But we are bound to give thanks always to God for you, brethren beloved of the Lord, because God hath from the beginning chosen you to salvation through sanctification of the Spirit and belief of the truth." In these scriptures we have God's purpose in the past—election and His choice. It is by sanctification of the Spirit that this is carried out in time. It was the Spirit of God working within us that showed us our need of a Saviour and led us to trust in Christ. Then the Spirit comes to dwell within us. He continues the work of sanctification all through our Christian lives.

Positional sanctification is absolutely complete from the moment we believe. We are then set apart to God in all the value of His precious blood. This sanctification is perfect. "By one offering He hath perfected forever them that are sanctified." Nothing can ever be taken from it; nothing can be added to it. Christ Himself is our sanctification, and we are complete in Him.

The third aspect is sanctification by the Word. Jesus prayed, "Sanctify them through Thy truth: Thy Word is truth." As we read and study the Word of God it opens up the wonderful truths which are there, and we learn from that Word what is in accordance with His will. As we obey the Word we are practically sanctified. This sanctification will never be complete until we reach the end of our pilgrimage. We are sanctified in Christ Jesus the moment we believe in Him, but as we feed upon the Word and apply it practically to our lives we are being sanctified by the truth.

People often tell me that they are sanctified completely. When I put the question to them, "Have you ever read through your Bible?" they often say, "No; I am afraid I cannot say that I have read it through all the way, but I have read a good deal of it." Then I reply, "How can you be sanctified completely if you have never read through your Bible, when sanctification is by the Word?"

When will our sanctification be complete? Note what we read here, "And the very God of peace sanctify you wholly; and I pray God your whole spirit and soul and body be preserved blameless unto the coming of our Lord Jesus Christ." Then we shall be wholly sanctified. "We know that, when He shall appear, we shall be like Him; for we shall see Him as He is" (1 John 3:2). Our entire spirit, the highest part of man; our soul, the seat of our emotional nature; and our bodies, then glorified, will be sanctified completely in that day, and we shall be altogether conformed to our Lord Jesus Christ.

This is the precious promise of ver. 24. "Faithful is He that calleth you, who also will do it." Do you know Him now as your own personal Saviour? Do you yearn for the day when you will be absolutely free from grief, pain, and sins? Do you long to become like Him? Well, God has called you for that

purpose. Think of His infinite faithfulness: He
guarantees to bring us to that desired end in Christ
Jesus. "He which hath begun a good work in you
will perform it until the day of Jesus Christ" (Phil.
1:6).

And now in the last four verses we have the concluding exhortation and salutation. "Brethren, pray
for us." That is, pray for us as servants of Christ,
missionaries of the cross, teachers of the Word of
God. Those who stand in places of public testimony
need the prayers of God's people, because they are
so likely to fail in some way. They need prayer that
they may be able to maintain a consistent testimony
for the glory of Christ as they seek to minister the
Word of God.

"Greet all the brethren with a holy kiss." The kiss
was the customary way to greet one another. The
emphasis here is not on the word "kiss" but on the
word "holy"—"Greet one another with a *holy* kiss."
If our method is to greet with a hand-shake, then
it should be a holy hand-shake. You have seen two
men talking unkindly about a third, and one of the
two will look up and see the third man coming suddenly and unexpectedly toward them. He grasps
the third man's hand and says, "Oh, dear brother,
I am so glad to see you!" That is an unholy hand-
shake. Or there may be two women—God forbid!
—but they are criticising another woman who appears suddenly, and one of the two will run up to

her and give her a good hearty kiss. That is a "Judas kiss." What the apostle is stressing here is the importance of reality as we greet one another. Let your attitude toward each other be holy, and you will never be embarrassed by the sudden meeting of a third person.

"I charge you by the Lord that this Epistle be read unto all the holy brethren." God has constituted believers holy before Him in Christ, and so He dares to use that term. The Epistle closes with the usual Pauline salutation or benediction, "The grace of our Lord Jesus Christ be with you all."

SECOND EPISTLE TO THE THESSALONIANS

DIVINE RETRIBUTION AT THE LORD'S RETURN

✓ ✓ ✓

"Paul, and Silvanus, and Timotheus, unto the church of the Thessalonians in God our Father and the Lord Jesus Christ: Grace unto you, and peace, from God our Father and the Lord Jesus Christ. We are bound to thank God always for you, brethren, as it is meet, because that your faith groweth exceedingly, and the charity of every one of you all toward each other aboundeth; so that we ourselves glory in you in the churches of God for your patience and faith in all your persecutions and tribulations that ye endure: which is a manifest token of the righteous judgment of God, that ye may be counted worthy of the kingdom of God, for which ye also suffer: seeing it is a righteous thing with God to recompense tribulation to them that trouble you; and to you who are troubled rest with us, when the Lord Jesus shall be revealed from heaven with His mighty angels, in flaming fire taking vengeance on them that know not God, and that obey not the gospel of our Lord Jesus Christ: who shall be punished with everlasting destruction from the presence of the Lord, and from the glory of His power; when He shall come to be glorified in His saints, and to be admired in all them that believe (because our testimony among you was believed) in that day. Wherefore also we pray always for you, that our God would count you worthy of this calling, and fulfil all the good pleasure of His goodness, and the work of faith with power: that the name of our Lord Jesus Christ may be glorified in you, and ye in Him, according to the grace of our God and the Lord Jesus Christ"—2 Thess. 1: 1-12.

✓ ✓ ✓

THE two letters to the Thessalonians, the first of which we have considered already, were written to the Church at Thessalonica from the city of Corinth, where Paul had gone after leaving Berea. The first letter dealt largely with the coming of the Lord Jesus Christ for His saints. It

is evident that some Christians in Thessalonica misunderstood the teaching given by the apostle in connection with this subject. They seemed to have come
to the conclusion that since the Lord's coming might
take place at any moment it was useless to work for
a living. Then, too, inasmuch as they were called
upon to go through some very trying and distressing experiences the notion had gotten abroad among
them that they were already entering the great tribulation. The apostle, hearing of these strange misunderstandings of the truth which he had sought to
set forth, wrote this second letter in order to correct these unwholesome views and to bring before
them more definitely and clearly what was really
involved as to their responsibility while they, as
Christians, waited for the coming of the Lord Jesus
Christ.

This first chapter naturally divides into three
sections. In the first two verses we have the apostolic salutation. In vers. 3-10 the apostle seeks to
comfort, cheer, and encourage these believers who
were enduring great suffering and persecution for
Christ's sake. He tells them that it is a token of
the righteous judgment of God that His saints are
counted worthy to suffer persecution for His Name;
for they will be rewarded when they return with
the Lord in the day when He will be manifested to
execute judgment upon those who rejected Him and
persecuted His people. In vers. 11, 12 we have the

2 Thess. 1:1-12 79

apostle's prayer for the saints that God might fulfil
His good pleasure in them.

Note the salutation in vers. 1, 2: "Paul, and Silvanus, and Timotheus, unto the church of the Thessalonians in God our Father and the Lord Jesus
Christ: Grace unto you, and peace, from God our
Father and the Lord Jesus Christ." The address
here is the same as in the first letter to the Thessalonians, and it is in these two letters only that you
find the church, a local church, spoken of in this
way: "the Church which is in God the Father and
the Lord Jesus Christ." The emphasis is upon family relationship. These were young believers, but
they knew God as Father. They were children, and
Jesus Christ was their Lord. The apostle wishes
them "Grace . . . and peace." Grace is needed for
every step of the way, and as we learn to trust in
the living Father we enjoy the peace of God which
garrisons the heart and gives quiet confidence as
we pursue our pilgrim journey through this troubled scene.

Beginning with ver. 3 Paul undertakes to console
and hearten the saints amidst their trials and perplexities. He says, "We are bound to thank God
always for you, brethren, as it is meet, because that
your faith groweth exceedingly, and the charity of
every one of you all toward each other aboundeth."
Our English word "love" is generally, I think, to be
preferred to the older rendering "charity," because

in some way, in the course of years, there has been attached to the word "charity" the thought of alms-giving rather than that of sincere affection. It is the latter of which Paul is speaking here. Yet real love is ever charitable, in the sense of kind consideration for others.

There are two things for which he gives the church credit: a growing faith and abounding love. It is a wonderful thing when Christians are characterized in this way. We often find believers, who have been on the road for many years, constantly looking back to early days. They are asking in the words of the old hymn:

> "Where is the blessedness I knew
> When first I saw the Lord?
> Where is that soul-refreshing view
> Of Jesus and His Word?"

They think of early raptures as they sing:

> "O happy day that fixed my choice
> On Thee, my Saviour and my God!"

But so many are not able to say at the present moment as in the last part of the verse:

> "Well may this glowing heart rejoice,
> And tell its raptures all abroad."

It is a pitiable thing when a Christian's present state is lower than it was years ago when he was first converted. The Lord had to say to the Ephesian Church, "I have somewhat against thee, because thou hast left thy first love." It was otherwise with these Thessalonian believers. Some little time had elapsed since they were converted, but their faith was growing exceedingly, and they were abounding in love. May we not search our own hearts to see if these things are true of us, and ask ourselves, Is our faith growing exceedingly? Have we more confidence in God today than we had when we came to Him in the beginning of our Christian life? Have we so proved and tested Him through the years that we can count on Him now in a larger and fuller way than we did when we were first brought to know Him? If this is not true then it is evident that we are in a backslidden condition. Declension has set in. We need to turn to God and cry unto Him, "Restore unto me the joy of Thy salvation," the joy of early days. It is written, "The path of the just is as the shining light, that shineth more and more unto the perfect day" (Proverbs 4: 18). Those who have known the Lord for years ought to be stronger in faith than ever before; we should be more characterized by abounding love each passing day.

As Paul noticed these evidences of the grace of God working in these believers, he said, "So that we ourselves glory in you in the churches of God for your patience and faith in all your persecutions and tribulations that ye endure." They were passing through a time of great suffering, tribulation and bitter anguish for Christ's sake; but they manifested the grace of God in their lives in a wonderful way. How they could be so joyous and so restful in spite of the persecutions which they were enduring was something their enemies could not understand. The apostle speaks elsewhere, in writing to the Philippians, of believers going on in holy, happy unity. The unbelievers could not understand it. They said, "How is it that these Christians do not seem to be moved by our efforts to upset them? They go right on rejoicing, returning love for hatred, kindness for malice, praying for those who persecuted them. We cannot understand it." This should ever be characteristic of those who are redeemed by the Lord Jesus Christ.

"Which is a manifest token of the righteous judgment of God, that ye may be counted worthy of the kingdom of God, for which ye also suffer." We are made heirs of the kingdom by the new birth, but we prove our worthiness of that kingdom by the readiness with which we endure suffering for Christ's sake down here. We are told that if we suffer with Him we shall also reign with Him. All believers suffer with Him in some sense. All do not suffer for Him in the same way. One could not be a Christian at all, could not be indwelt with the Holy Spirit, and not suffer with Christ. The very fact that we belong to Him and have received a new and divine nature makes us suffer as we go through this world which has rejected Him. But to suffer for Him is something more than that. It is to take so definite a stand for Him that we become the objects of the world's hatred, and it is as we are thus prepared to endure grief and wrong in faithfulness to Christ that we have the opportunity to prove ourselves worthy of the kingdom of God to which we belong by the new birth.

The apostle goes on to speak of the coming of the Lord Jesus Christ in retributive judgment, and he shows that a great distinction will be made in that day between those who knew and loved the Saviour and those who refused to believe the gospel, who persisted in their sins and wickedness in utter indifference to the God who created them. He says, "It is a righteous thing with God to recompense tribulation to them that trouble you." We are to love our enemies; we are to bless them that curse us, and pray for them that despitefully use us. But in His own due time God will deal with those who have persecuted His Church. At the second coming of the Lord Jesus Christ to set up His glorious kingdom He will visit such with judgment who are living on this earth. Those who have died are reserved until the last great assize. When He descends to recompense tribulation to them that have troubled His people He will take care of those they have sought to injure, "To you who are troubled rest with us, when the Lord Jesus shall be revealed from heaven with His mighty angels;" that is, when He is manifested in the clouds with power and in great glory, He will recompense tribulation, trouble, and anguish to those who have deserved His wrath, but He will recompense with rest, joy, and comfort all who are His own. When thus shown with His mighty angels, in flaming fire taking vengeance on them that know not God, and that obey not the gospel of our Lord Jesus Christ," this is not the coming of the Lord for His own, of which we read in chapter 4 of the first Epistle. This is the manifestation, the day of the Lord, of chapter 5. It is the appearing of the Lord Jesus Christ to the world as we get in Revelation 1: 7, "Behold, He cometh with clouds; and every eye shall see Him, and they also which pierced Him: and all kindreds of the earth shall wail because of Him." He then comes as Judge to destroy out of the earth those who have spurned His grace. This great event will usher in that glorious era when the Lord Jesus will reign in righteousness from sea to sea and from the river to the ends of the earth. He shall be revealed in flaming fire, taking vengeance and visiting with retributive judgment them that know not God, and those who obey not the gospel. These are two classes of people: Those who know not God are the heathen who have lived in ignorance of the gospel but in definite rebellion against God their Creator; the second class will be those who have heard but have rejected the truth.

People ask, "Is God going to deal in judgment with the heathen? Is He going to send them to hell for rejecting Jesus Christ when they have never heard of Christ?" No; He is not going to send them to hell for rejecting Jesus Christ, but He is going to judge them for their own sins. We read in the first chapter to the Romans that they have been given up to uncleanness, because they have sinned against their own conscience and against the God they once knew. So whether or not the Word has ever been taken to them by missionaries, they are sinning against the light which God has given them. When the Lord Jesus returns He will visit judgment on all them that know not God. The guiltier class or whom He will pour out His wrath are those who obey not the gospel of our Lord Jesus Christ. This is something which those who live in this favored land should look upon with intense solemnity. When I hear people talking so glibly about the heathen and what God will do with them, I feel they had far better be thinking about themselves. What will God do with those who have heard the message over and over again and have spurned it, who have known of Christ all their lives and have rejected His love and grace? One of the saddest things I know is to see young men and young women growing up in Christian homes where they have had an example of piety in a godly father or mother, where family worship has been maintained; and yet they go out of those Christian homes to live careless, indifferent lives; sometimes using the stupid expression that they had religion enough when they were young and do not want it now. How it tells out the rebellion of the heart and hardness of conscience! For such there is nothing but judgment unless there be repentance, a breaking down before God, a confession of sins and turning to the Christ who has been rejected.

When the Lord Jesus comes in the clouds, in flaming fire, He will visit with judgment those who have sinned with no knowledge of Christ; but with more intense wrath those who have sinned against the light and knowledge that God has given them concerning His beloved Son. They "shall be punished," we read, "with everlasting destruction from the presence of the Lord, and from the glory of His power." What solemn words! What terrible warnings God has given us in order that men might face the question of their guilt and turn to Him in repentance. It is like the often-seen railroad warning —"Stop! Look! Listen!" How sad to be found in one's sin "When He shall come to be glorified in His saints, and to be admired in all them that believe (because our testimony among you was believed) in that day." What a great separation there will be: those gathered about Christ who have believed the message, trusted Him as Saviour, maintained a testimony for Him on earth, but who were misunderstood and persecuted for His name's sake—they will rejoice with Him in that day of His power. On the other hand, those who have spurned His loving-kindness will experience the awfulness of retributive judgment in that day.

Closing the chapter we have the apostle's prayer for the saints. We may well take these very expressions on our own lips and pray that we may have grace to act accordingly: "Wherefore also we pray always for you, that our God would count you worthy of this calling, and fulfil all the good pleasure of His goodness, and the work of faith with power." It is a privilege to be allowed to walk with Him through a world that rejects Him; it is a privilege to bear His name when that name is despised by the godless. How many of us look upon it as a privilege to be thus counted worthy of this calling? As our love abounds there will be increased power in the life to witness for Christ and to glorify Him. "That the name of our Lord Jesus Christ may be glorified in you, and ye in Him, according to the grace of our God and the Lord Jesus Christ."

This is the Christian's path of rejection as he goes through the world with a glorious prospect ahead of joy with Christ at His return; but for the unsaved there is nothing but judgment in that day when the Lord Jesus will be revealed from heaven in flaming fire taking vengeance on them that know not God and obey not the gospel.

THE RISE OF THE ANTICHRIST

✦ ✦ ✦

"Now we beseech you, brethren, by the coming of our Lord Jesus Christ, and by our gathering together unto Him, that ye be not soon shaken in mind, or be troubled, neither by spirit, nor by word, nor by letter as from us, as that the day of Christ is at hand. Let no man deceive you by any means: for that day shall not come, except there come a falling away first, and that man of sin be revealed, the son of perdition; who opposeth and exalteth himself above all that is called God, or that is worshipped; so that he as God sitteth in the temple of God, showing himself that he is God. Remember ye not, that, when I was yet with you, I told you these things? And now ye know what withholdeth that he might be revealed in his time. For the mystery of iniquity doth already work: only He who now letteth will let, until He be taken out of the way. And then shall that Wicked be revealed, whom the Lord shall consume with the spirit of His mouth, and shall destroy with the brightness of His coming: even him, whose coming is after the working of Satan with all power and signs and lying wonders, and with all deceivableness of unrighteousness in them that perish; because they received not the love of the truth, that they might be saved. And for this cause God shall send them strong delusion, that they should believe a lie: that they all might be damned who believed not the truth, but had pleasure in unrighteousness"—2 Thess. 2: 1-12.

✦ ✦ ✦

AS we undertake to consider the special line of truth brought before us in this chapter we need again to remind ourselves that the great outstanding theme of the first Epistle is the coming of the Lord Jesus Christ to receive His own to be with Him before that awful period of judgment which will come upon the earth, designated in the Old Testament as "The day of the Lord," "A time

of trouble," and "The time of Jacob's trouble." Our
Lord Jesus spoke of it as "the great tribulation."
The Thessalonian believers were looking forward
to the appearing of the Lord. It was this aspect of His coming which had made the deepest
impression on their hearts. They were looking for
Him to return to earth to execute judgment on the
wicked, and to set up His kingdom in this very scene
where He had been rejected and crucified. In his
first letter Paul shows that first He will come in the
air for His saints.

Sometimes believers have very poor memories,
and these Thessalonians seemed to have forgotten
this truth which Paul had endeavored to make so
clear. When they found themselves going through
a period of bitter persecution and trouble they began to wonder if the day of the Lord had begun:
that is, they thought they might be already in the
great tribulation. They lost sight altogether of the
truth that had been revealed concerning the catching up first of the Church. It would seem that someone had misled them into believing that they had
entered into the throes of that time of Jehovah's
wrath. Presumably it had been asserted that a special revelation from God had been given as to this,
and so many of the brethren had been deceived. It
would seem also as though someone had forged a
letter in the name of the Apostle Paul in which he
had definitely declared that the day of the Lord

really had begun, and the Church was going through the great tribulation. It was in order to correct this that the apostle wrote this second letter. In the first chapter, as we have seen, he set forth the truth of the Lord's judgment to take place at His manifestation when He shall be "revealed from heaven with His mighty angels, in flaming fire taking vengeance on them that know not God, and that obey not the gospel of our Lord Jesus Christ." Believers of this Church age will have been "caught up in the clouds, to meet the Lord in the air," ere this, but will appear with Him in glory when He descends as here depicted.

In the present section the apostle emphasizes this, and stresses the fact that the day of the Lord cannot begin while the Church is still on the earth. He says, "Now we beseech you, brethren, by the coming of our Lord Jesus Christ, and by our gathering together unto Him, that ye be not soon shaken in mind, or be troubled, neither by spirit, nor by word, nor by letter as from us, as that the day of Christ is at hand." He would have them remember that our hope is that of being gathered together unto the Lord, ere these judgments fall upon the earth. Even though some professed to speak by the Spirit, or to have discovered such teaching in the Word, or even to have received a letter from him asserting it, they were not to give heed to the theory that they were entering the great tribulation era.

"The day of Christ" is a faulty rendering. The best manuscript authority gives "the day of the Lord." The two refer to very different events. "The day of Christ" is the day of manifestation when believers receive their rewards at the judgment-seat of Christ. This is immediately after the rapture. "The day of the Lord," as we have tried to make clear, is the day when Jehovah's judgments will be poured out, culminating in the literal return of the Lord Jesus to this world where He will set up the kingdom of God in manifested glory. The day of Christ is always imminent. There are no signs to be looked for: we are to wait for the Son from heaven, who may return at any time. But that day of which we read here refers not to this precious and glorious event, but to the next stage of Christ's second advent and those judgments immediately preceding it.

Almost invariably when the Church is called upon to go through a time of great suffering, there are those who leap to the conclusion that it must be the beginning of "the hour of temptation which is come upon the whole world to try them that dwell on the earth." In our own generation we have passed through two world wars, and in each of these awful conflicts, great suffering came to a large part of the professing Church of Christ. Following on this many teachers began to assert that we were entering the great tribulation. Some have held that the

Church must go through the entire tribulation
period which, according to the Book of Daniel, is
to take place in the last and unfulfilled seventieth
week of the great prophecy of chapter 9. This
seven-week period is divided in Scripture into two
parts: it is all a time of tribulation, but the first
three-and-one-half years will be given up to pre-
liminary and largely providential judgment; the
last three-and-one-half years cover the great tribulation proper when the wrath of the Lamb and the
wrath of God will be poured out upon the world, and
Satan himself will be cast down from the heavens,
having great wrath. Some who realize that the
Church is to be saved from the wrath, and therefore cannot fall in with the idea that it will go
through the entire seven-week period of judgment,
nevertheless have held and taught that it will go
into at least the first half of the week. This, however, would involve two companies of saints on
earth at the same time: the heavenly company, the
Church which is the Body of Christ, and the remnant of Israel who are to be gathered out from the
apostate nation at the beginning of that time. This
is unthinkable if one but weighs the scriptures relating to each company. God has both a heavenly
and an earthly election. For instance, in our Lord's
great prophetic discourse as recorded in Matthew
24, the elect to be gathered out from all the nations,
when He descends to set up His kingdom, is Israel;

and those of the Gentiles who will come up out of
the great tribulation, having washed their robes and
made them white in the blood of the Lamb. The
elect of the Epistles are a heavenly company the
church of the firstborn whose names are written in
heaven.

It is for us as Christians to realize that ours is
indeed a heavenly hope. We are not to be occupied
with events and conditions down here, but we should
be looking for our blessed Lord Himself to snatch
us away from the wrath to come.

The day of the Lord cannot begin until after this
has taken place. That is why the apostle says, "We
beseech you, brethren, by the coming of our Lord
Jesus Christ, and by our gathering together unto
Him, that ye be not soon shaken in mind, or be
troubled, neither by spirit, nor by word, nor by letter as from us, as that the day of Christ is at hand."
We have already noticed that it should be "the day
of the Lord." Actually the thought that was in their
minds was that the day of the Lord had begun
already.

Paul says, "For that day shall not come, except
there come a falling away first, and that man of sin
be revealed, the son of perdition." The man of sin
is undoubtedly the same as the personal Antichrist
of whom the Apostle John speaks in his epistles,
and who is known also as the king who "shall do
according to his own will" in Daniel's great proph-

ecy. The day of the Lord cannot come until he has
been made manifest; he will not be made manifest prior to the rapture. But after the Church has
been caught away then the apostasy of Christendom and Judaism will be complete: the vast throng
of unconverted professors left on earth will throw
off all pretension of allegiance to Christ and to God.
That will be the complete falling away or apostasy,
which will be the preparation for the reception of
the Antichrist. "Who opposeth and exalteth himself
above all that is called God, or that is worshipped;
so that he as God sitteth in the temple of God, showing himself that he is God." We, therefore, are
never instructed to look for the rising up of this
sinister personage who occupies such a large place
in those prophecies that relate to the last days.
When Israel will be gathered back to their own land
in unbelief the words of the Lord Jesus, spoken
when He was here before, will be fulfilled. He said,
"I am come in My Father's name, and ye receive
Me not: if another shall come in his own name, him
ye will receive" (John 5:43). This one who comes
in his own name is the man of sin, the son of perdition. It is evident that this man of sin proclaims
himself the incarnation of God; he exalts himself
above all that is called God or that is worshipped.
The temple in which he will sit will be that which
the returning Jews will build in the land of Palestine. Antichrist will take his place there, and to

him will be rendered the worship that belongs to God alone.

I have already referred to Daniel's prophecy, but let me here quote the passage in question, "And the king shall do according to his will; and he shall exalt himself, and magnify himself above every god, and shall speak marvellous things against the God of gods, and shall prosper till the indignation be accomplished: for that that is determined shall be done. Neither shall he regard the God of his fathers, nor the desire of women, nor regard any god: for he shall magnify himself above all." This mysterious king will be a Jew. We get that from the fact that he is said not to regard the God of his fathers. In Scripture this refers invariably to the God of Abraham, the God of Isaac, and the God of Jacob. The desire of women undoubtedly refers to Messiah Himself. Every Jewish woman hoped to be the mother of the Deliverer of Israel. So the man of sin will be the son of Jewish parents; he will present himself to Israel as God manifest in the flesh, the Messiah for whom they have waited.

It is evident that Paul had given certain instruction concerning this when he was in Thessalonica, for he says, "Remember ye not, that, when I was yet with you, I told you these things?" Of course, in the short time that he was in that city he could not make everything clear, and even though he had done so, much would be forgotten. When circumstances arose that filled them with fear and dread they became so occupied with these conditions that they lost the hope of the return of Christ Himself to take His people away before the judgments began.

In the verses that follow the apostle put something before these Thessalonian Christians which every believer ought to understand, and yet it has been misunderstood by a great many prophetic students and even teachers. He says, "And now ye know what withholdeth that he might be revealed in his time. For the mystery of iniquity doth already work: only He who now letteth will let, until He be taken out of the way." This is another case where words have changed their meaning in the course of the centuries. When our English version was made "let" meant "to hinder;" now it means "to permit." What the apostle was really saying is this: "Ye know what restrains that he might be revealed in his own time. For the mystery of lawlessness doth already work: only there is One who now hindereth, until He be taken out of the way." Observe he suggests that they should "know what hindereth." Some have supposed that he referred to the Roman Empire whose downfall he had told the Thessalonians privately would take place before the second coming of Christ. It has been said that he spoke in a cryptic way, because to have made clearer his teaching as to this matter would have endangered both himself and other Christians and subjected them to suspicion on the part of the ruling powers. Others have thought that he was referring to orderly government as such; in other words, that a state of anarchy must prevail throughout the world before the manifestation of the Antichrist and the revelation of the Lord from heaven. But all such speculation seems needless in view of the fact that Paul was writing not merely for the Thessalonians or other believers living at that time, but also for Christians to the end of the dispensation. He speaks to us all when he says, "Ye know what restraineth." Let me put the question definitely: My reader, are you a Christian? If so, you ought to know what restrains the full manifestation of evil. Do you know? I have put this question to Christian audiences many times, and I have never failed to get the answer. Yes, it is the Holy Spirit who restrains. This is exactly what we are told in Isaiah 59:19, "When the enemy shall come in like a flood, the Spirit of the Lord shall lift up a standard against him." Or as it has been translated, "The Spirit of the Lord shall restrain him." The Holy Spirit is in the world working in and through the Church of God; He indwells every believer individually, and the Church collectively; therefore, as long as the Church of God is in the world the Antichrist will not be revealed. Of course, as the Apostle John tells us, "Even now are there many antichrists." Every denier of the

Father and the Son is an antichrist. But we are
speaking here of the man of sin, the son of perdition, the one who comes in his own name, the arch-
deceiver who will appear at the end of the age. This
one will not be manifest so long as the Spirit of God
is in the world. He came to abide with the Church
forever. So as long as the Church is here He will
be here, but when the Church is caught up to be
with the Lord then the Spirit of God will no longer
be in the world in the sense in which He has been
here during the Christian era. We sing sometimes:

> "The Holy Ghost is leading
> Home to the Lamb His Bride."

Like Abraham's servant, the Spirit of God has come
down into this far country to find a Bride for the
Son. It is He who works in the hearts of men and
women, leading them to Christ. When His work is
completed He will go up with the Church "and then
shall that wicked (*one*) be revealed, whom the Lord
shall consume with the spirit of His mouth, and
shall destroy with the brightness of His coming:
even him, whose coming is after the working of
Satan with all power and signs and lying wonders,
and with all deceivableness of unrighteousness in
them that perish; because they received not the love
of the truth, that they might be saved." This law-
less one who sets himself up to be God incarnate
will be the special object of Divine judgment; he

will be destroyed by the Lord Himself when He returns in power and glory. We learn from the Book of Revelation that he will be cast alive into the lake of fire.

During his brief time of power on earth he will deceive the nations by all manner of false miracles and lying wonders. Jesus says that if it were possible the very elect would be deceived; but, thank God, that is not possible: they know not the voice of strangers, but will hear the voice of the Good Shepherd. It is those who receive not the love of the truth that they might be saved who will be carried away by the propaganda of the Antichrist: in fact, it is God Himself who, in righteous judgment, will give them up to this. We read in vers. 11, 12: "And for this cause God shall send them strong delusion, that they should believe a lie: that they all might be damned who believed not the truth, but had pleasure in unrighteousness." We might read, "That they should believe *the* lie"—the lie that the man of sin is the Christ of God. This is a solemn word indeed for those who hear the gospel in our day and definitely reject it. It tells us that if they should be found in that condition when the rapture of the Church takes place and they pass into the last solemn period of tribulation, there will be no hope of their turning to Christ in that day, but they will believe this lie and thus be judged with all those who have apostatized from the truth.

No doubt many of you who are unsaved are children of Christian parents. You have heard the name of Christ all your lives; yet you have never definitely decided for Christ. If Jesus should come today you would be among the number who will receive the Antichrist. You say, "Impossible! I have been too well-taught for that; I have heard the gospel too many times. I have learned the great outlines of prophecy, and I know something of the Divine program. I would not be deceived in that way. I would turn immediately to the Lord after He had taken His own out of the world, and so I should be prepared to welcome Him at His glorious appearing." No; according to the Word of God that will never be true. If you reject Christ now you will have no desire to accept Him in that coming day. You are in the most dangerous position in which anyone could be. The Word of the Lord says, "He, that being often reproved hardeneth his neck, shall suddenly be destroyed, and that without remedy" (Proverbs 29:1). Some of the saddest funerals I have ever had to conduct in my life have been funerals of young men or young women who were members of Christian families, who had often been pleaded with to come to Christ; but they had gone on in carelessness, hoping that everything would come out all right in the end. Then suddenly they were struck down, perhaps by accident, and they went out into eternity leaving no testimony. Young

men and young women, I plead with you, do not
allow another day to pass without coming to Christ,
lest the near future find you forever beyond all hope
of mercy. God has given you the opportunity to
believe the truth. He has presented His Word, but
if you turn away from that truth and refuse to believe the gospel, then God Himself may give you up
to judicial judgment that you should believe the lie
of the man of sin and so be forever lost.

EVERLASTING CONSOLATION

✶ ✶ ✶

"But we are bound to give thanks alway to God for you, brethren beloved of the Lord, because God hath from the beginning chosen you to salvation through sanctification of the Spirit and belief of the truth: whereunto He called you by our gospel, to the obtaining of the glory of our Lord Jesus Christ. Therefore, brethren, stand fast, and hold the traditions which ye have been taught, whether by word, or our epistle. Now our Lord Jesus Christ Himself, and God, even our Father, which hath loved us, and hath given us everlasting consolation and good hope through grace, comfort your hearts, and stablish you in every good word and work"—2 Thess. 2: 13-17.

✶ ✶ ✶

THE apostle has spoken of the apostasy of the last days, and the coming of the man of sin when the Hinderer, the Holy Spirit, will no longer be working on the earth. It is noticeable that he then turns to comfort the saints with the assurance that they are the special objects of the divine care. To all who have put their trust in Christ, he writes, "But we are bound to give thanks alway to God for you, brethren beloved of the Lord, because God hath from the beginning chosen you to salvation through sanctification of the Spirit and belief of the truth." These words apply to Christians everywhere for all such are "brethren beloved of the Lord," and everyone of them has been chosen by God from the beginning to salvation. This was brought about "through sanctification of the Spirit and belief of the truth." We read in Romans

8:29, "For whom He did foreknow, He also did predestinate to be conformed to the image of His Son." Looking down through the ages God foreknew all who would ever put their trust in the Lord Jesus Christ, and He chose them to be conformed to Christ. If you are a believer in the Lord Jesus Christ you need never worry about your election. The very fact that you are a believer, redeemed by Christ, assures you that you are among the elect of God.

Notice three things: He has chosen you to *salvation* through *sanctification*. That means we were aroused to realize our lost condition and our need of a Saviour by the direct work of the Holy Spirit; and so we were led to trust in the Lord Jesus Christ. Sanctification of the Spirit is the initial work of God in the soul. When we believe the gospel we have the assurance of salvation.

Paul told the Romans that he was a minister of God to the nations in order "that the offering up of the Gentiles might be acceptable, being sanctified by the Holy Ghost" (Romans 15:16). One may preach the Word with ever so great liberty and power, but unless the Holy Spirit applies the Word to the hearts, illumines the minds, and exercises the consciences of the hearers, it will never convert a single person. Those who are saved can look back and recall how the work of the Holy Spirit began in their own souls. We remember the time when we were just part and parcel of the world around us, and then there came an awakening. Perhaps at first we could not understand it. We became unhappy and dissatisfied; there was a desire for something we had never known before; we became conscious of our sinfulness and guilt, and we cried out in our hearts for cleansing and purity—that was the sanctification of the Holy Spirit. There is a beautiful illustration of this in Genesis 1: 1, 2. We read, "In the beginning God created the heaven and the earth." That creation, we learn from Isaiah 45, was absolutely perfect, like everything else that comes from God's hand. But in the second verse we read, "The earth was without form, and void." Or as most Hebrew scholars feel that it might be better rendered, "The earth became without form, and void." Whether or not this had to do with the fall of angels we cannot be sure, but a tremendous catastrophe took place, and the earth was plunged into chaos. "And darkness was upon the face of the deep." It was a scene of gloom and desolation. Then we read that "The Spirit of God moved upon the face of the waters." The word translated "move" is a word that is used for brooding, as a hen brooding over her nest. "The Spirit of God *brooded* upon the face of the waters." This suggests the Holy Spirit brooding over fallen man in order that he might be reached for God and saved. A brooding hen, although she seems quiet and inert, is actually in constant motion, every muscle quivering. This generates the warmth needed to hatch the eggs. So we see the Holy Spirit brooding, moving over the waste of waters, preparatory to the reorganization of the earth, in order to fit it for man's dwelling-place. That same blessed Holy Spirit does His brooding, sanctifying work in the sinner's heart, then, when the light shines in, the soul is saved. "And God said, Let there be light: and there was light." This was the beginning of the new order. "The entrance of Thy Words giveth light" (Ps. 119:130). But no man sees the light till he has been awakened from his sleep by the Holy Spirit.

We are chosen "to salvation through sanctification of the Spirit and belief of the truth." Notice a passage in the first Epistle of Peter (1:1, 2), "Peter, an apostle of Jesus Christ, to the strangers scattered throughout Pontus, Galatia, Cappadocia, Asia, and Bithynia, elect according to the foreknowledge of God the Father, through sanctification of the Spirit, unto obedience and sprinkling of the blood of Jesus Christ: Grace unto you, and peace, be multiplied." What does he tell us? That the Spirit's sanctification leads us into the obedience of faith which brings us to the sprinkling of the blood of Jesus Christ. When we take our place in faith beneath that sprinkled blood, like Israel on the Passover night, we become absolutely secure.

Jehovah said, "When I see the blood, I will pass over you" (Exodus 12: 13).

There is another passage of deep interest. It is found in 1 Corinthians 6: 9, 10. There we have a list of evil characters, many of them so vile and unclean that we feel almost like refraining from reading them in a mixed audience. "Know ye not that the unrighteous shall not inherit the kingdom of God? Be not deceived: neither fornicators, nor idolators, nor adulterers, nor effeminate, nor abusers of themselves with mankind, nor thieves, nor covetous, nor drunkards, nor revilers, nor extortioners, shall inherit the kingdom of God." But the apostle adds, "And such were some of you: but ye are washed, but ye are sanctified, but ye are justified in the name of the Lord Jesus, and by the Spirit of our God." Some of the Corinthians had lived such lives as are depicted here, but they had been washed by the application of the Word of God, sanctified by the Holy Spirit and justified in the name of the Lord Jesus. This is the order in Scripture. The Word of God is proclaimed, heard or read, the Spirit of God sanctifies—convicts the sinner, bringing him to the place where he desires to be saved, and is ready to receive Christ. Believing the gospel he is justified by faith.

Let me give a word to those who seek to win souls: Do not try to rush people into confessing Christ; do not try to make them say they are saved.

Endeavor to find out if there is any real exercise about their sins, if the Spirit of God has awakened them. The reason a great many people make a profession of Christianity and appear to come out for Christ in revival meetings, and then soon afterward drift back into their former ways, is that there is no real work of God in the soul. They have never been sanctified by the Holy Spirit; they have never known divine conviction. The first consideration is that men might be awakened to see their need of Christ. Then give the gospel to them. That is the divine order: Sanctification by the Spirit which leads to belief of the truth. "Whereunto He called you by our gospel, to the obtaining of the glory of our Lord Jesus Christ." The purpose for which God is sending His gospel out into the world is that the Holy Spirit might awaken men and lead them to believe it. When they believe the gospel message they may be assured of eventually sharing the glory of our Lord Jesus Christ. When people have been really born again they will go on in the Christian life. We hear a great deal about backsliders. But some one has well said that many who are designated as backsliders have never been frontsliders; they have never been born again. In Philippians 1:6 we read, "He which hath begun a good work in you will perform it until the day of Jesus Christ."

"Therefore, brethren, stand fast, and hold the traditions which ye have been taught, whether by word, or our epistle." They were not to let anything turn them aside from the truth which had been proclaimed. Do not misunderstand what the apostle says as to traditions. Paul did not add human traditions to the Word of the Lord; but he had told these Thessalonians certain things by word of mouth, and he urged them to "hold fast these teachings," as well as those he committed to them in writing. Today we no longer have inspired apostles proclaiming the Word. Nothing is left for us but the written Word. We have no need of traditions: we have the Scriptures complete. "All Scripture is given by inspiration of God, and is profitable for doctrine, for reproof, for correction, for instruction in righteousness: that the man of God may be perfect, throughly furnished unto all good works" (2 Timothy 3:16, 17). When on earth our Lord told the scribes and Pharisees that they made the Word of God of none effect through their traditions. There are those today who have added a great many human traditions to the Word and have utterly confused their followers. But those who honor the Scriptures need no human traditions. These Thessalonians had listened to the apostle and had also received his written word, and they were exhorted to stand fast in all that they had received. "Now our Lord Jesus Christ Himself, and God, even our Father, which hath loved us, and hath given us everlasting consolation and good hope through

grace:"—Everlasting consolation is comfort which
will go on throughout eternity. Our hope will never
be disappointed.—"Comfort your hearts, and stablish you in every good word and work." We are not
saved by good works, nor by any effort or behavior
of our own; but because we have been saved through
the sanctification of the Spirit of God and belief of
the truth, we are responsible to maintain good
works. Thus we adorn the gospel of Christ.

CHRISTIANITY IN PRACTICE

✦ ✦ ✦

This third chapter is divided into three distinct sections, which we will take up one at a time.

"Finally, brethren, pray for us, that the Word of the Lord may have free course, and be glorified, even as it is with you: and that we may be delivered from unreasonable and wicked men: for all men have not faith. But the Lord is faithful, who shall stablish you, and keep you from evil. And we have confidence in the Lord touching you, that ye both do and will do the things which we command you. And the Lord direct your hearts into the love of God, and into the patient waiting for Christ"—2 Thess. 3: 1-5.

✦ ✦ ✦

IN these five verses the apostle seeks to impress upon the hearts of these young Christians, and of everyone of us, things which I want to bring before you under five terms.

The first one is *Prayerfulness*. "Finally, brethren, pray for us, that the Word of the Lord may have free course, and be glorified, even as it is with you." That is, the Thessalonians were asked to remember the one who wrote this letter. He was the mightiest evangelist, missionary, and teacher of the Word that the Church of God has ever known, and yet he felt the need of the prayers of these converts in order that he might the better fulfil his ministry. How often do you pray for those who are called to preach the Word to others? When alone with God do you remember to pray for Christ's under-shepherds who seek to care for His flock? Do you pray for missionaries who have gone forth into the regions beyond for the Lord Jesus? Do you remember those who labor in the home fields, many of them working in hard places where they find very little to cheer and encourage? Many of God's people cannot preach; many cannot teach, nor travel abroad to take the Word to distant lands; but all can pray. People say sometimes to me, "I do not know for what I should pray. I get down on my knees, thinking I shall spend some time in prayer, but in a few moments I have said everything that is on my heart, and there seems to be nothing else about which to pray." At such time why not wait quietly before God, and ask Him to bring before your mind those who are laboring in word and doctrine, and as they come before you mention them individually before God? Pray that they may be sustained and kept from discouragement. There is no one who needs prayer more than those who are bearing the burden and heat of the day in the terrific battle for righteousness. Paul and his companions had preached the Word to these Thessalonians, and he called upon them to pray for blessing as the witnesses went on elsewhere to preach. In this way believers may cooperate with those who are engaged in public ministry. Then in that coming day of manifestation, when we all appear before the judgment-seat of

Christ, and the Lord gives out rewards for faithful
service, He will see to it that recognition will be
given not only to those who preach the Word, but
also to those who back up His servants in prayer.
You may not be qualified to go to the mission-field,
but as you remain at home and give of your means
to help support a missionary in Africa, China, South
America, or in the isles of the sea, you will have a
large part in these things. You may never stand in
a pulpit to preach the Word, but by your prayers
and intercessions you can bear up before Him those
who minister it. This is a very real thing. I am
sure of this: if we prayed more for God's messengers we would criticize them less. Some are constantly finding fault with servants of Christ. They
never do just the right thing from the standpoint
of these critics. If one says much about sin he is
too stern; if he says more about the comfort and
consolation that is in Christ he is too soft; if he
speaks specially to the unsaved he is neglecting the
saints; if he addresses himself particularly to Christians he is not sticking to the gospel. It is easy to
get into a criticizing mood. But when we are bearing up God's servants in prayer the spirit of criticism gives way to one of loving helpfulness.

The second word I desire to stress is *Preserva-
tion.* The apostle and his companions were exposed
to great dangers. He says, "Pray that we may be
delivered from unreasonable and wicked men: for

all men have not faith." It is a sad fact that some men will never believe, no matter how clearly and tenderly the gospel is preached. There are many unreasonable and wicked men who have not faith, because they have closed their hearts and minds to the Word of God. There are those who say, "I have heard the gospel message over and over, and I cannot believe the Bible; I cannot believe in the virgin birth of Christ; I cannot believe that He was the Son of God; I cannot believe in His physical resurrection from the dead; I cannot believe in His ascension to heaven, and that He is coming again. I cannot believe all this." I can tell you why you cannot believe. It is because you have no desire to be free from your sins. You are rolling sin as a sweet morsel under your tongue, and as long as your sin means more to you than a place in heaven you will never be able to believe. Such are the people to whom the apostle refers here, and whom he describes as wicked. God's gospel is reasonable. He says, "Come now, and let us reason together, saith the Lord: though your sins be as scarlet, they shall be as white as snow; though they be red like crimson, they shall be as wool" (Isaiah 1: 18). He wants to reason with men; He wants them to sit down and face thoughtfully these great eternal truths that are presented in His Word. In writing to the Corinthians (1 Cor. 10: 15) the Apostle Paul said, "I speak as to wise men; judge ye what I say." That is, *exercise reason* as to what I say; think it through. Some people will never do that; they are determined not to believe. They do not wish to be delivered from their evil habits; therefore, they are unreasonable; they reject the gospel. Unreasonableness itself is wickedness. God says, "Let the wicked forsake his way, and the unrighteous man his thoughts: and let him return unto the Lord, and He will have mercy upon him; and to our God, for He will abundantly pardon" (Isaiah 55:7). But if men have no desire to turn from their sins and be delivered from their unrighteousness they will never be forced to do so. God commands all men to repent; if they refuse they must be dealt with in judgment.

These unreasonable and wicked men have not faith. These words have troubled some people. They have been misinterpreted and made to mean that there are people to whom it does not please God to give faith, and therefore they cannot believe. Scripture says, "For by grace are ye saved through faith; and that not of yourselves: it is the gift of God" (Eph. 2:8). Those words declare plainly that the very faith by which we are saved is the gift of God. But some will say that if the gift is not given by God then they cannot believe, and so they should not be held responsible for the loss of their soul. That interpretation is very unsound. The Word says, "So then faith cometh by hearing, and hearing by the Word of God" (Romans 10:17). Faith is founded upon hearing, and if men give attention and hear the voice of God and desire to be delivered from their sins, then faith springs up in their souls, and they are enabled to lay hold of Christ and be saved. But where men deliberately spurn the Word of God and persist in their sinfulness, they are numbered among those of whom the apostle writes here: "All men have not faith." They have not faith because they will not give heed to the message.

The third word I want to stress is *Protection.* "But the Lord is faithful, who shall stablish you, and keep you from evil." This is a wonderful promise for young Christians—and old ones too— but here Paul is thinking particularly of these young believers in Thessalonica. They were very much on his heart. He knew they were exposed to all kinds of danger; he knew Satan would do all he could to turn them away from the simplicity of the gospel of Christ. Paul had asked them to pray for him, even as he had prayed for them. He had confidence in the faithfulness of God: "The Lord is faithful!" He gives eternal life to all who believe in Him and He has promised that none shall pluck them from His hand (John 10:27-29). Nothing shall separate us from the love of Christ. The life that the believer receives is not conditional but eternal, and therefore can never be lost. Those who reason otherwise show that they never have understood the meaning of salvation by pure grace. They still think of human merit as a condition for final salvation. This is the very essence of Roman Catholic theology; but many Protestants never have been delivered from it.

The instructed Christian rests, not upon any fancied faithfulness of his own, but upon the faithfulness of God whose gifts and callings are without repentance. He can be depended upon to establish us and to keep us from all evil, as we seek to walk in obedience to His revealed will. If at times our feet slip through self-confidence or lack of watching unto prayer, like Peter in the high priest's porch, He knows just how to restore our souls and bring us back to the path of obedience.

The fourth word is *Perseverance*, as in verse 4: "And we have confidence in the Lord touching you, that ye both do and will do the things which we command you." The apostle believed always in the saints. They had believed in Christ, and he believed in them. If they trusted Christ, Paul knew they were saved, and he counted on seeing them come out on top. It is a bad thing to get into the habit of underrating and misunderstanding God's people. I know that many of God's dear children become enthused about certain things for a time, and then they drift away from their first love, and their keen interest seems to be dissipated. But the very fact that the Spirit of God dwells in them is good reason for confidence that they will be recovered and will come at last to the path of subjection to the will of the Lord.

The last word is *Patience*. Oh, how much we need patience. The apostle says, "And the Lord direct your hearts into the love of God, and into the patient waiting for Christ." A better rendering is, "The Lord direct your hearts into the love of God, and into the *patience* of Christ." You remember that James (5:7) says, "Be patient therefore, brethren, unto the coming of the Lord. Behold, the husbandman waiteth for the precious fruit of the earth, and hath long patience for it, until he receive the early and latter rain." The Husbandman sits at God's right hand in heaven, and He is waiting for the precious fruit of the earth. What does this mean? He is waiting until the last soul is saved in order to complete the Body of Christ. Then the Man of Patience, who has been sitting at the right hand of God during all these centuries, as we count time on earth, will rise from the throne and "shall descend from heaven with a shout, with the voice of the archangel, and with the trump of God: and the dead in Christ shall rise first: then we which are alive and remain shall be caught up together with them in the clouds, to meet the Lord in the air: and so shall we ever be with the Lord." We need patience as we wait for Him. This patience rests upon our realization of the unchanging love of our Heavenly Father. "The Lord direct your hearts into the love of God." What does he mean? In Jude 21 we read, "Keep yourselves in the love of God." How can I keep in the love of God? Am I responsible to keep God loving me? He says, "I have loved thee with an everlasting love." Does it mean that I am to keep loving God? No; "We love Him because He first loved us." But I am to keep in the realization of His love; the constant enjoyment of it. I have often illustrated it in this way. Suppose my child has been ill, and during dark and murky weather he has to be kept in the house. Then one day the sun shines brightly, and the doctor says, "He can go out today for a few hours, but be sure to warn him to keep in the sunshine." I say to my boy, "Son, you may go out and enjoy yourself, but the doctor says you are to keep in the sunshine." The boy asks, "How can I keep the sun shining?" I explain, "I did not tell you to keep the sun shining; I am telling you to keep in the sunshine." This, I think, makes clear what is meant here—keep in the love of God. "The Lord direct your hearts into the love of God." As we enjoy His love and learn to rely upon it, we can wait in patience for the day when all our trials will be ended, and the Lord Jesus will come to take us to be forever with Himself.

In the next section of our Epistle, verses 6-15, we have a warning against idleness and presumption.

"Now we command you, brethren, in the name of our Lord Jesus Christ, that ye withdraw yourselves from every brother that walketh disorderly, and not after the tradition which he received of us. For yourselves know how ye ought to follow us: for we behaved not ourselves disorderly among you; neither did we eat any man's bread for nought; but wrought with labor and travail night and day, that we might not be chargeable to any of you: not because we have not power, but to make ourselves an ensample unto you to follow us. For even when we were with you, this we commanded you, that if any would not work, neither should he eat. For we hear that there are some which walk among you disorderly, working not at all, but are busybodies. Now them that are such we command and exhort by our Lord Jesus Christ, that with quietness they work, and eat their own bread. But ye, brethren, be not weary in well doing. And if any man obey not our word by this epistle, note that man, and have no company with him, that he may be ashamed. Yet count him not as an enemy, but admonish him as a brother" (vers. 6-15).

Evidently the precious truth of the second coming of our Lord had gripped the hearts of these Thessalonians so that they were fully expecting Him to return in their lifetime. I gather from this passage and the corresponding verses in the first Epistle that some of the members of the Church at Thessalonica who did not particularly enjoy hard work, were saying, "Well, if the Lord is coming soon what is the use of our working? Why not take it easy? Others of our brethren have enough laid up for the future; let them divide with us. There is no necessity for our working." The apostle rebukes such a thing. He says, "God has ordained that if a man will not work, neither shall he eat." Work may be of one kind or another; it may be mental or physical. But everyone in this world is expected to do work of some kind. God said to Adam, "In the

sweat of thy face shalt thou eat bread." God could
provide for us without our working, but it might
not be good for us. We derive physical and intellectual help as we use the muscles and mind which
God has given us. Professor Henry Van Dyke's
lines are thoroughly *apropos* here:

> "The blessing of heaven is perfect rest,
> But the blessing of earth is work."

These men to whom Paul refers were simply ignoring the divine plan, for honest labor has a very
prominent place in Christianity. Every Christian
mechanic or professional man knows that he is expected to give his very best service in return for
the remuneration he receives. It is God who has
ordained that men should support themselves by
their labor. When men are not employed properly
there is always the danger that they will busy themselves in matters in which they ought not to inter-
fere. So they become a nuisance and are used of
Satan to disturb the peace of the Church, or of
those to whom they look for their support. The
tongue does not offend so seriously when the hands
are kept busy.

The apostle adds, "And if any man obey not our
word by this Epistle, note that man, and have no
company with him, that he may be ashamed. Yet
count him not as an enemy, but admonish him as
a brother." That is, such an one is not to be treated

unkindly, but it is only right to let him see that his behavior does not meet with the approval of his brethren.

The last section of three verses gives us the benediction and concluding salutation.

"Now the Lord of peace Himself give you peace always by all means. The Lord be with you all. The salutation of Paul with mine own hand, which is the token in every epistle: so I write. The grace of our Lord Jesus Christ be with you all. Amen"— (vers. 16-18).

Every authentic epistle by Paul closes with a similar message about grace. Saved by grace and sustained by grace himself, he ever commended that grace to others.